Your Pe
HOROS
—1995—

Your Personal HOROSCOPE 1995

Month-by-Month Forecasts for Every Sign

Joseph Polansky

Aquarian
An Imprint of HarperCollins*Publishers*

Aquarian
An Imprint of HarperCollins*Publishers*
77–85 Fulham Palace Road,
Hammersmith, London W6 8JB
1160 Battery Street,
San Francisco, California 94111-1213

Published by Aquarian 1994
1 3 5 7 9 10 8 6 4 2

Joseph Polansky asserts the moral right to
be identified as the author of this work

A catalogue record for this book
is available from the British Library

ISBN 1 85538 376 4

Typeset by Harper Phototypesetters Limited
Northampton, England
Printed in Great Britain by
HarperCollinsManufacturing Glasgow

Contents

Introduction

This book is written for those of you who would like to reap the benefits of astrology and who would like to learn more about how this vast, intricate and incredibly deep science is influencing your everyday life. My hope is that after reading the book you will see some of the possibilities that a knowledge of astrology brings, and be inspired to further explore this fascinating world.

I consider you, the reader, to be my personal client. By studying your Solar horoscope I gain an awareness of what is going on in your life – what you are feeling and striving for – and the challenges you face. I then do my best to address these concerns. Consider this book the next best thing to having your own personal astrologer!

I write to you as I would to a personal client. Thus, the section on each sign includes a Personality Profile, a look at the trends for 1995 and in-depth month-by-month forecasts. Every effort has been made to keep things simple and useful – we've even included a glossary section to help you with unfamiliar terms. The Personality Profiles will help you understand your own nature and the nature of those around you. This knowledge will make you more open-minded of both yourself and others. For the first law of the universe is that people must be true to themselves. The Personality Profile sections of the book are designed to foster 'self-acceptance' and 'self-love'. Without these, it is very difficult – to say the least – to accept and love others.

If this book gives you greater self-acceptance and self-knowledge, then it has done its job. But astrology has other practical applications in daily life. It shows the trends of your life and in the lives of those around you. By reading this book you will understand that, although the Cosmic Currents don't compel you, they do impel you in certain directions. The 'Horoscopes for 1995' and the 'Month-by-Month Forecasts' are designed to guide you through the planetary movements and influences, so that you can more easily steer your life in the desired direction and make the most of the year ahead. These forecasts include specific guidance on issues like health, love, finance, home, career and self-improvement – the areas we all are most interested in. If a co-worker, child or spouse is unusually irritable or cantankerous in a given month, you will see why when you read their monthly forecasts. This will make you more tolerant and understanding.

One of the many helpful features of this book is the 'Best and Worst Days' section at the beginning of each monthly forecast. This section will further help you schedule your plans and ride the Cosmic Currents to your advantage. If you try to schedule things on your best days – the days when you are stronger and more magnetic – you will achieve more with less effort and your chances of success will be greatly increased. Similarly, it is best to avoid important meetings or taking major decisions on these days, as important planets in your horoscope are retrograde (moving backwards in the zodiac).

The 'Major Trends' section for your sign lists those days when your vitality is strong or weak, or when relationships with your co-workers or loved ones may need a bit more effort on your part. The 'At a Glance' section of your Personality Profile details the gems, colours, scents, needs, virtues and other interesting information. You can enhance your energy, improve your creativity and general sense of well-being by using this knowledge in creative ways, such as wearing the scents, colours and gems of your sign, decorating your house in these colours, and even visualizing your colours around you before you go to sleep.

It is my sincere hope that *Your Personal Horoscope 1995* will enhance the quality of your life, make things easier, illuminate the way forward, banish the obscurities and make you more aware of your personal connection to the universe. Astrology – understood properly and used wisely – is a great guide to understanding yourself, the people around you and the events in your life – but remember that what you do with these insights – the final result – is up to you.

Astrological Terms

Ascendant

We experience day and night because the Earth rotates on its axis once every 24 hours. It is because of this rotation that the Sun, Moon and planets seem to rise and set. The Zodiac is a fixed belt (imaginary, but very real in spiritual terms) around the Earth. As the Earth rotates, the different Signs of the Zodiac seem to the observer to rise on the horizon. During a 24-hour period every Sign of the Zodiac will pass this horizon point at some time or another. The Sign that is at the horizon point at any given time is called the Ascendant, or Rising Sign. The Ascendant is the Sign denoting a person's self-image, body and self-concept – the personal ego, as opposed to the spiritual ego which is indicated by a person's Sun Sign.

Aspects

Aspects are the angular relationships between planets, the way in which one planet stimulates or influences another. If a planet makes a harmonious aspect (connection) to another, it tends to stimulate that planet in a positive and helpful way. If it makes a stressful aspect to another planet, the stimulation is stressful and uneasy, causing disruptions in the planet's normal influence.

Astrological Qualities

There are three astrological qualities into which all the 12 Signs are divided: *cardinal, fixed* and *mutable.*

The cardinal quality is the active, initiating principle. Cardinal Signs (Aries, Cancer, Libra and Capricorn) are good at starting new projects.

Fixed qualities are stability, persistence, endurance and perfectionism. Fixed Signs (Taurus, Leo, Scorpio and Aquarius) are good at seeing things through.

Mutable qualities are adaptability, changeability and balance. Mutable Signs (Gemini, Virgo, Sagittarius and Pisces) are creative, if not always practical.

Direct Motion

When the planets move forward – as they normally do – through the Zodiac they are said to be going 'direct'.

Houses

There are 12 Signs of the Zodiac and 12 Houses of experience. The 12 Signs are personality types and ways in which a given planet expresses itself. The Houses show 'where' in your life this expression takes place. Each House has a different area of interest (see the list, opposite). A House can become potent and important – a House of power – in different ways: if it contains the Sun, the Moon or the Ruler of your chart, if it contains more than one planet, or if the Ruler of the House is receiving unusual stimulation from other planets.

1st House of Body and Personal Image

2nd House of Money and Possessions

3rd House of Communication

4th House of Home and Family, Domestic Life

5th House of Fun, Entertainment, Creativity, Speculations and Love Affairs

6th House of Health and Work

7th House of Love, Romance, Marriage and Partnership

8th House of Elimination, Transformation and Other People's Money

9th House of Travel, Education, Religion and Philosophy

10th House of Career

11th House of Friends, Group Activities and Fondest Wishes

12th House of Spiritual Wisdom and Charity

Karma

Karma is the law of cause and effect which governs all phenomena. We are all in the situation in which we find ourselves because of Karma – because of actions we have performed in the past. The universe is such a balanced instrument that any unbalanced act immediately sets corrective forces into motion – Karma.

Long-term Planets

The planets that take a long time to move through a Sign are considered long-term planets – these planets are Jupiter (which stays in a Sign for about a year), Saturn (which stays in a Sign for two and a half years), Uranus (seven years), Neptune (14 years) and Pluto (15 to 30 years). These planets show the long-term trends in a given area of life and thus they are important when astrologers forecast the prolonged view of things. Because these planets stay in one Sign for so long, there are periods in the year when the faster-moving (short-term) planets will join them, further activating and enhancing the importance of a given House.

Lunar

Relating to the Moon.

Natal

Literally means 'birth'. In Astrology this term is used to distinguish between planetary positions that occurred at birth (natal) and transiting (current) ones. For example, Natal Sun refers to where the Sun was when you were born; the transiting Sun refers to where the Sun's position is currently at any given moment – which usually doesn't coincide with your birth, or Natal, Sun.

Out of Bounds

The planets move through our Zodiac at various angles relative to the celestial equator (if you draw an imaginary extension of the Earth's equator out into the universe you will have the celestial equator). The Sun – being the most dominant and powerful influence in the Solar system – is the measure astrologers use as a standard. The Sun never goes more than approximately 23 degrees north or south of this celestial equator. At the winter solstice the Sun reaches its maximum southern angle of orbit (declination) and at the summer solstice it reaches its maximum northern angle. Any time a planet exceeds this Solar boundary – and occasionally planets do – it is said to be 'out of bounds'. This means that the planet exceeds or trespasses into strange territory – beyond the limits allowed by the Sun, the Ruler of the Solar system. The planet in this condition becomes more emphasized and exceeds its authority, becoming an important influence in a forecast.

Phases of the Moon

After the full Moon, the Moon seems to shrink in size (as perceived from the Earth), gradually growing smaller until it is virtually invisible to the naked eye – at the time of the next new Moon. This is called the *waning* Moon phase – or the waning Moon.

After the new Moon, the Moon gradually gets bigger in size (as perceived from the Earth), until it reaches its maximum size at the time of the full Moon. This period is called the *waxing* Moon phase – or waxing Moon.

Retrogrades

The planets move around the Sun at different speeds. Mercury and Venus move much faster than the Earth, while Mars, Jupiter, Saturn, Uranus, Neptune and Pluto move more slowly. Thus there are times when, relative to the Earth, the planets appear to be going backwards. In reality they are always going forward, but relative to our vantage point on Earth they seem to go backwards through the Zodiac for a period of time. This is called 'retrograde' motion and it tends to weaken the normal influence of a given planet.

Short-term Planets

These are the fast-moving planets: the Moon (which stays in a Sign for only two and a half days), Mercury (20 to 30 days), the Sun (30 days), Venus (approximately a month) and Mars (approximately two months). Since these planets move so quickly through a Sign their effects are generally of a short-term nature. They show the immediate, day-to-day trends in a Horoscope.

Transits

This refers to the movements or motions of the planets at any given time. Astrologers use the word 'transit' to make the distinction between a birth or Natal planet and its current movement in the heavens. For example, if at your birth Saturn was in the Sign of Cancer in your 8th House, but is now moving through your 3rd House, it is said to be 'transiting' your 3rd House. Transits are one of the main tools with which to forecast trends.

Aries

♈

THE RAM

Birthdays from
21st March
to 20th April

Personality Profile

ARIES AT A GLANCE

Element – Fire

Ruling planet – Mars
Career planet – Saturn
Love planet – Venus
Money planet – Venus
Planet of home and family life – Moon
Planet of wealth and good fortune – Jupiter

Colours – carmine, red, scarlet

Colours that promote love, romance and social harmony – green, jade green

Colour that promotes earning power – green

Gem – amethyst

Metals – iron, steel

Scent – honeysuckle

Quality – cardinal (= activity)

Quality most needed for balance – caution

Strongest virtues – abundant physical energy, courage, honesty, independence, self-reliance

Deepest need – action

Characteristics to avoid – haste, impetuousness, over-aggressiveness, rashness

Signs of greatest overall compatibility – Leo, Sagittarius

Signs of greatest overall incompatibility – Cancer, Libra, Capricorn

Sign most helpful to career – Capricorn

Sign most helpful for emotional support – Cancer

Sign most helpful financially – Taurus

Sign best for marriage and/or partnerships – Libra

Sign most helpful for creative projects – Leo

Best Sign to have fun with – Leo

Signs most helpful in spiritual matters – Sagittarius, Pisces

Best day of the week – Tuesday

Understanding the Aries Personality

Aries is the activist *par excellence* of the Zodiac. The Arien need for action is almost an addiction and those who do not really understand the Arien personality would probably use this hard word to describe it. In reality 'action' is the essence of the Arien psychology – the more direct, blunt and to-the-point the action, the better. When you think about it, this is the ideal psychological makeup for the warrior, the pioneer, the athlete or the manager.

Ariens like to get things done and in their passion and zeal often lose sight of the consequences for themselves and others. Yes, they often *try* to be diplomatic and tactful, but it is hard for them. When they do so they feel that they are being dishonest and phony. It is hard for them even to understand the mind-set of the diplomat, the consensus builder, the front office executive. These people are involved in endless meetings, discussions, talks and negotiations – all of which seem a great waste of time when there's so much work to be done – so many real achievements to be gained. An Aries can understand, once it is explained to him to her, that talks and negotiations – the social graces – lead ultimately to better, more effective actions. The interesting thing is that an Aries is rarely malicious or spiteful – even when waging war. Aries people fight without hate for their opponents. To them it is all good-natured fun; a grand adventure; a game.

When confronted with a problem many people will say 'Well, let's think about it, let's analyse the situation.' But not an Aries. An Aries will think 'Something must be done. Let's get on with it.' Of course neither response is the total answer. Sometimes action is called for, sometimes cool thought. But an Aries tends to err on the side of action.

Action and thought are radically different principles. Physical activity is the use of brute force. Thinking and deliberating require one not to use force – to be still. It is not good for the athlete to be deliberating the next move; this will only slow down his or her reaction time. The athlete must act instinctively and instantly. This is how Aries people tend to behave in life. They are quick, instinctive decision-makers and their decisions tend to be translated into actions almost immediately. When their intuition is sharp and well tuned, their actions are powerful and successful. When their intuition is off, their actions can be disastrous.

Don't think this will scare an Aries. Just as a good warrior knows that in the course of combat he or she might acquire a few wounds, so too does an Aries realize – somewhere deep down – that in the course of being true to oneself, one might incur a disaster or two. It's all part of the game. An Aries feels strong enough to weather any storm.

There are many Aries people who are intellectual: Ariens make powerful and creative thinkers. But even in this realm they tend to be pioneers – outspoken and blunt. These types of Ariens tend to elevate (or sublimate) their desire for physical combat with intellectual, mental combat. And they are indeed powerful.

In general, Aries people have a faith in themselves that others could learn from. This basic, rock-bottom faith carries them through the most tumultuous situations of life. Their courage and self-confidence make them natural leaders. Their leadership is more by way of example than by actually controlling others.

Finance

Aries people often excel as builders or estate agents. Money in and of itself is not as important as are other things – action, adventure, sports, etc. They are motivated by the need to support their partners and to be well thought of by partners. Money as a way of attaining pleasure is another important motivation. Ariens function best in their own businesses or as managers of their own departments within a large business or corporation. The less orders they have to take from higher up the better. They also function better out in the field rather than behind a desk.

Aries people are hard workers with a lot of endurance; they can earn large sums of money due to the strength of their sheer physical energy.

Venus is their Money Planet, which means that Ariens need to develop more of the social graces in order to realize their full earning potential. Just getting the job done – which is what an Aries excels at – is not enough to create financial success. The co-operation of others needs to be attained. Customers, clients and co-workers need to be made to feel comfortable. Many people need to be treated properly in order for success to happen. When Aries people develop these abilities – or hire someone to do this for them – their financial potential is unlimited.

Career and Public Image

One would think that a pioneering type would want to break with the social and political conventions of society. But this is not so with the Aries-born. They are pioneers within conventional limits, in the sense that they like to start their own businesses within an established industry rather than to work for someone else.

Capricorn is on the 10th House (of Career) cusp of Aries' Solar Horoscope. Saturn is the planet that rules their life's work and professional aspirations. This tells us some interesting things about the Arien character. First off, it shows that in order for Aries people to reach their full career potential they need to develop some qualities that are a bit alien to their basic nature. They need to become better administrators and organizers. They need to be able to handle details better and to take a long-range view of their projects and their careers in general. No one can beat an Aries when it comes to a short-range objective, but a career is long term, built over time. You can't take a 'quickie' approach to it.

Some Aries people find it difficult to stick with a project until the end. Since they get bored quickly and are in constant pursuit of new adventures, they prefer to pass the old project or task to somebody else in order to start something new. Those Ariens who learn how to put off the search for something new until the old gets done will achieve great success in their careers and professional lives.

In general, Aries people like society to judge them on their own merits, on their real and actual achievements. A reputation acquired by 'hype' feels false to them.

Love and Relationships

In marriage and partnerships Ariens like people who are more passive, gentle, tactful and diplomatic – people who have the social grace and skills they sometimes lack. Our partners always represent a hidden part of ourselves – a self that we cannot express personally.

An Aries tends to go after what he or she likes aggressively. The tendency is to jump into relationships and marriages. This is especially true if Venus is in Aries as well as the Sun. If an Aries likes you, he or she will have a hard time taking no for an answer; many attempts will be made to sweep you off your feet.

Though Ariens can be exasperating in relationships – especially if they are not understood by their partners – they are never consciously or wilfully cruel or malicious. It is just that they are so independent and sure of themselves that they find it almost impossible to see somebody else's viewpoint or position. This is why an Aries needs someone with lots of social grace to be his or her partner.

On the plus side, an Aries is honest, someone you can lean on, someone with whom you'll always know where you stand. What he or she lacks in diplomacy is made up for in integrity.

Home and Domestic Life

An Aries is of course the ruler at home – the Boss. The male will tend to delegate domestic matters to the female. The female Aries will want to rule the roost. Both tend to be handy around the house. Both like large families and both believe in the sanctity and importance of the family. An Aries is a good family person, although he or she doesn't especially like being home a lot, preferring instead to be roaming about.

For natures that are so combative and wilful, Aries people can be surprisingly soft, gentle and even vulnerable with their children and partners. The Sign of Cancer, ruled by the Moon, is on the cusp of their Solar 4th House of Home and Family. When the Moon is well aspected – under favourable influences – in the birth chart an Aries will be tender towards the family and want a family life that is nurturing and supportive. Ariens like to come home after a hard day on the battlefield of life to the understanding arms of their partner and the unconditional love and support of a family. An Aries feels that there is enough 'war' out in the world – and he or she enjoys participating in that. But when Aries comes home, comfort and nurturing are key.

Horoscope for 1995

Major Trends

In 1994, Aries, you prospered and expanded by eliminating the old and the useless from your life. This applied to possessions, debts, expenses and even friendships. Though you may not have understood the reasoning for this last year, in 1995 it becomes abundantly clear. You needed to weed out the old in order to make room for the new. Two important – and very positive – long-term transits occur in 1995 and bring a new sense of health, well-being, happiness and prosperity. You certainly deserve it! If you got through 1993 with your health and confidence intact, you did extremely well. That was the low point. 1994 was a lot easier and happier than 1993, and 1995 is going to be even more easy than 1994 was.

You can expect significant improvements in almost every major area of your life this year. Most importantly, joy and optimism return to you. You had almost forgotten what they were like. All the changes that you made in the past few years, many of which were forced upon you, now seem to have been orchestrated by a wise and benevolent power. A power that saw your Destiny and knew what it was doing. Whereas for years you railed and complained about all these changes, now you are grateful for them.

Health

Though your 6th House of Health is not a House of Power this year, other factors in your Horoscope show a tremendous increase in your vitality and stamina. Jupiter in the Sign of Sagittarius all year makes beautiful aspects to your Sun. This not only increases the general Life-Force, but brings optimism and a sense of well-being as well. Mars, your Ruling Planet, makes an unusually long four-month transit in Leo this year – further enhancing your vitality. And, towards the end of the year – 10th November, specifically – Pluto moves into harmonious aspect to you for many, many years to come. There's no question that you are more illness-resistant now than you have been for the past few years. Naturally you will have your low periods during the year, but the lows will never be as low as they have been in the past – especially those you experienced in 1993. The overall trend is towards abundant health and vitality.

The situation with your partner however, is another story. Your partner definitely needs to rest and relax more this year and to take drug-free non-surgical preventives. Luckily, your superabundant vitality will help get your partner through this low-energy year. The health of your parents also seems delicate as they are moving around a lot and changing their diets. Perhaps they are experimenting with diets too much and being erratic in their physical behaviour. At times they overwork and at other times do nothing. They need to slow down and find a middle ground. Radical dietary changes will cause them to feel uneasy.

This is a year when exercise regimes are fun for you. You naturally do well at these kind of things, but this year you excel at them. Your athletic skills get sharpened.

Home and Domestic Life

Your 4th House of Home and Domestic interests is not a House of Power this year. The Cosmos is neither obstructing nor aiding your domestic plans and family relationships. You have unusual latitude to make of this aspect of your life what you will. Actually, you are much more preoccupied with your career and with faraway places and climes really to care much about what occurs close to home. Your family seems tolerant about this. You are much more concerned with religious and philosophical issues than with emotional ones. You've gone through your domestic battles in the past; this year you want 'outside' action.

The Moon is the Ruler of your Home and Family Life. It is a good Ruler to have, as the home and family are her natural sphere. If you follow the Lunar movements month to month – especially the lunar phases – you can understand your moods and your ability to handle family situations better. You will always be in a better mood and have more enthusiasm for domestic projects and for mingling with the family when the Moon is waxing than when it is waning. You are more likely to express negative emotion when the Moon is waning than when it is waxing. Schedule yourself accordingly. These Lunar movements are detailed in the month-by-month forecasts below.

Love and Social Life

Your 7th House of Love and Marriage is not a House of Power this year. Therefore you are being given the latitude to make what you like of your social life. Many astrologers consider 'empty' Houses, i.e. non-active Houses, to be fortunate. An empty House creates a feeling of being free and unbound, whereas when a House is strong there is a sense of coercion and compulsion involved. The fact that your 7th House is not powerful this year doesn't mean that you won't have a social life. Of course you will. Only that other things take priority over it in your thinking – most notably 'outer', objective achievement.

An empty, non-active House tends to foster the status quo. Thus marrieds will tend to stay married and singles will tend to stay single. For those of you who have been married once and are planning to get married again, the situation is different. This will be an unusually active social year and a happy second marriage is very likely. The new love interest is rich, generous, probably religious, likes to travel, wants to teach you things and hates details and being on time as much as you do.

Your social life will tend to be most active from 22nd July to 8th September and from 23rd September to 24th October. This latter period seems especially romantic.

A sibling will probably get married this year – or be involved in a significant love affair. Your parents' marriage is stormy and fraught with changes. Uncles and aunts are also having marital difficulties.

Career and Finance

There's no question that career and finance are – as they have been for many years now – among your most important priorities in 1995. The cosmic signals are good, better than last year and infinitely better than 1993. Though you are earning more this year, money *per se* is not that important to you. Obviously it's nice to have money, but you are much more concerned with your career and life's work than with mere cash. So, though the pay rises, travel and various corporate perks come, you are blasé about them. And that's just perfect. Your previous anxieties were just blocking you anyway, delaying the financial good that wanted to come to you. Now that you are relaxed, it comes in with fabulous ease and abundance. You earn money easily and you spend it easily.

The real news is the progress you are making on the career front. Your increased self-esteem has made you in turn more valuable to your employers and customers. You rise in the corporate hierarchy suddenly and unexpectedly. Superficial observers think that you've got 'lucky' or that you've become an overnight success, but you know differently. You've worked long and hard, endured many trials and tribulations to get where you are now. This is no fluke. You've earned your place in the world.

Saturn, your Career Planet, is in your 12th House of Spiritual Wisdom and Idealism all year. This further reinforces the career idealism that you've had for the past few years. You want power and authority so that you can help others and do good in the world. You don't want power merely for power's sake. Also, very unlike your normal character, you wield power gently and compassionately. You are the perfect boss. Your superiors are also more gentle with you. But question their motives: it is not idealism that motivates them but their need for control. This year they feel they can get more out of you by being gentle. Now that you're rising in the corporate ranks you must be even more careful of secret manipulations. This will be a real eye-opener for you, as you are not like those who scheme and conspire. You are well-equipped to handle obstacles or enemies that you can see – few are better at this than you. But it's the invisible enemies, the things that you can't confront openly, that you can hardly detect, that give you problems. Cleave to your open and honest self, watch and observe, for this will be a real revelation for you.

In spite of all this you will advance this year. If you are a corporate employee you will rise in the hierarchy. You will do this both by 'luck' and by sheer hard work. With Mars making a four-month transit in Leo and with Jupiter in

Sagittarius you simply outwork and outperform your competitors. If you are self-employed your business will also grow.

Involvement in charitable activities definitely boosts your career and professional image this year. Many of you might even enter this field on a full-time, professional level.

Mars in Leo from 23rd January to 26th May also shows that you are a lucky speculator during this period. The entire year is good for this sort of thing, but this period is exceptionally so.

Those of you who write for a living are likely to get published this year. Interest income from an inheritance or jointly held property will exceed expectations.

The income of your partner is steady and stable this year. He or she rather plugs away and makes steady, if unspectacular, progress. Your partner is also much more serious about money this year than you are. You seem 'laissez faire' about it all.

Your partner will acquire a new car and probably new communication equipment this year – computers, fax machines, telephones, modems and the like. Friends are hard pressed financially but you seem unaware of it. When things go well for a person it seems that everyone else is doing well – everything seems rosy. Be careful that your contentedness doesn't cause secret resentments.

The income of one of your parents – your father if you are a man, your mother if you are a woman – undergoes some upheavals. They are on a financial roller-coaster ride. They feel financially ruined one day and as rich as Croesus the next. They are being led – through trial and error and experimentation – to economic freedom and liberation. Your personal financial life is much more stable than theirs.

Self-improvement

Two areas of life that have not been fully discussed yet are prominent in your Horoscope this year: your 9th House of

Religion and Higher Education and your 12th House of Spiritual Wisdom, Sacrifice and Charity. Both of these Houses deal with 'Higher Knowledge', the attempt to align more perfectly with the 'spiritual self', but in different ways. The 9th House deals with higher knowledge of an intellectual nature, while the 12th House deals with profound psychological experience. The power in the 9th House is going to increase your religious knowledge. You will probably get involved in bible studies or courses on religion. You will expand your knowledge of what others have written about the nature of the universe and God. But the power in the 12th House is not satisfied with this alone. It wants direct, personal experience of the realities that you are studying. In order to get this direct experience you need to discipline yourself and make modifications in your lifestyle. You need to practise meditation, prayer and spiritual disciplines – not just read about them or talk about them. A little bit of meditative contemplation is called for this year.

Many other Signs have no problem with this, but you, Aries, have. You are such an activist by nature that the practice of stillness, quietude and receptivity is difficult for you. Indeed this is not your true spiritual path. Your path to spiritual reality is through good works. Nevertheless, a little stillness and silence is good for you – especially this year. Mastering a hot, fidgety body that wants to run around all over the place is harder than conquering a thousand cities. And while it would be cruel and unusual punishment to make this your entire life, a little is good. If you persist you will experience the understanding and peace that you have read about.

Opportunities for higher education are going to come to you this year, and by all means take them. You also have an interest in foreign cultures and lifestyles, which you will experience through travelling to various countries and mixing with natives of different cultures. This too is right and proper. Anything that makes you more valuable to life is good for you.

Month-by-month Forecasts

January

Best Days Overall: 7th, 8th, 17th, 18th, 26th, 27th

Most Stressful Days Overall: 1st, 2nd, 15th, 16th, 22nd, 23rd, 28th, 29th

Best Days for Love: 5th, 6th, 7th, 8th, 17th, 18th, 19th, 22nd, 23rd, 26th, 27th

Best Days for Money: 5th, 6th, 7th, 8th, 10th, 11th, 17th, 18th, 26th, 27th

Don't let temporary setbacks or conflicts get you down, Aries; you are in a period of long-term good. It's quite all right now to sacrifice personal interests and desires in favour of far-reaching benefit. Look at the big picture and make your decisions accordingly.

This is a powerful career month. Upheavals in the power structure of your company or industry are working in your favour. They create opportunities for your advancement. Your creativity in promoting yourself works wonders. If you are in the creative or performing arts your popularity with the public is very much enhanced. Your work finds favour also with the powers that be.

With Mars, your Ruling Planet, retrograde (moving backwards) all month you feel less powerful than usual. You feel you are going backwards instead of forwards. But this is only the surface appearance. You don't need to be personally strong – in an egotistical way – right now; others are promoting you and your interests. You will understand the scripture 'my strength is made perfect in your weakness' this month.

Though your health is excellent over the long term this is not one of your better health months. Rest and relax more, especially until the 20th. After that your vitality surges once more.

Seldom have you been so creative, Aries. Truly creative and original. Take advantage of this period now to express this creativity in art, writing or wherever your interests happen to lie. The muses are all around you now.

Love, too, is all around. Singles find abundant romantic opportunities, especially from the 14th to the 16th when Venus and Jupiter conspire to bring love to you. Love with a big L. Singles are very likely to find that 'significant other' this period. Marrieds become unusually romantic in their relationship. Your partner in particular is unusually affectionate, optimistic, fortunate and probably generous. Some major stroke of good luck befalls your partner – both in financial and in communication endeavours. A romantic adventure to some foreign paradise is very much on the cards this month. You could use a holiday this month in any case.

Finances are unusually good. Money is earned pleasantly and you make the lucky breaks. Windfall earnings come to you from the 14th to the 16th.

February

Best Days Overall: 3rd, 4th, 5th, 13th, 14th, 15th, 22nd, 23rd

Most Stressful Days Overall: 11th, 12th, 18th, 19th, 24th, 25th

Best Days for Love: 4th, 5th, 6th, 7th, 16th, 17th, 18th, 19th, 24th, 25th

Best Days for Money: 3rd, 4th, 5th, 6th, 7th, 13th, 14th, 15th, 16th, 17th, 22nd, 23rd, 24th, 25th

With 80 to 90 per cent of the planets at the top half of your Solar Horoscope the drive to outer success and career achievement is intense indeed. Much more important than domestic or emotional harmony. Combine this with the fact that after the 16th, 90 per cent of the planets will be in forward motion and you have the recipe for an active, ambitious, forward-moving career. Career plans move ahead with great speed – which is just the way you like things, Aries.

There is another potent signal for career achievement this month: Venus, your Planet of both Money and Love, moves into your Career House after the 4th. Not only does your pursuit of status and prestige bring money and financial opportunity, it brings love as well. Venus' position also shows where you most find happiness and harmony. No question about it – follow your star and promote yourself.

Other paths to happiness and harmony are shown by Jupiter's position and the position of the Moon's North Node. Judging by their placement this month, higher education, religious and philosophical studies, foreign travel, physical intimacy and the elimination of undesirable conditions are also paths of fulfilment for you now.

With Venus being the most elevated planet in your Solar Horoscope, love and money are top priorities in your life. Your general popularity makes you feel rich and lovable. Romantic and financial opportunities come via those involved with promoting your career, via elders and via your superiors. That special someone could cross your path in the oddest places this month – at a government office, at a driving test centre or at the tax office, for example.

Those of you who have their hearts set on an Aries need to understand that Ariens is likely to be turned on by those who support their careers and who are in a position to help them go further in their professions. Power and status are Aries' aphrodisiacs now.

Though you will be very active this month, don't get so active that you ignore your own spiritual needs. This becomes especially important after the 19th when the Sun moves into your 12th Solar House. While you are unlikely to remove yourself to a mountain-top to commune with your inner being, you still need to set aside some time for this kind of thing. Review the past year – beginning with your last birthday – see how far you've come and where you want to go from here. Correct any mistakes in your actions and attitudes. Then you'll be ready to move forward even more rapidly next month when the Sun enters your own Sign.

Your health is excellent all month.

March

Best Days Overall: 3rd, 4th, 5th, 13th, 14th, 21st, 22nd, 30th, 31st

Most Stressful Days Overall: 10th, 11th, 12th, 17th, 18th, 24th, 25th

Best Days for Love: 8th, 9th, 17th, 18th, 26th, 27th, 28th

Best Days for Money: 3rd, 4th, 8th, 9th, 13th, 14th, 17th, 18th, 21st, 22nd, 26th, 27th, 28th, 30th, 31st

For the past few months you have made many personal sacrifices in order to pursue career interests. Now, though you are still ambitious, you're getting close to the time when you can start to shape events as you like. There will be less of having to obey orders and more of doing what you want. There will be less enforced diplomacy and toadying to others and more self-assertion. This has not happened yet but it's about to. Take this month (especially since Mars, your Ruler, is retrograde until the 24th) to consider the kind of conditions and circumstances you would wish to create. This is an activity well worth the time. When the moment of 'liberation' comes you will be ready.

Though your ambitions are still strong this is a more spiritual month for you. Meditation, charitable and volunteer activities are favourable and profitable. Pay off old debts this month, whether they are financial or emotional. Clear the mental and psychological decks for the coming spring.

You won't believe the inrush of energy and vitality that comes to you after March 21st. And while the spring season always brings you added energy, this is unique. This spring there is a Heavenly Grand Formation in Fire Signs (and Aries is one). People will look at you and say: 'Now there's a person who has got *it*'. Your health is, needless to say, very good. And when Mars, your Ruler, starts going forward after the 24th it will get even better. You can do the work of 10 people, with plenty of energy left over for fun and games.

This is basically a fun month, especially after the 21st. Schedule joyful, fun activities – you deserve a holiday.

Money and romance come to you but they are not priorities right now. You seem calm and dispassionate about these things. Financial dreams are coming true, yet you are nonchalant about them. You just want to have fun. Truthfully, you are more interested in friendship than in romance; friendship is less complicated and less time-consuming. Those of you who fancy an Aries take note. Be their friend and you will endear yourselves to them.

April

Best Days Overall: 1st, 9th, 10th, 18th, 19th, 26th, 27th, 28th

Most Stressful Days Overall: 7th, 8th, 14th, 15th, 20th, 21st

Best Days for Love: 7th, 8th, 14th, 15th, 16th, 17th, 26th, 27th, 28th

Best Days for Money: 1st, 2nd, 3rd, 7th, 8th, 9th, 10th, 16th, 17th, 18th, 19th, 26th, 27th, 28th

Most of the planets have shifted now to the Eastern sector of your Horoscope. This is the sector that emphasizes self-assertion, getting one's way, self-indulgence and the power to create conditions and circumstances. Being naturally an 'Eastern sector' type, you feel very comfortable about things now. This is how you like to operate. 'I will be true to myself, do what I want to do, and let the chips fall where they may.' Yes, with the Sun in your own Sign and with Mars, your Ruler, in Fire Signs, you are a 'super' Aries this month – with all the wonderful virtues (and problems) that go with it.

Your personal confidence is so strong now that it is difficult for you to see another's point of view or position on things. This could cause some trouble with a partner or lover later in the month – around the 15th – triggered by the Lunar Eclipse in your 7th House of Love. This will be a real test to your relationship – a 'make-or-break' point. Whether or not this particular relationship survives is up to you, but you will have love in your life either way.

Crises for you are merely 'dangerous opportunities'. Those of you involved with Ariens should understand that they are not really responsible for being overbearing and for having apparently domineering tendencies. With all this fire around they just can't help themselves. There is no malice intended on their part. If you truly love your Aries partner or lover, roll with the punches now, and give in on the little things. Don't escalate the problem. It's not a question of who is right or wrong, but of understanding the forces you are dealing with.

The positive side to all of this is that Aries is going to accomplish 10 times what the normal person accomplishes this month – so long as the energy is directed constructively. The energy of Aries is equal to any task, even the labours of Hercules.

This is a month of personal pleasure and indulgence, a month of unusual physical activity when you excel at sports and exercise regimes. You are truly who you are, without compromise, this month.

Finances become important later in the month as both the Sun and Mercury move into your 2nd House of Money. Earning power is strong. Money is made through lucky speculations and through sales activity. The Solar Eclipse of the 29th also occurs in your Money House, foreshadowing a major change in your financial life. A short-term upheaval – caused perhaps by your new-found financial strength – leads to long-term adjustments that were long overdue. Financial attitudes and the financial picture in general will improve.

May

Best Days Overall: 6th, 7th, 8th, 15th, 16th, 24th, 25th

Most Stressful Days Overall: 4th, 5th, 11th, 12th, 17th, 18th

Best Days for Love: 6th, 7th, 8th, 11th, 12th, 15th, 16th, 17th, 26th, 27th, 28th

Best Days for Money: 6th, 7th, 8th, 15th, 16th, 17th, 24th, 25th, 26th, 27th, 28th

The planets are evenly dispersed between the top and bottom halves of your Solar Horoscope this month, showing that you've got your career and emotional life in the proper perspective. You are neither overly ambitious nor overly family-orientated: a very balanced attitude. Most of the planets are now concentrated in the East – a very comfortable pattern for you – giving you freedom to be who you are and to create the conditions and circumstances that you desire. You have scope now to express your natural sense of independence and initiative. All of this bodes well for you this month, Aries – only remember that 40 per cent of the planets are now retrograde, making other people more cautious and less prone to action. Be patient with them.

Your paths of greatest fulfilment this month involve

enhancing your personal image, detoxification regimes, exercise, religious studies and money-making.

Venus, the planet that rules both your love life and finances, is in your own Sign of Aries until the 17th. This lends glamour to your personal appearance and makes you more attractive to others. It also tends to soften your self-assertiveness, which can be a turn-off to potential partners. You are less brash about getting your own way. You can achieve as much with charm as with brute force. In love, it shows that your partner is catering to your wishes – putting your interests ahead of his or her own. You call the shots in the relationship now.

Union with your beloved is exceptionally close and intimate. After the 17th your partner becomes more financially supportive. Singles will tend to look for someone who can do them some good financially, and they are likely to find such a person.

Finances are positive all month, but especially after the 17th when your Money Planet (Venus) moves into your (2nd) Money House. It is not only more comfortable there, but operates near the peak of its power. You will have unusual control of your spending and your earnings. You will create financial circumstances rather than be their victim. Money will come to you in pleasurable ways. Thus you will earn more and enjoy the way you earn it as well.

Your health is excellent all month, and when Mars, your Ruler, moves into Virgo on the 25th you are going to start becoming exceptionally health- and diet-conscious.

June

Best Days Overall: 3rd, 4th, 12th, 13th, 20th, 21st, 30th

Most Stressful Days Overall: 1st, 2nd, 7th, 8th, 9th, 14th, 15th

Best Days for Love: 5th, 6th, 7th, 8th, 9th, 16th, 17th, 25th, 26th

Best Days for Money: 3rd, 4th, 5th, 6th, 12th, 13th, 16th, 17th, 20th, 21st, 22nd, 23rd, 24th, 25th, 26th, 30th

Though you are making good progress towards your goals, the fact that 50 per cent of the planets are retrograde this month shows that most of the people around you are experiencing delay and being inactive. You need to be patient with all these slow pokes, especially if you are in a leadership position. In general – because you are so action-orientated – you are not comfortable with this kind of inertia. Victory over frustration this month is the greatest triumph you can achieve.

The planets are evenly balanced in the different sectors of your Horoscope this month, creating in you a nice balanced perspective on things. You are neither overly self-assertive nor too eager to please others, neither overly ambitious nor a couch potato. You seem able to give to each area of life its due.

Your paths of greatest fulfilment and happiness this month lie in money-making, physical intimacy, religious studies, higher education and – after the 10th – intellectual pursuits and sales projects.

Happily most of your important planets are moving forward this month. Mars (your Ruler), Saturn (your Career Planet) and Venus (your Love and Money Planet) are all moving ahead. Therefore you are miraculously succeeding and moving forward while all around you are standing still. Of course you are affected by the general climate to some degree, but nowhere near to the extent other people are.

Earnings are very strong until the 10th. On the 10th a sudden financial windfall comes through a friend or through some political or professional organization to which you belong. Money is earned pleasurably and you may buy some luxury item that you've coveted for a while. After the 10th you must work harder for your money, which comes through sales and communication activities. But take note: Mercury, the Lord of Communication, is retrograde. You are not in a position to avoid communication projects but must take more care with them. Nail down all details. Check your phones and equipment so that they don't fail you when you really need them. Be more conscious and careful when you handle computers, phones, faxes, copiers and the like. They are more likely to be temperamental than usual now. Make sure other parties get your true message, and when customers respond to you make sure that you understand them completely. A little extra care will prevent a lot of wasted time later on.

Your love life also goes smoothly – until the 10th; after then, be ultra careful of how you communicate with your lover. Misunderstandings can cause real spats. All of this gets resolved after the 17th, when Mercury goes direct again. Rest and relax more after the 22nd.

July

Best Days Overall: 1st, 9th, 10th, 17th, 18th, 27th, 28th, 29th

Most Stressful Days Overall: 5th, 6th, 11th, 12th, 25th, 26th

Best Days for Love: 5th, 6th, 7th, 8th, 15th, 16th, 25th, 26th

Best Days for Money: 1st, 7th, 8th, 9th, 10th, 15th, 16th, 17th, 18th, 20th, 21st, 25th, 26th, 27th, 28th

The Heavenly Grand Square that dominated the past month is dissipating this month. By the 11th it will be gone, easing the general sense of crisis in the air. Fifty per cent of the planets are retrograde, so the feeling of inertia is still very strong. You need patience and an ability to relax and 'not do'.

By the 11th, the overwhelming percentage of planets will

be in the Western sector of your Solar Horoscope, joining Mars, your Ruling Planet, which has been there for a quite a while now. You are going to have to temper your fiery, independent Aries nature a bit. You are not as independent as you'd like to be. You must adapt yourself – however difficult this may be for you – to the needs and whims of others and to conditions set by others. If you fight this, as you are likely to do, the consequences could be quite traumatic. Better to go with the flow of events and not 'kick against the pricks'. Master the social graces and put others ahead of yourself and your own needs and desires will naturally be fulfilled. Make special efforts to understand where others are coming from and what their needs are. You can't do it on your own right now; you need them.

You are the type of person who believes that strength comes from personal power, but this month you will learn that there is a strength in 'weakness' as well. This is quite evident in your social life. Your inability to assert yourself the way you usually do makes you unusually popular with your partner. This is understandable, for you are catering to his or her every whim. You are also pursuing social objectives with great vim and vigour after the 22nd. You are on a 'charm offensive', determined to sweep the object of your desire off his or her feet. Only remember to use charm, not brute force. Your partner or lover will enjoy the pleasures of the home and hearth during this period. Entertain him or her at home in intimate and comfortable surroundings. Eat in. Watch films on video. Make your partner feel emotionally secure, particularly because he or she is unusually sensitive this month. Little things hurt a lot, so take care.

Finances don't seem a great priority this month. Financial opportunities do present themselves, however, from your family or from real estate deals. People from your early childhood reappear to offer financial openings. Best to make your home base secure this month and let your career develop as it will. There's not much you can do about your career situation until Uranus and Neptune start going forward again. But you can take positive steps to make your home base more perfect and more secure. Rest and relax more until the 22nd.

August

Best Days Overall: 5th, 6th, 14th, 15th, 24th, 25th

Most Stressful Days Overall: 1st, 2nd, 7th, 8th, 21st, 22nd, 28th, 29th

Best Days for Love: 1st, 2nd, 5th, 6th, 14th, 15th, 26th, 27th, 28th, 29th

Best Days for Money: 5th, 6th, 14th, 15th, 16th, 17th, 26th, 27th

Some of the obstacles of recent months are disappearing now but it is unwise to think that you can go it alone just yet. The planetary power is still overwhelmingly focused in the Western half of your chart. With Mars, your Ruler, in your 7th House of Social Activities all month, you are still very much dependent on others and their good will. This is a difficult pill for you to swallow, but it does have its good points. You are involved in 'people-pleasing' and putting other people ahead of yourself, and this is making you more popular. Your love life gets better and better as the months go by. Also you are learning that there are other ways of getting things done than by using brute force and energy, such as consensus, discussion and negotiation.

As the month begins there is only a slight dominance of the upper half of your Horoscope, but towards the end the upper half gets increasingly empowered. Thus your ambitions in the world become activated, though you are still confronted with inertia in this department. The Cosmos is signalling that you should prepare now for career expansion later on. Develop the social contacts you need and do all the work assigned to you with zest, gusto and perfectionism, even if some of the work is menial. More important assignments will come later on.

Your paths of greatest fulfilment this month are religious studies, foreign travel, love and romance, personal creativity, parties and fun.

Talking of fun, this month seems like one long party. You are in such high spirits that a spontaneous jaunt to a foreign land could happen out of the blue. All the goods of the Cosmos are constantly being offered us, but if we are not in the right mood – the right frame of mind – we have difficulty accepting them. But now you *are* in the right frame of mind. And you should enjoy yourself now, for after the 23rd the demands of work call you and you will heed them. You become very busy at work.

Your health is very good all month. You can enhance it even further by expressing yourself creatively, keeping harmony with your children and lover and maintaining a purer diet.

Finances are much better now than they have been in recent months. Speculations are favourable. Your creativity translates into cash. Money is earned in pleasurable ways, by doing things that you love. Until the 23rd money comes easily and is spent easily. Your financial optimism is sky high. Prudence comes after the 23rd.

September

Best Days Overall: 2nd, 10th, 11th, 20th, 21st, 29th, 30th

Most Stressful Days Overall: 4th, 5th, 17th, 18th, 19th, 24th, 25th

Best Days for Love: 4th, 5th, 12th, 13th, 14th, 24th, 25th

Best Days for Money: 2nd, 4th, 5th, 10th, 11th, 12th, 13th, 14th, 20th, 21st, 24th, 25th, 29th, 30th

The weight of planetary power in the Western sector of your Horoscope – though unnatural for you – is having many positive side-effects. Your concern for others, willingness to put their interests ahead of your own and great adaptability to situations are making you popular indeed. More than that, by transcending your natural inclinations you are becoming a deeper, more perceptive person. You can see now which areas of your character need to be transformed, and you are ready and willing to do so. This will be a good part of your work for the next few months.

The planetary power is becoming increasingly weighted above the horizon of your chart. Your ambitions in the world are becoming ever more important. And since these ambitions can only be realized through other people, you are learning patience. This is important, for you can't – at least not now – make it all happen. You have to let career success take its own course – as it will. You are learning the miracle of detachment, another trait that is basically uncharacteristic of you.

Your paths of greatest happiness this month are your love and social life, the achievement of work goals, being of practical service to others, religious studies, higher education and foreign travel.

You are very much in social demand this month. A current relationship is unusually romantic and, after the 7th, very physically passionate as well. Singles find serious romantic love this month. Until the 16th romantic rendezvous occur in some odd places – doctors' surgeries, hospitals – and in the workplace. After the 16th, love comes through parties and social functions. Art galleries, jewellery shops and places that market fashionable clothes and accessories are likely meeting places. Those of you involved in serious, long-term relationships will find this a good month to pop the big question. Marriage is very much on your mind.

As mentioned earlier, your financial success seems totally dependent on your social success, especially after the 16th. Before then you earn money in the usual way, through your work. Your social contacts are a secret form of wealth that doesn't appear in any financial statement, yet is working in your favour. If you are rich in real friends you are rich indeed.

Rest and relax more after the 23rd.

October

Best Days Overall: 7th, 8th, 9th, 17th, 18th, 26th, 27th

Most Stressful Days Overall: 1st, 2nd, 15th, 16th, 22nd, 23rd, 28th, 29th

Best Days for Love: 3rd, 4th, 15th, 16th, 22nd, 23rd, 24th, 25th

Best Days for Money: 3rd, 4th, 7th, 8th, 9th, 10th, 11th, 15th, 16th, 17th, 18th, 24th, 25th, 26th, 27th

The planetary power is still very much in the Western sector of your chart and three powerful planets activate your 7th House of Love, Marriage and Social activities. You are in one of the social peak periods of your year, with all the happiness and the challenges that go with this. Nothing is ever black or white. Every positive has a negative and every negative its positive. Duality is built into the very fabric of our universe. Thus you are now socially popular, very much in demand and basically getting on with others. You are forced to exercise your social gifts rather than your normal martial gifts. You get to perceive the universe as others perceive it. You get a glimpse of yourself through other people's eyes – and the result of this can be quite shocking. For others see you very differently from the way you see yourself. You can now see the power in powerlessness and the advantages of weakness. A whole new vista of understanding opens up to you.

As in previous months, this is not a time to go it alone. Get things done through partnerships and co-operative efforts.

Look for consensus wherever possible and avoid acting without consulting partners and interested parties. Put other people ahead of yourself and fulfil their needs before you fulfil your own. Before trying to change anything, do your best to adapt to existing conditions. Play out the hand that the Cosmos has dealt you as skilfully as possible. The time for personal creation will come in due course.

Though you are unlikely to let others define your personality - - you are much too centred and strong to fall into that trap – it is nevertheless healthy to see the dichotomy between your perception of yourself and other people's perception of you. Your own sense of self will thus tend to be enlarged.

Rest and relax more until the 24th. Social harmony and harmony with your partner will actually enhance your physical well being. Work towards harmony.

Your paths of greatest happiness are your love life, romance, physical intimacy, elimination and transformation, religious studies, higher education and foreign travel.

November

Best Days Overall: 4th, 5th, 14th, 15th, 23rd

Most Stressful Days Overall: 11th, 12th, 18th, 19th, 25th

Best Days for Love: 2nd, 3rd, 4th, 14th, 15th, 18th, 19th, 23rd, 24th

Best Days for Money: 2nd, 3rd, 4th, 5th, 6th, 7th, 14th, 15th, 23rd, 24th

A very interesting, happy and active month. The universe speeds forward, and you along with it. It's almost as if you are not doing it – a strange feeling for you – but are simply swept up by events. Rest assured that the cosmic currents are pulling you to a happier shore.

The planetary power is still mostly in the Western sector of your chart, further reinforcing the changes and events of last month. Your good is coming through others; your job is to adapt yourself to conditions as best you can. No need to assert yourself or force things. Just let things happen.

Between 90 and 100 per cent of the planets - an incredible percentage - are above the horizon of your chart, continuing to spur your ambitions and your need for outward, career security.

Your paths of greatest happiness are elimination and transformation, physical intimacy, religious studies, foreign travel, higher education, love and romance.

Overall you are in one of the happiest and most fortunate periods of your year, perhaps your life. Your health is excellent and your vitality supercharged. The Fire element dominates the month, which suits you just fine. Great expansion is occurring for you on many levels: in your philosophical understanding, your love life and in your financial life. New vistas open up to you in all these areas.

In both love and finance matters, spend the early part of the month paying off debts, getting rid of any excess possessions and romantic prospects that drain you, and cut expenses. In love focus on quality rather than quantity. This will prepare you for the great expansion that occurs after the 3rd. Huge and happy financial windfalls are coming to you. Great earning opportunities are in the works. Your entire financial and social life is being changed.

This is a month of boundless optimism. A foreign trip is very likely and very favourable. Singles meet that special someone this month, someone wealthy, prominent, refined and educated. Marrieds make fortunate business connections. People who are ready, willing and able to make your financial goals come true. Earnings come easy and spending seems lavish.

December

Best Days Overall: 1st, 2nd, 11th, 12th, 20th, 21st, 28th, 29th

Most Stressful Days Overall: 8th, 9th, 16th, 17th, 22nd, 23rd

Best Days for Love: 3rd, 4th, 13th, 14th, 16th, 17th, 24th

Best Days for Money: 1st, 2nd, 3rd, 4th, 11th, 12th, 13th, 14th, 20th, 21st, 24th, 28th, 29th, 31st

You are still in one of the happiest periods of what is essentially a happy year. Your strength and vitality are strong – especially until the 23rd – and your mind is being expanded in extraordinary ways. You're nearly ready to enter the heights of career success and public acclaim. The planets are making a major shift from the Western sector of your chart – an inherently uncomfortable position for you – into the Eastern sector. Moreover, all the planets are going forward. What more can an Aries ask for? You are back in charge, acting with little obstruction, achieving what you set out to achieve and having plenty of energy with which to achieve it. Your days of people-pleasing and dependency are over. You can and should assert yourself now and have things your way. You can be yourself without compromise or apology.

Ninety to 100 per cent of the planets (all of them except the Moon) are above the horizon of your chart this month. Thus you are unusually career-driven and unusually conscious of your duty to life and to the world. You dare not look back this month but must keep your eyes fixed on the goal. You will have plenty of time to reminisce and to come to terms with the past in future months. This month think only of the future. Great career activity and success are taking place. Changes in the corporate set-up or hierarchy are leaving openings and opportunities that you are uniquely qualified to fill. You are called upon to exercise just and legitimate power, both over yourself and over others. You are the born leader this month and your administrative skills are sharper now.

Your paths of greatest fulfilment are your love life, religious studies, foreign travel, higher education, the career and, towards the end of the month, friendships and group activities.

Unusually high career demands tend to drain your superabundant vitality after the 23rd. Try to rest and relax more and plan your activities more efficiently. Your health can be enhanced by a better understanding of the philosophy of health and disease, prayer and metaphysical studies and by keeping things harmonious with parents and superiors.

Taurus

♉

THE BULL

Birthdays from
21st April
to 20th May

Personality Profile

TAURUS AT A GLANCE

Element – Earth

Ruling planet – Venus
Career planet – Uranus
Love planet – Pluto
Money planet – Mercury
Planet of wealth and good fortune – Jupiter

Colours – earth tones, green, orange, yellow

Colours that promote love, romance and social harmony – red-violet, violet

Colours that promote earning power – yellow, yellow-orange

Gems – coral, emerald

Metal – copper

Scents – bitter almond, rose, vanilla, violet

Quality – fixed (= stability)

Quality most needed for balance – flexibility

Strongest virtues – endurance, loyalty, patience, stability, a harmonious disposition

Deepest needs – comfort, material ease, wealth

Characteristics to avoid – rigidity, stubbornness, tendency to be overly possessive and materialistic

Signs of greatest overall compatibility – Virgo, Capricorn

Signs of greatest overall incompatibility – Leo, Scorpio, Aquarius

Sign most helpful to career – Aquarius

Sign most helpful for emotional support – Leo

Sign most helpful financially – Gemini

Sign best for marriage and/or partnerships – Scorpio

Sign most helpful for creative projects – Virgo

Best Sign to have fun with – Virgo

Signs most helpful in spiritual matters – Aries, Capricorn

Best day of the week – Friday

Understanding the Taurus Personality

Taurus is the most earthy of all the Earth Signs. If you understand that Earth is more than just a physical element, that it is a psychological attitude as well, you will get a better understanding of the Taurus personality.

A Taurus has all the power of action that an Aries has. But Taureans are not satisfied with action for its own sake. Their actions must be productive, practical and wealth-producing. If Taureans cannot see a practical value in an action they will not bother taking that action.

Taureans' forte lies in their power to make real their own or other people's ideas. They are generally not very inventive but they can take another's invention and perfect it, make it more practical and useful. The same is true for all projects. Taureans are not especially keen on starting new projects, but once they get involved they will bring these projects to completion. A Taurus carries everything through. He or she is a finisher and will go the distance as long as no act of God intervenes.

Many people find Taureans too stubborn, conservative, fixed and immovable. This is understandable, because Taureans dislike change – in their environment or in their routine. Taureans even dislike changing their minds! On the other hand, this is their virtue. It is not good for a wheel's axle to waver. The axle must be fixed, stable and unmovable. Taureans are the axle of the wheel of society and the heavens. Without their stability and so-called stubbornness, the wheels of the world (and especially the wheels of commerce) wouldn't turn.

Taureans love routine. A routine, if it is good, has many virtues. It is a fixed – and, ideally, perfect – way of taking care of things. When one allows for spontaneity mistakes can happen, and mistakes cause discomfort and uneasiness – something almost unacceptable to a Taurus. Meddling with Taureans' comfort and security is a sure way to irritate and anger them.

While an Aries loves speed, a Taurus likes things slow. They are slow thinkers – but don't make the mistake of assuming they lack intelligence. On the contrary, Taureans are very intelligent. It's just that they like to chew on ideas, to deliberate and weigh them up. Only after due deliberation is an idea accepted or a decision taken. Taureans are slow to anger – but once aroused, take care!

Finance

Taureans are very money-conscious. Wealth is more important to them than it is to many other Signs. Wealth to a Taurus means comfort and security. Wealth means stability. Where some Zodiac Signs feel that they are spiritually rich if they have ideas, talents or skills, Taureans only feel their wealth when they can see and touch it. Taurus' way of thinking is 'What good is a talent if it has not been translated into a home, furniture, car and swimming pool?'

These are all reasons why Taureans excel in estate agency and agricultural industries. Usually a Taurus will wind up owning land. They love to feel their connection to the Earth. Material wealth began with agriculture, the tilling of the soil. Owning a piece of land was humanity's earliest form of wealth: Taureans still feel that primeval connection.

It is in the pursuit of wealth that Taureans develop their intellectual and communication abilities. Also, in this pursuit of wealth and need to trade with others Taureans are forced to develop some flexibility. It is in the quest for wealth that they learn the practical value of the intellect and come to admire it. If it weren't for the search for wealth and material things Taureans might not try to reach a higher intellect.

Some Taureans are 'born-lucky' people who usually win in any gamble or speculation they make. This luck is due to other factors in their Horoscope and is not part of their essential nature. By nature they are not gamblers. They are hard workers and like to earn what they get. Taureans' innate conservatism makes them abhor unnecessary risks in finance and in other areas of their lives.

Career and Public Image

Being essentially down-to-earth people, simple and uncomplicated, Taureans tend to look up to those who are original, unconventional and inventive. Taureans like their bosses to be creative and original – since they themselves are content to perfect their superiors' brain-waves. They admire people who have a wider social or political consciousness and they feel that someday (when they have all the comfort and security they need) they too would like to be involved in these big issues.

In business affairs Taureans can be very shrewd – and that makes them valuable to their employers. They are never lazy; they enjoy working and getting good results. Taureans don't like taking unnecessary risks and do well in positions of authority, which makes them good managers and supervisors. Their managerial skills are reinforced by their natural talents for organization and handling details, their patience and thoroughness. As mentioned, through their connection with the earth Taureans also do well in farming and agriculture.

In general a Taurus will choose money and earning power over public esteem and prestige. A position that pays more – though it has less prestige – is preferred to a position with a lot of prestige but fewer earnings. Many other Signs do not feel this way, but a Taurus does, especially if there is nothing in his or her personal birth chart that modifies this. Taureans will pursue glory and prestige only if it can be shown that these things have a direct and immediate impact on their wallet.

Love and Relationships

In love, the Taurus-born likes to have and to hold. They are the marrying kind. They like commitment and they like the terms of a relationship to be clearly defined. More importantly, Taureans like to be faithful to one lover and they expect that lover to reciprocate this fidelity. When this doesn't happen the whole world comes crashing down. When they are in love Taureans are loyal, but they are also very possessive. They are capable of great fits of jealousy if they are hurt in love.

Taureans are satisfied with the simple things in a relationship. If you are involved romantically with a Taurus there is no need for lavish entertainments and constant courtship. Give them enough love, food and comfortable shelter and they will be quite content to stay home and enjoy your company. They will be loyal to you for life. Make a Taurus feel comfortable and – above all – secure in the relationship and you will rarely have a problem.

In love, Taureans can sometimes make the mistake of trying to take over their partners, which can cause great pain on both sides. The reasoning behind their actions is basically simple. Taureans feel a sense of ownership over their partners and will want to make changes that will increase their own general comfort and security. This attitude is OK when it comes to inanimate, material things but it can be dangerous when applied to people, so Taureans should be careful and attentive.

Home and Domestic Life

Home and family are vitally important to Taureans. They like children. They also like a comfortable and perhaps glamorous home – something they can show off. They tend to buy heavy, ponderous furniture – usually of the best quality. This is because Taureans like a feeling of substance in their environment. Their house is not only their home but their place of creativity and entertainment as well. The Taureans' home tends to be truly their castle. If they could choose, Taureans would prefer living in the countryside to being city-dwellers. If they can't do so during their working lives, many Taureans like to holiday in or even retire to the country, away from the city and closer to the land.

At home a Taurus is like a country squire – the lord of the manor. They love to entertain lavishly, to make others feel secure in their home and encourage them to derive the same sense of satisfaction as they do from it. If you are invited for dinner at the home of a Taurus you can expect the best food and best entertainment. Be prepared for a tour of the house – which the Taurus treats as a castle – and expect to see your Taurus friend exhibit a lot of pride and satisfaction in his or her possessions.

Taureans like children but they are usually strict with them. The reason for this is they tend to treat their children – as they do most things in life – as their possessions. The positive side to this is that their children will be well cared for and well supervised. They will get every material thing they need to grow up properly. On the down-side, Taureans can get too repressive with their children. If a child dares to upset the daily routine – which Taureans love to follow – he or she will have a problem with a Taurus parent.

Horoscope for 1995

Major Trends

1994, though good and productive, was active, hectic and fraught with changes. And change is not something you are very comfortable with, Taurus. Every time you thought you had a comfortable routine something happened to disturb it. But this year the quickness of change slows down a bit so you feel more at ease. You can proceed at your own pace in life. 1994 was primarily a social and career year. Many of you got married or involved in a significant relationship. Many of you achieved career peaks through considerable effort. It was hard work to manage a love relationship with a demanding partner, and a career with demanding bosses, at the same time. By now you have mastered the juggling act and are ready for new challenges and opportunities.

This year you are less concerned with romance and more concerned with sensual passion. You are less concerned with friends of the heart and more concerned with friends of the mind. The need to weed out the useless and outdated is still as prominent this year as it was last year. But it should go easier for you this year as you have more experience. In terms of your career you have more freedom to experiment this year than you did last year. It is much easier to make changes, to innovate and explore new career paths than it was last year. The truth is that you've been longing to try these things out for years now, but felt inhibited and perhaps afraid. This fear leaves you now and you are free to survey the 'undiscovered territory' of the future.

Health

Your 6th House of Health is not especially prominent this year, Taurus. You are not overly concerned with health issues; this should be interpreted as a good sign. In the case of health, no news is good news. Few of us ever think about our health unless something is amiss. When things are going right we just take good health for granted – this is how it should be. And this is the message of your 1995 Horoscope.

There are other positive health signals in this year's Horoscope as well. Saturn, which for two years has been making stressful aspects to you, has (at the end of 1994) finally moved away. Now it is actually helping you, increasing your vitality and supporting your interests. Uranus and Neptune continue to make spectacular aspects to you for the next few years. And, by the end of the year, Pluto moves away from its long-term stressful aspect to you as well. By the end of the year you will feel as if mighty burdens have been lifted off you. You will brim over with vitality and well-being.

You are in better shape than last year, and next year will be even better than this. The long-term trends are spectacular.

The health of a partner also seems good – much improved over last year. A sibling might undergo some medical procedure – probably at the end of the year – but it all works out well. The health of a parent – your mother if you are a man, your father if you are a woman – is somewhat delicate. He or she should be encouraged to try out new forms of therapy and new approaches to healing.

Home and Domestic Life

Mars makes an unusually long transit through your 4th House of Home and Family interests this year. Aside from this, the domestic scene is relatively quiet and serene. The Cosmos neither helps nor obstructs your plans. There is freedom in the home and with family members.

Mars' four-month transit occurs from 23rd January to 26th May. This signals the paying off of old debts to family members. Past promises should now be fulfilled. These may involve money, service or health care. Clear up your debts and you can proceed with a clear conscience. This is also a time when you are likely to make major renovations in the home, or even move to another place.

It will be hard work to manage your temper and to control emotional outbursts with your family. But you should try. Family disputes are more likely during this four-month period, but they are short term and will blow over quickly.

Your home is likely to be used as a place for meditation or for some spiritual gathering. Astrologers and psychics frequent your home.

The home and family will again become prominent in your life from 23rd July to 23rd August. You will want to stay home more, spend more time with your family and give and receive emotional support. Your home and family become sources of particular pleasure this period. In addition, many psychological areas become illuminated during this time. This will increase your emotional well-being.

You are much more focused on friendships and career than on family issues this year, and the wonderful thing is that your family doesn't obstruct you in these pursuits.

Love and Social Life

Your 7th House of Love and Marriage is emphasized in this year's Horoscope, Taurus. Not as much as last year to be sure, and not as strongly as other areas, but it is still prominent. 1994 was a year of great social expansion; many new friends came into your life and romance blossomed. Many of you married or remarried. Yet Pluto, the Lord of Transformation and Elimination, is still in your House of Love for most of the year. The message here is that there is unfinished business with old relationships that needs to be taken care of. Yes, you have a new marriage, romance and social life, but you still need to sever ties with an old romantic partner. You have been clinging to old connections, and this is no longer necessary. By the time the year is out and Pluto finally finishes the job in your Love House, these old connections, bonds and attachments will be gone.

The need to focus on quality over quantity – which was important last year – continues to be important. You don't need a whole lot of second-rate friends. A few first-rate ones are sufficient.

By nature you are a sensually-orientated person – perhaps the most sensually-orientated of the entire Zodiac. You appreciate things that are tangible and real, that you can feel, see and touch. This sensuality becomes even more prominent in your love and romantic life this year. You are more concerned with physical intimacy within a relationship than with romantic niceties. You show your love in physical, sensual ways rather than with flowers or gifts. (Those of you involved with a Taurus should take note.)

Unlike in previous years, your partner is becoming

progressively less demanding as the year goes on. He or she shifts focus, with ever increasing intensity, away from you and onto finances.

Those of you who are looking for a second marriage have the most interesting love life of all. It is filled with ups, downs, sudden changes, idealism and experimentation. 'Experimental' is indeed the best way to describe your love life this year. It is as if you are striking out into the unknown. You know that the old ways of relating are no longer valid for you. You know you want love, but you're not exactly sure of what you're looking for. You try this and that, you make discoveries and suffer a few failures. Every failure brings you closer to your heart's desire, for you learn what it is you don't want. You find love suddenly, unexpectedly, out of the blue -- and break-ups can happen just as suddenly. But as the process continues you will find the perfect partner, perhaps by the time the year is out.

Those of you working towards a third marriage are also experimenting this year, but you need to exercise some caution. Don't be reckless with your feelings. Experiment by all means, but do so within safe and traditional boundaries. A current love affair needs more time to mature, so delay marriage until you're absolutely sure of things in your own mind. Don't marry while there are doubts.

Career and Finance

Your career and your place in society definitely take priority over mere money-making this year, Taurus. Of course money-making – your earning ability – is always important to you, for this is your nature. But it is less important this year. On the career front much of the stress and pressure has been lifted this year. You have much more freedom and leeway to explore different career paths and to examine different techniques within your field. Bosses, elders and superiors are more laid-back towards you than they have been in the past. You've demonstrated your worth and abilities in the past two years and they seem satisfied.

You've had the urge to experiment with your career for many years now. However, in the past two to three years this urge has been thwarted, either by others or by your own fears. These blockages are now removed and you are free to discover your ideal. Make no mistake, you are idealistic about your career now. You want the highest and the best, but are not quite sure what it is. Trial and error will be your teacher. Mistakes have nowhere near the dreaded consequences that you once thought they would have. Your falls are cushioned by a higher power and you just pick yourself up and try again. You are being led to a public success that is beyond your fondest dreams. Keep the faith.

Your 2nd House of Money is not a House of Power this year, thus there is great freedom and latitude in your earnings. You have more personal control over your possessions than usual. The Cosmos neither helps nor obstructs your earning talents. But you would much rather have the respect of your peers and of society at large than a big bank account.

Whether you are earning money personally or not, you find yourself supplied. In fact, you might do better just to focus your efforts on making money for other people – enhancing the prosperity of others, especially your partner – than thinking about your own earnings. Your own will just come to you naturally. A deeper law of the universe is being revealed to you through this.

A partner is really prospering this year and is very generous with you. Money comes to you from insurance settlements and law suits that work in your favour. Stocks, bonds or mutual funds that you own rise of their own accord and with little effort on your part. You are remembered in someone's will. Writers and inventors get larger than expected royalty checks. Money comes to you, but not so much through your own personal effort – lest your ego get overly swollen.

This is a happy financial year in many other ways as well. Debts are paid off rather easily. If you are looking for investors for your projects, you attract them quite effortlessly. Your credit rating gets a boost and you have greater access to other people's capital.

Mercury is the Lord of Taurus' finances and its movements and positions should be followed with special care – especially its retrogrades (travels backward) – before financial actions are planned or taken. You can follow these ever-changing fluctuations by looking at the month-by-month forecasts, below.

Self-improvement

You can improve your intellectual abilities (not only this year but in any year) by observing the phases of the Moon. Following these lunar phases will clear up a lot of mystery about your intellectual abilities. In the past when you may have underperformed you were probably in a waning lunar cycle, or perhaps the Moon was receiving stressful aspects. Had you known when the Moon was waxing instead of waning you would have done better. Your intellectual rhythms follow the Moon. Try to do your communications, studies and exam-taking when the Moon waxes and you will always do better. There is more intellectual energy available to you at these times.

Your interest in dreams and in-depth psychology is very much stimulated and expanded this year. Your understanding of these subjects will grow with almost no effort on your part. The opportunities to delve into these things will come to you. You are learning how to re-invent yourself this year. This ability enables you to discard outmoded patterns of behaviour and to create new ones that are happier for you. If you follow the process of re-invention to its logical conclusion, you will ultimately discover the secrets of life. It all depends on how deep you choose to go.

Your 11th House of Friends and Scientific Interests is an important area this year. But this area is going to require some work and discipline on your part. Many improvements are going to be made this year – and for the long term – but you have to co-operate and whip this part of your life into shape. You are forced to study and master complex technological subjects. You are also forced to 'weed out' old friends and to focus on quality rather than quantity, for you cannot be a social butterfly this year and still give all your friends their due. If they are truly your friends they will understand this 'neglect'. If they are not, you will have to deal with their resentment. You will be forced to learn the art of forgiveness when friends disappoint your expectations, and you will learn to forgive yourself as well.

Month-by-month Forecasts

January

Best Days Overall: 1st, 2nd, 10th, 11th, 19th, 20th, 21st, 28th, 29th

Most Stressful Days Overall: 3rd, 4th, 17th, 18th, 24th, 25th, 30th, 31st

Best Days for Love: 5th, 6th, 7th, 8th, 15th, 16th, 17th, 18th, 19th, 24th, 25th, 26th, 27th

Best Days for Money: 1st, 2nd, 7th, 8th, 12th, 13th, 17th, 18th, 22nd, 23rd, 26th, 27th, 30th, 31st

This is a powerful and good month for you, Taurus, but most of the action comes from other people and not so much through your own efforts. Though you go 'out of bounds' in your pursuit of earnings and financial opportunities (especially early in the month), the real money doesn't come from this gargantuan effort. Rather it comes from business or romantic partners, from outside investors and from the fortuitous settlement of insurance claims or legal cases. Focus on helping others to prosper – especially from the 14th to the 16th – and your own prosperity will follow naturally. You have a real knack right now for assisting others in their pursuit of wealth – use it.

Those of you who are in debt will find these debts paid off easily and pleasantly. Your credit rating is boosted as well. Only be careful not to create new debts as other people's money seems so easy to attain. A partner is unusually prosperous this month and unusually generous with you. You are remembered in someone's will.

Your love life is especially good this month as well. Your interests have shifted, however, from courtship and romance to the exploration of physical intimacy with your partner. It's as if you have entered a new stage in your relationship. Physical intimacy is unusually thrilling.

Until the 20th give your attention to travel opportunities that come your way and to higher educational pursuits. After the 20th focus on both your career and your home. This will be the time – if you choose – to make your home a showcase you can be proud of. This doesn't mean that you have to emulate the 'rich and famous' – just bring your home up to your personal expression of what is best. Your family is very supportive of your career after the 20th. You can go ahead with your plans assured of their backing. The New Moon of the 30th, which occurs in your 10th House of Career, will clear up any confusion you have about your work.

Your health is unusually good until the 20th, but after that rest and relax more. Be careful of over-eating and other forms of personal over-indulgence. Enjoy life by all means, but don't overdo it.

February

Best Days Overall: 6th, 7th, 16th, 17th, 24th, 25th

Most Stressful Days Overall: 13th, 14th, 15th, 20th, 21st, 26th, 27th, 28th

Best Days for Love: 3rd, 4th, 5th, 6th, 7th, 13th, 14th, 16th, 17th, 20th, 21st, 22nd, 23rd, 24th, 25th

Best Days for Money: 3rd, 4th, 5th, 8th, 9th, 10th, 13th, 14th, 15th, 18th, 19th, 22nd, 23rd, 26th, 27th, 28th

Eighty to 90 per cent of the planets are clustered at the top half of your Solar Horoscope, denoting an intense drive for career success and, consequently, less interest in family and emotional concerns. Have no fear about this. There are times in life when we do need to emphasize one thing over another – not for too long, mind you, but for a while. This is one of those times. By all means push for that promotion, reach out for more responsibility and advance yourself or your business. Take steps to increase your status and prestige in your company or industry.

Outside the business world, the world of politics might beckon. You seem called upon to exercise power and authority in order to serve the public good. You might do this directly or by getting involved with – on a supportive level – those who are doing this.

All of this ambition can be tiring, especially since so much of it involves a sacrifice of domestic and personal interests. Try to rest and relax more until the 20th. After that your vitality returns, stronger than ever.

Don't ignore your social life either, which seems happy and filled with passion. A partner or lover continues to prosper this month and continues his or her generosity towards you. Investments continue to be profitable as well. Your lover or partner is intensely focused on money matters, while you are focused on career and higher education. In spite of this divergence of interests there is still harmony between you.

In your personal finances you still need to exercise caution, as Mercury, your Money Planet, is retrograde until the 16th. Avoid making long-range financial commitments, signing contracts or making major purchases until after the 16th. Do all the leg-work but withhold any commitments. Tradition holds that Mercury in the Sign of Aquarius (where it will be all month) is in its 'exaltation'. That is, it reaches its highest and most powerful expression. This is a wonderful financial signal for you, especially after the 16th. Your financial judgement will be sound and trustworthy. You will be able to conceive of very big ideas. You will have special abilities to communicate your financial ideas or plans to others, especially to groups or to your elders. Your fondest financial dreams come true this month, only to be replaced by new dreams.

March

Best Days Overall: 5th, 6th, 15th, 16th, 24th, 25th

Most Stressful Days Overall: 7th, 13th, 14th, 19th, 20th, 26th, 27th

Best Days for Love: 3rd, 4th, 8th, 9th, 13th, 14th, 17th, 18th, 19th, 20th, 21st, 26th, 27th, 28th

Best Days for Money: 3rd, 4th, 8th, 9th, 13th, 14th, 19th, 20th, 21st, 22nd, 28th, 29th, 30th, 31st

As has been the case for the past few months, the overwhelming majority of the planets are clustered in the upper hemisphere of your Solar chart, denoting ambition and the drive for social and professional recognition. These drives remain basically unchanged. What is changing is the planetary shift over to the Eastern sector of your Horoscope.

This is giving you a greater amount of self-assertiveness and greater control over circumstances. You are beginning to call the shots now and others will have to adjust to you rather than vice versa.

Whether you create your own conditions or are forced to adapt to conditions, you have certain perks and challenges. When you are forced to adapt you feel less empowered but there is also less responsibility. When you create conditions you feel more empowered but along with this comes increased responsibility. As you make this shift now to greater empowerment make sure that the conditions and circumstances that you create are desirable not only for yourself but for others as well. Inadequate planning can be disastrous and you will have to live with the consequences.

In addition to all the planets at the top of your chart, Venus, your Ruler, also moves into the most elevated position of the chart. This reinforces your ambition and drive for recognition. And since the aspects are kind to Venus, you will succeed and have plenty of help. This is the time to push for promotions and pay rises. If you are politically active, this is the time to begin a campaign for office. This is a period when you are uniquely qualified to exercise lawful and legitimate administrative or political power.

Now that Mercury is speedily moving forward, finances are much improved over last month. Sound financial judgement – which is basically normal for you – has returned. Financial confidence and faith in the future have returned. Go forward with your deals, investments and financial goals. Until the 15th money comes to you through pay rises or promotions at work. Your willingness to assume responsibility and authority brings more money to you. Elders and superiors help you meet your financial goals. Your partner is still prospering – he or she will prosper all year – and is still generous with you. Your partner is starting to rethink his or her focus on financial matters and wants to concentrate more on your relationship. After the 15th financial opportunities come through friends. You are more generous to your friends and to charities after the 15th as well. Your 'financial intuition' – as opposed to logic – is especially strong after the 15th.

Your health is excellent all month.

April

Best Days Overall: 2nd, 3rd, 11th, 12th, 13th, 20th, 21st, 29th, 30th

Most Stressful Days Overall: 9th, 10th, 16th, 17th, 22nd, 23rd

Best Days for Love: 1st, 7th, 8th, 9th, 16th, 17th, 18th, 25th, 26th, 27th, 28th

Best Days for Money: 1st, 4th, 5th, 6th, 9th, 10th, 18th, 19th, 26th, 27th, 28th

With most of the planets in the Eastern sector of your Horoscope, showing your command over events and circumstances, this is the month for you to make long overdue changes in important aspects of your life. Best to make them now while you are more in control of things than to be forced to make them later on through pressure from others.

Though your physical vitality is strong right now – especially after the 20th – a health check or a complete physical would be prudent. Both the Solar and Lunar Eclipses this month occur in Houses that deal with health – the 1st and the 6th. So, unresolved problems could come to the fore for permanent cleansing. Best to nip them in the bud before they get out of hand. Chances are that you will get a clean bill of health.

Uranus, your Career Planet, makes a major move into your Career House (10th) this month. And though it is not yet ready to abide there permanently – it will retrograde back out in June – it is still a signal for career change. Yes, you are ready to break out of your present career situation and your present status. You want sudden and absolute change. You want more independence in your career – more power to create your own employment conditions and circumstances. And you are getting this independence and power. As a Taurus these feelings are highly unusual, because you are generally conservative and resistant to change. These feelings must have been brewing for a long time. Changes in your corporate structure will help you in your desire for change. You need more freedom and space in your work.

Career changes will not come without cost, however. You are going to have to sacrifice some personal desires and pleasures. You will need to make major changes in the way you look, dress and otherwise 'package' yourself. If you are going to occupy a 'higher' status before the world you will have to look and dress the part.

Finances are wonderful this month. Earnings are strong and your financial confidence is high. Mercury, your Money Planet, moves forward speedily and is involved in a blessed and fortunate Heavenly Grand Aspect until the 17th, making your financial intuition uncanny and revealing much financial help from the celestial powers. Your financial gifts and business abilities are highlighted. After the 17th you become more conservative with money – less intuitive and more careful. Until the 17th you are more generous, giving lavishly to worthy causes. After the 17th you spend more on yourself and your personal needs.

May

Best Days Overall: 9th, 10th, 17th, 18th, 26th, 27th, 28th

Most Stressful Days Overall: 6th, 7th, 8th, 13th, 14th, 19th, 20th

Best Days for Love: 4th, 5th, 6th, 7th, 8th, 13th, 14th, 15th, 16th, 17th, 21st, 22nd, 23rd, 26th, 27th, 28th

Best Days for Money: 1st, 2nd, 3rd, 6th, 7th, 8th, 11th, 12th, 15th, 16th, 19th, 20th, 24th, 25th, 29th, 30th

Career changes initiated last month might be delayed a bit now as Uranus (your Career Planet) goes retrograde. With the Sun moving through your own Sign – the conservative Sign of Taurus – the need for caution is especially great. Change, though desirable, must not be made for its own sake. Change must lead you in the direction you want to go.

But Uranus' retrograde is only part of the story this month. Three other planets are also going retrograde this month, creating a general climate of caution, delay and sometimes stalemate. While other Zodiac Signs might chafe at this you are calm and placid about it. You kind of like a stalemate. You tend to be comfortable with the status quo. And with the favourable aspects you are receiving this month, who could blame you?

You seem exceptionally well balanced this month. The planets are more or less evenly dispersed in the different sectors of your Horoscope. Neither emotional security nor ambitions are overly emphasized. Your personal interests and social urges are in the correct perspective as well.

You are in a period of personal pleasure and self-indulgence now. And few know how to self-indulge as well as a Taurus. Try not to overdo it.

Your health and vitality are superabundant now. You get what you want in charming ways – by hard work and persistence – and in ways that do not turn others off. Your personal magnetism and glamour are strong. Even though your partner may not notice this, other members of the opposite sex do.

In spite of the fact that your partner or lover is in a long-term trend of prosperity, at present there are financial and business delays going on. Your partner is reviewing and remaking his or her own self-image as well. Business ventures need more thought and clarification. These delays no doubt affect his or her generosity towards you – but have no fear, your personal earning power is exceptionally strong now and you make it on your own.

Image and appearance are particularly important in your financial life until the 24th. Sales prospects and others in a position to bring money your way are judging the package rather than what's inside it. Be aware and 'dress for success'. After the 24th, you have more personal control over earnings. You are in a position to create your financial conditions and circumstances and spend and invest as you see fit. Your net worth increases by the time the month is over.

June

Best Days Overall: 5th, 6th, 14th, 15th, 22nd, 23rd, 24th

Most Stressful Days Overall: 3rd, 4th, 10th, 11th, 16th, 17th, 30th

Best Days for Love: 2nd, 5th, 6th, 10th, 11th, 16th, 17th, 19th, 25th, 26th

Best Days for Money: 3rd, 4th, 7th, 8th, 9th, 12th, 13th, 16th, 17th, 20th, 21st, 25th, 26th, 30th

Though there are slightly more planets above the horizon than below it, this could not be considered a terrible imbalance. It reflects a slight bias towards the career and 'outer' ambitions and away from family and emotional security. The Eastern and Western sectors of the chart are also evenly balanced, showing that you are neither overly self-assertive nor overly concerned with others. You have a knack for balancing your own interests with other people's. You achieve your goals this month through both personal creativity and the co-operation of others.

Fifty per cent of the planets are retrograde this month, Taurus – including some of your own very important Lords. Caution, patience and more caution and patience are called for. Of all the Signs you are best equipped to handle bottlenecks and delays. You even feel comfortable with them, as they foster the status quo.

Your paths of greatest happiness and fulfilment involve the enhancement of your appearance, buying clothes and personal accessories, love and romance, physical intimacy, making money for others and – after the 10th – the pursuit of personal wealth.

With Venus, your Ruler, in your own Sign until the 10th you are personally glamorous, magnetic and charismatic. Your appeal to the opposite sex is strong. One would think that your love life would sparkle because of this, but this is not the case now. Your partner is rethinking the current relationship and is unsure where things will go. Moreover, your personal desires and inclinations conflict with those of your partner. You are pulled in opposite directions and this creates a distance between you. Each of you wants to do different things this month. A compromise will solve things. One day do what your partner wants and the next do what you want. This conflict is short term.

Your earning power is very strong all month but especially after the 10th – only you need to work hard, overcome obstacles, deal with the resistance of a friend and possibly a religious organization and be ultra-careful in communicating. Mercury, your Money Planet, is retrograde until the 17th. Do all your financial homework until then but don't sign contracts, make major purchases or commit yourself financially over the long term. Wait till after the 17th. Your review and caution about a career proposal now is very wise. Change will come, but slowly.

Your health is excellent all month.

July

Best Days Overall: 2nd, 3rd, 4th, 11th, 12th, 20th, 21st, 30th, 31st

Most Stressful Days Overall: 1st, 7th, 8th, 13th, 14th, 27th, 28th

Best Days for Love: 7th, 8th, 15th, 16th, 25th, 26th

Best Days for Money: 1st, 5th, 6th, 9th, 10th, 15th, 16th, 17th, 18th, 22nd, 23rd, 26th, 27th, 28th

Most of the planets are still retrograde this month creating a general climate of delay and inaction. The status quo is fostered. Needed changes will probably be delayed because of the necessity for further study, but they will come eventually.

You still have a nice balance between the upper and lower halves of your Solar Horoscope. You continue to keep your career and family life in exactly the right perspective.

Until the 23rd there is a nice balance between the Eastern and Western sectors of your chart. You have an uncanny knack for balancing your own interests with those of others. There is great freedom and flexibility with others. For, if you choose, you can create your own circumstances if other people get too unreasonable, or adapt to the needs of others when they are reasonable. After the 23rd, however, the planets shift into the Western sector of the Horoscope, making you more dependent on others for your success. Thus you have less personal freedom and more of a need to please others.

Your personal earning power is unusually strong during this period and your financial judgement is keen. Mercury, your Money Planet, moves very speedily through three different Signs and Houses this month. This shows financial confidence and different approaches being taken in money-making. Until the 11th you will need your good financial judgement, as there are many obstacles to be dealt with. You have to work harder for your earnings but you are also given the energy and the genius to overcome difficulties. After the 11th, money comes through sales and marketing projects and through neighbours. After the 26th it comes through family connections. Real estate investments seem to attract you all month.

Your love life is much improved over last month – especially until the 23rd. Differences with a lover which have sprung up of late are now resolved. Communication with him or her is much improved. After the 23rd your relationship is stressed due to family matters. Your lover resents you paying so much attention to other family members. Parents object to a current relationship and vice versa. You may tend to side with your family or parents on this issue.

Your health is excellent until the 23rd, but after then rest and relax more.

August

Best Days Overall: 7th, 8th, 16th, 17th, 26th, 27th

Most Stressful Days Overall: 3rd, 4th, 9th, 10th, 24th, 25th, 31st

Best Days for Love: 3rd, 4th, 5th, 6th, 12th, 13th, 14th, 15th, 21st, 22nd, 26th, 27th, 31st

Best Days for Money: 5th, 6th, 14th, 15th, 16th, 17th, 19th, 20th, 26th, 27th

All the slow-moving planets are above the horizon of your chart, while all the short-term, fast-moving planets are below. This shows that over the long term you are ambitious and working to make your mark on the world. But for the short term – especially this month – you are giving much-needed attention to your family and to domestic life. You can't ignore them completely.

This month you are not only interested in your own career but in other people's careers as well. You can promote your own ambitions by fostering the ambitions of others.

The past is very much with you now. Old friends, old lovers and acquaintances – and also old memories – come to you now so that you can better digest past events and move on to the new. Have no fear, you are not living in the past, you are viewing it from a new perspective and putting it all in its proper context. This promotes psychological health and will help you in your career later on. Sudden bursts of nostalgia always have their cosmic purposes.

The planets are overwhelmingly concentrated in the Western half of your chart. Let's face facts, you need other people and their good opinion. You can't allow others to form an incorrect or distorted view of you now, as your key to success lies in what they think of you. Correct false impressions or slanders quickly.

Your paths to greatest fulfilment are the home, family interests, psychological studies, fun activities, parties, personal creativity, achieving work goals and helping others prosper – in their careers and financially.

When you come to terms with your personal past and history you will be in a better position to enjoy all the fun and games that the Cosmos has in store for you after the 23rd. Singles become less marriage-conscious and more fun-orientated. Marrieds become more playful with each other. Personal creativity leads to unexpected earnings. You make money in ways that you love. Speculations are favourable. You have lucky financial breaks and your financial confidence and judgement is strong. Your partner's or lover's income begins to skyrocket this month.

Your love life is also starting to improve this month. Pluto, your Love Planet, finally goes forward after many months of retrograde motion. Your social charisma and confidence are restored. If breaking off with a current love is needed you are not afraid to make the break. You are bolder now. You do what needs to be done.

September

Best Days Overall: 4th, 5th, 12th, 13th, 22nd, 23rd

Most Stressful Days Overall: 6th, 7th, 20th, 21st, 27th, 28th

Best Days for Love: 4th, 5th, 9th, 12th, 13th, 14th, 18th, 19th, 24th, 25th, 27th, 28th

Best Days for Money: 2nd, 6th, 7th, 10th, 11th, 15th, 16th, 20th, 21st, 24th, 25th, 29th, 30th

The planetary power is overwhelmingly in the Western sector of your Horoscope this month. You have to face the facts: you are temporarily dependent on other people for your well-being right now. Though you are not known for being adaptable, this month you must become more so. It is difficult, but at least try. Put other people first; let their interests and desires take precedence over your own. Don't try to make things happen, just let them happen. Do your best to understand other people's feelings, thoughts and positions on things and you will go through this period with flying colours. This is not a month to go it alone.

On the positive side, you are becoming socially more popular and in demand. Career vistas are opening up to you – because of your social popularity – that were not available before. You are becoming less interested in your own family and more interested in other people's families.

Your paths of greatest fulfilment this month are parties, fun activities, personal creativity, the achievement of work goals, being of practical service to others and enhancing the income of others.

Mercury, your Money Planet, moves slowly and cautiously this month and on the 22nd starts to go retrograde. This movement is a reflection of your financial affairs. You are more cautious – perhaps insecure – where finances are concerned. You take longer to decide things. Earnings come in more slowly than usual. This is quite all right – not a financial disaster or collapse but a temporary breathing spell. Use the time, especially after the 22nd, to rethink and perfect your products, services and financial goals. Though you are sorely tempted, avoid rash speculation after the 22nd. Before that, modest speculations could prove profitable.

Whatever your personal financial shortcomings may be, your partner has taken up the slack. He or she has been experiencing financial delays and setbacks of late, but is now back on track. Your partner prospers and is generous with you. In spite of all the delays you can expect an increase in your net worth this month.

Your health is very good all month and you can enhance it even more by maintaining harmony with children and by expressing yourself creatively. Creativity is not only an outlet for all kinds of pent-up emotions, it also lifts you to a higher and healthier energy level. Purity of diet and the right exercise also bolster your health after the 16th.

October

Best Days Overall: 1st, 2nd, 10th, 11th, 20th, 21st, 28th, 29th

Most Stressful Days Overall: 3rd, 4th, 17th, 18th, 24th, 25th, 30th, 31st

Best Days for Love: 3rd, 4th, 5th, 6th, 15th, 16th, 24th, 25th

Best Days for Money: 3rd, 4th, 7th, 8th, 9th, 12th, 13th, 17th, 18th, 22nd, 23rd, 26th, 27th, 30th, 31st

Like last month, the planetary powers – Venus, your Ruler, among them – are overwhelmingly focused in the Western sector of your chart. Moreover, your 7th House of Love, Marriage and Social Activity becomes unusually activated after the 11th. You are less self-assertive, independent and concerned with yourself. Your good comes to you through other people. You put other people ahead of yourself and are perhaps even overly concerned with how other people see you. You value the good opinion of others. It is not enough for you to feel good about yourself or to have a positive opinion of yourself, others must think highly of you as well. Herein lies the difficulty with this kind of configuration, for it is rare for anyone to be universally approved of. There is bound to be some rejection and loss of self-esteem. When others approve of you, your self-esteem is strong; when they disapprove, your self-esteem sinks. This is the down side. On the up side, you are socially popular, well liked and in demand. People enjoy co-operating with you. You can achieve much more through co-operation with others than you ever could on your own, thus your potential for success is greater. And the main asset – though perhaps the most shocking – is that you get to see yourself as others see you.

Seek consensus in all your actions and projects. Consult with people before venturing into anything new. Be aware of how others are likely to react to a given line of action. With Venus as your Ruler you will have an easier time of this than your Arien brothers and sisters (who are also going through similar experiences).

Your health is excellent until the 24th, but after then rest and relax more. Your health and vitality can be enhanced through harmony at your workplace, social accord and peace in your marriage or partnerships. A purer diet will not hurt you, either.

The planetary power is shifting with ever greater intensity above the horizon of your chart, making you more ambitious and worldly. And with Uranus, your Career Planet, finally going direct this month, much positive change is starting to happen there.

By the 14th, 90 per cent of the planets will be going forward. Much of the blockage of recent months is over with. You are in a month of achievement and action – but, as mentioned earlier, consult with others before you act.

November

Best Days Overall: 6th, 7th, 16th, 17th, 25th

Most Stressful Days Overall: 14th, 15th, 21st, 22nd, 27th, 28th

Best Days for Love: 1st, 2nd, 3rd, 4th, 13th, 14th, 15th, 21st, 22nd, 23rd, 24th

Best Days for Money: 4th, 5th, 8th, 9th, 10th, 11th, 12th, 14th, 15th, 21st, 22nd, 23rd

The planets are still concentrated in the Western sector of your chart; 80 to 90 per cent of them are there now. Your social life takes priority over your personal life and desires. Other people's needs come before your own. Conditions created by others are stronger than the conditions that you create. Adapt, adapt, adapt.

Your social life is active, happy and changing. Pluto, your Love Planet, makes a major move – and for good this time – into the Sign of Sagittarius, your 8th Solar House. This has long-term implications for your social life, marriage and romantic interests. Passion and physical intimacy become more important than courtship and romantic niceties. Socially, the need is to eliminate false friends and irrelevant romantic partners and focus on the real and the true. Quality, not quantity, is what counts. Your partner or lover becomes almost totally involved in money-making and prospers greatly. You will be remembered in someone's will. Major long-term changes are taking place in your investments and in your dealings with investors. Those of you who have no investment portfolio will now start to acquire one; those of you who have one will change its contents radically. Debts are paid easily this month and investors attracted effortlessly. Your credit line (or your ability to borrow in other ways) is probably increased.

The planets are now mostly above the horizon of your chart, fostering your ambitions and your need for outward, career security. You want to feel confident in your niche in society.

Your paths of greatest fulfilment this month are your love life, physical intimacy, helping others prosper, elimination and transformation and the achievement of work goals.

Your finances are getting better, though perhaps they are not as strong as your partner's. The earnings of your partner are simply stupendous and difficult to match. But your personal financial confidence is strong and your financial judgement is sound. Early in the month money is earned through work. After the 4th, money comes through your partner and through social contacts. Your ability to unite different people – to bring divergent factions together – means money in the bank for you.

Rest and relax more until the 23rd.

December

Best Days Overall: 3rd, 4th, 13th, 14th, 22nd, 23rd, 31st

Most Stressful Days Overall: 11th, 12th, 18th, 19th, 24th, 25th

Best Days for Love: 1st, 3rd, 4th, 11th, 13th, 14th, 18th, 19th, 20th, 24th, 28th

Best Days for Money: 1st, 2nd, 6th, 7th, 11th, 12th, 13th, 20th, 21st, 22nd, 23rd, 28th, 29th, 31st

All the planets (with the exception of the Moon) are above the horizon of your chart, making you more ambitious and less family-orientated this month. This trend towards the career has not even peaked yet and gets ever stronger for the next two months. Outward security takes priority over inner security, other people's families take precedence over your own, the future is more important than the past and your head tends to override your heart.

Most of the planets are still in the Western sector of your chart (though this is soon to change), making you more 'other-orientated' than 'self-orientated'. Though adapting is not one of your strong points, this is still what is required of you. Though you can plan your future conditions and circumstances it is unwise to put these plans into motion just yet. Give yourself a few months. In the mean time continue to put others ahead of yourself – and especially to put their needs before your own. Your good will come through the grace of others.

Your paths of greatest fulfilment now are the achievement of work goals and creating harmony at the workplace, helping others to prosper, attracting investors, paying debts, religious studies, physical intimacy, foreign travel and your career.

Your health is good all month and can be enhanced even further by a deeper understanding of the philosophy of health and disease, prayer, religious illumination and maintaining harmony with parents, elders and superiors.

Pluto's permanent move into the Sign of Sagittarius has a long-term impact on your love life or marriage. It shows that your partner now makes a long-term commitment to wealth and financial goals. Money-making dominates his or her mind. There is great success here now and great generosity towards you. Pluto's shift also shows that you are remembered in someone's will and will inherit substantial sums of money in future years. Your own earning power is strong this month as well, though you are less interested in personal earnings than in making money for others. Your personal philosophy of wealth is changing and new financial vistas open up – intellectually. This may sound odd, but don't discount it. All wealth begins in the mind.

Your public popularity and esteem get a boost after the 22nd.

Gemini

♊

THE TWINS

Birthdays from

21st May

to 20th June

Personality Profile

GEMINI AT A GLANCE

Element – Air

Ruling planet – Mercury
Career planet – Neptune
Health planet – Pluto
Love planet – Jupiter
Money planet – Moon

Colours – blue, yellow, yellow-orange

Colour that promotes love, romance and social harmony – sky blue

Colours that promote earning power – grey, silver

Gems – agate, aquamarine

Metal – quicksilver

Scents – lavender, lilac, lily of the valley, storax

Quality – mutable (= flexibility)

Quality most needed for balance – deep rather than superficial thought

Strongest virtues – great communication skills, quickness and agility of thought, ability to learn quickly

Deepest need – communication

Characteristics to avoid – gossiping, hurting others with harsh speech, superficiality, using words to mislead or misinform

Signs of greatest overall compatibility – Libra, Aquarius

Signs of greatest overall incompatibility – Virgo, Sagittarius, Pisces

Sign most helpful to career – Pisces

Sign most helpful for emotional support – Virgo

Sign most helpful financially – Cancer

Sign best for marriage and/or partnerships – Sagittarius

Sign most helpful for creative projects – Libra

Best Sign to have fun with – Libra

Signs most helpful in spiritual matters – Taurus, Aquarius

Best day of the week – Wednesday

Understanding the Gemini Personality

Gemini is to society what the nervous system is to the body. It does not introduce any new information but is a vital transmitter of impulses from the senses to the brain and vice versa. The nervous system does not judge or weigh these impulses – this function is left to the brain or the instincts. The nervous system only conveys information. And does so perfectly.

This analogy should give you an indication of a Gemini's role in society. Geminis are the communicators and conveyors of information. To Geminis the truth or mendacity of the information is irrelevant, they only transmit what they see, hear or read about. They teach what the textbooks say or what their managers tell them to say. Thus they are capable of spreading the most outrageous rumours as well as conveying truth and light. Geminis sometimes tend to be unscrupulous in their communications and they can do great good or great evil with their power. This is why the Sign of Gemini is called the Sign of the Twins. They have a dual nature.

Their ability to convey a message – to communicate with such ease – makes Geminis ideal teachers, writers and media and marketing people. This is helped by the fact that Mercury, the Ruling Planet of Gemini, also rules these activities.

Geminis have the gift of the gab. And what a gift this is! They can make conversation about anything, anywhere, at any time. There's almost nothing that is more fun to Geminis than a good conversation – especially if they can learn something new as well. They love to learn and they love to teach. To deprive a Gemini of conversation, or of books and magazines, is cruel and unusual punishment.

Geminis are almost always excellent students and take well to book learning. Their minds are generally stocked with all kinds of information, trivia, anecdotes, stories, news items, rarities, facts and statistics. Thus they can support any intellectual position that they care to take. They are awesome debaters and, if involved in politics, make good orators.

Geminis are so verbally smooth that even if they don't know what they are talking about they can make you think that they do. They will always dazzle you with their brilliance.

Finance

Geminis tend to be more concerned with the wealth of learning and ideas than with actual material wealth. As mentioned they excel in professions that involve writing, teaching, sales and journalism – and not all of these professions pay very well. But to sacrifice intellectual needs merely for money is unthinkable to a Gemini. Geminis strive to combine the two.

Cancer is on Gemini's Solar 2nd House (of Money) cusp, which indicates that Geminis can earn extra income (in a harmonious and natural way) from investments in residential property, restaurants and hotels. Given their verbal skills, Geminis love to bargain and negotiate in any situation, but especially when it has to do with money.

The Moon rules Gemini's 2nd Solar House. The Moon is not only the fastest-moving planet in the Zodiac but actually moves through every Sign and House every 28 days. No other heavenly body matches the Moon for swiftness or the ability to change quickly. An analysis of the Moon – and lunar phenomena in general – describes Gemini's financial attitudes very well. Geminis are financially versatile and flexible. They can earn money in many different ways. Their financial attitudes and needs seem to change daily. Their moods about money change. Sometimes they are very enthusiastic about it; sometimes they couldn't care less.

For a Gemini, financial goals and money are often seen only as means of supporting a family; they have little meaning otherwise.

The Moon, as Gemini's Money Planet, has another important message for Gemini financially: in order for Geminis to realize their financial potential fully they need to develop more of an understanding of the emotional side of life. They need to combine their awesome powers of logic with an understanding of human psychology. Feelings have their own logic; Geminis need to learn this and apply it to financial matters.

Career and Public Image

Geminis know that they were given the gift of communication for a reason, that it is a power that can achieve great good or cause unthinkable distress. They long to put this power at the service of the highest and most transcendental truths. This is their primary goal, to communicate the eternal verities and prove them logically. They look up to people who can transcend the intellect – to poets, artists, musicians and mystics. They may be awed by stories of religious saints and martyrs. A Gemini's highest achievement is to teach the truth, whether it is scientific, inspirational or historical. Those who can transcend the intellect are a Gemini's natural superiors – and a Gemini realizes this.

The Sign of Pisces is in Gemini's Solar 10th House of Career. Neptune, the planet of spirituality and altruism, is Gemini's Career Planet. If Geminis are to realize their highest career potential they need to develop their transcendental – their spiritual and altruistic – side. They need to understand the larger cosmic picture, the vast flow of human evolution – where it came from and where it is heading. Only then can a Gemini's intellectual powers take their true position and he or she can become the 'messenger of the Gods'. Geminis need to cultivate a facility for 'inspiration', which is something that does not originate *in* the intellect but which comes *through* the intellect. This will further enrich and empower a Gemini's mind.

Love and Relationships

Geminis bring their natural garrulousness and brilliance into their love and social life as well. A good talk or a verbal joust is an interesting prelude to romance. Their only problem in love is that their intellect is too cool and passionless to incite passion in others. Emotions sometimes disturb them, and their partners tend to complain about this. If you are in love with a Gemini you must understand why this is so. Geminis avoid deep passions because these would interfere with their ability to think and communicate. If they are cool towards you, understand that this is their nature.

Nevertheless, Geminis must understand that it is one thing to talk about love and another to actually love – to feel it and radiate it. Talking about love glibly will get them nowhere. They need to feel it and act on it. Love is not of the intellect but of the heart. If you want to know how a Gemini feels about love you shouldn't listen to what he or she says but rather observe what he or she does. Geminis can be quite generous to those they love.

Geminis like their partners to be refined, well educated and well travelled. If their partners are more wealthy than them, that is all the better. If you are in love with a Gemini you'd better be a good listener as well.

The ideal relationship for the Gemini is a relationship of the mind. They enjoy the physical and emotional aspects, of course, but if the intellectual communion is not there they will suffer.

Home and Domestic Life

At home the Gemini can be uncharacteristically neat and meticulous. They tend to want their children and partner to live up to their idealistic standards. When these standards are not met they moan and criticize. However, Geminis are good family people and like to serve their families in practical and useful ways.

The Gemini home is comfortable and pleasant. They like to invite people over and they make great hosts. Geminis are also good at repairs and improvements around the house – all fuelled by their need to stay active and occupied with something they like to do. Geminis have many hobbies and interests that keep them busy when they are home alone.

Geminis understand and get along well with their children, mainly because they are very youthful people themselves. As great communicators, Geminis know how to explain things to children; in this way they gain their children's love and respect. Geminis also encourage children to be creative and talkative just like they are.

Horoscope for 1995

Major Trends

1994 was primarily a work year. You enhanced your ability to serve and became a more valuable and productive worker. There was great satisfaction at the workplace. This trend continues in 1995 but you are more focused on your professional status. Whereas in 1994 you worked for the joy of service, now you are working for promotions and professional esteem.

On the social front there is much more expansion this year. Last year you were primarily weeding out undesirable friends and lovers. This year you do this to some degree but you are more concerned with expanding your social sphere. Your love and romantic life is especially prominent in 1995. The need to eliminate old and useless things from your life and character – which was so important in 1994 – continues to be so this year. It is a long-term trend. Saturn, which for two years has been making harmonious aspects to you, begins making stressful aspects this year. This forces you to become more realistic about your life's work, your intellectual interests and your energy in general. Your feelings of confidence and self-esteem will be subject to some shocks. If these feelings were healthy to begin with, Saturn will confirm and affirm you. If your ego is out of joint –

either too humble or too swollen – Saturn will reveal it to you. Rejoice in this, for it brings long-term, ultimate good.

Health

Your Solar 6th House of Health continues to be a House of Power this year, as it has been for many years now. By the time Pluto, the Lord of this House, leaves in November you will have revamped all of your attitudes to health, diet, nutrition and physical fitness. All that you need to know about regenerating your body will be revealed to you in very personal ways. Pluto as Health Lord in the Sign of Scorpio shows that for you the road to good health consists not in adding new things to the body but rather through the elimination of the poisonous and unfruitful from the system. In short, 'detoxification' will be your byword. Sickness is caused by the accumulation of toxins the body can't handle. Toxins can be removed in various ways – through fasting, taking herbs and maintaining a purer diet. Consult a health professional on these matters.

Many of you have undergone or will undergo some form of surgery this year – this has been a long-term trend. Sometimes these things are necessary and called for and sometimes not. Be sure to get a few opinions on these things before rushing into any procedures. For, in truth, your tendency is to be radical with your health. You are uncompromising and want instant results.

Saturn has now come into a more difficult alignment for you, Gemini. Your general vitality, while basically strong, is not what you are used to. You feel the limits on your physical energy. You cannot do everything, be everywhere and please everyone. You have a certain quota of energy on any given day, and you must use it wisely. A little planning and priority-setting will save you from any major health disasters. Speak less and listen more. Learn to turn off your restless mind when it isn't needed. Look more and think less. If you practise these things you will save enormous amounts of energy that can be used to prevent any form of ailment.

The health of your partner is basically strong all year, though there are some problems from 23rd January to 26th May. Your partner might contemplate surgery at this time, but second opinions should be sought. The health of your mother (or mother figure) if you are a man, or father (or father figure) if you are a woman, also seems delicate this year. He or she is making radical dietary changes and experimenting with all kinds of faddish regimes – taking a trial-and-error approach to a health problem. Ultimately success is likely. The same sort of thing is going on with the health of one of your siblings.

On 10th November Pluto makes a major long-term move into Sagittarius – a stressful alignment for you. Be sure to rest and relax more after this period. You have all the energy necessary to prevent health problems as long as you are not wasteful with it. Life-force (energy) is the strongest of medicines.

Home and Domestic Life

Though at various times during the year your 4th House of Home and Family will get activated by the fast-moving planets, overall this department of life is not a priority. The Cosmos is neither helping nor obstructing your domestic plans and projects. You have freedom in this area, though it is unlikely that you will use this freedom. When Mars moves through this House from 26th May to 22nd July you will feel the need to do some work around the house – construction and the like. When the Sun and Venus move through it beginning 23rd August you will want to stay home more and to entertain from home. This will help mend fences with disgruntled relatives.

Every month the Moon spends two days in this House, activating your urge to spend time with your family and to take care of domestic chores. But these are short-term trends which pass relatively quickly. (You can follow these trends by reading the month-by-month forecasts.)

Aside from this sense of freedom in the home there is other good news. Your family is not obstructing your real interests – career, social life and higher education plans. They give you the freedom to do what you want in these areas.

Your father or mother seems overly strict and exacting with you. This parent is urging you to duties that you don't really want to perform. This doesn't involve domestic concerns but rather debts or lawsuits. The legacy is used as a tool for control. This parent – though probably well meaning – is not helping your self-esteem and perhaps should be confronted about it.

Love and Social Life

This area of life has become very prominent in your 1995 Solar Horoscope. Jupiter, your Lord of Love, stays in his own House – your (7th) Marriage House – all year. This is an unusually long transit for Jupiter because usually this planet stays in a Sign or House for 11 months. This year it stays in Sagittarius for 12 months. Jupiter is very powerful in his own Sign and House – doing mighty works for your social benefit, with plenty of time to do so. Singles are likely to get married or involved in a serious committed relationship – fortunate and blessed. Marrieds are likely to become more romantic with partners. All of you will definitely expand your social sphere and meet all kinds of new and important people. These are not superficial contacts, either, but real friends who have both the power and the inclination to help and promote you. Singles marry someone richer than they are. Those already married see their partners becoming much more prosperous and happy.

One of Jupiter's many titles is that of 'Guru' – the teacher. So Jupiter's move through your House of Marriage shows that your partner has deep urges to guide and teach you. He or she does have much to share, so be open to it. Close-mindedness can thwart the relationship.

For most of the year you are socially expanding – and

expanding and expanding. But after 10th November you'll have to consolidate and become more selective. You can't socialize with everybody or accept every romantic opportunity. Be aware of your limits. Too much of a good thing can cause stress.

Those of you looking towards a second marriage have a more turbulent time of it. Your love life is a roller-coaster with wild highs and profound lows. Experimentation brings unexpected bliss but a few embarrassing failures as well. Keep right on experimenting, though – the right partner is out there for you – and you are likely to meet him or her suddenly, unexpectedly and when you've given up all hope.

Those who are hoping for a third marriage need patience this year. Though your social life is expanding and happy, Mr or Ms Right seems to lurk in the shadows. If you've met him or her, there is a coyness about commitment. Enjoy the relationship for what it is and let go. Marriage is not necessarily called for this year.

Career and Finance

Your Solar 2nd House of Money and Possessions is not a House of Power this year, Gemini. Mere money-making takes a back seat to many other things, most notably your career and professional esteem and your love life. You would much rather have professional and public esteem than a big bank account right now. This will change in the future, but for now this is how you feel.

Having said this, your interest in money-making and personal earning power will peak during the summer – from 22nd June to 30th July. This is when the Sun, Venus and Mercury move through your Money House, practically simultaneously. You will earn more during this period and probably get involved in a conflict with your partner about it. Your financial interests or opportunities will conflict with those of your partner at this time. Whether you are male or female you are better off fostering the income of your partner than promoting your own. Your own will come to you naturally when you need it.

Your partner or lover is very much involved with money-making this year as well. Money is earned through high technology or through real estate. Your partner does a lot of his or her work from home. At times he or she is wildly generous and then (apparently) maniacally mean. Ride the roller-coaster. It might help you if you understand that your partner is striking out into the 'unknown', economically, being very experimental in business. Earnings come to him or her in fits and starts and therefore any generosity is erratic. Your partner is being led to economic liberation – complete financial freedom. In order to attain this there is a need to break with tradition and smash old barriers in the business world. Your partner is a real risk-taker – a swashbuckling entrepreneur – therefore your emotional support is critical to his or her success.

Basically, your money comes to you through others – through enhancing the prosperity of others, through royalties, lawsuits, legacies and/or insurance payments. An idea you have for a new invention is good. Not only are the investors out there for you but royalty payments can come through licensing your idea to others. You have a few ways you can go with this. The world is ready for the bold, the new and the innovative, now.

Self-improvement

The Moon is Lord of Gemini's financial life. Following the Moon and its phases can help you achieve financial goals more easily. You are always financially stronger when the Moon is waxing than when it is waning. It is always better to make investments – things that you want to grow in value – when the Moon is waxing. It is also much better to pay off debts and bills (things that you want diminished in your life) when the Moon is waning. This is good guidance for everyone, but especially good for a Gemini. You can get information about the lunar phases from any newspaper, from some calendars or by following the month-by-month forecasts below.

Your social life is going to improve almost by itself. You can just sit back and enjoy it, for the opportunities will come. You can, however make things even easier and better by weeding out the unnecessary – those friends or romantic partners who do not truly have your best interests at heart. The friends that take you closer to where you want to go in life are the ones you should socialize with. Those of you who know your goals will be able to judge this more easily. Those of you who don't should perhaps spend time sorting this out. Your friends are those who want for you what you want for yourself.

Your career prospects will improve this year, but there is more work and discipline involved than you are used to. Saturn is subjecting your career goals to a 'reality check' – just as it is doing to your ego and self-esteem. Saturn is very just – beautifully and marvellously so – have no fear of that. But if you think of yourself as Chairman and Managing Director even though you are as yet a filing clerk – Saturn will remind you of this fact. By all means dream on, but let Saturn guide you to the practical steps needed to transform the filing clerk into the MD. Real achievement and ability are what's demanded of you now. You will rise accordingly. This is not the year to take career short-cuts. Dot your 'I's and cross your 'T's. Do everything by the book. Avoid playing fast and loose with the law of the land or the rules and regulations of your company, no matter how ridiculous they may seem. In some years you can get away with this, but this is not one of those years.

Month-by-month Forecasts

January

Best Days Overall: 3rd, 4th, 12th, 13th, 22nd, 23rd, 30th, 31st

Most Stressful Days Overall: 5th, 6th, 19th, 20th, 21st, 26th, 27th

Best Days for Love: 5th, 6th, 7th, 8th, 17th, 18th, 19th, 26th, 27th

Best Days for Money: 1st, 2nd, 7th, 10th, 11th, 15th, 16th, 17th, 18th, 22nd, 23rd, 26th, 27th, 30th, 31st

Between 70 and 90 per cent of the planets, including Mercury, your Ruler, are clustered in the Western half of your Solar Horoscope this month, Gemini. This shows that you are focused on other people this month. Your social life is active and you attain your ends through the grace of others rather than through your personal efforts. Thus it is wise for you to hone your social skills now.

You are very much involved in earning money for others for most of the month by going to unusual lengths on their behalf. And you seem successful at it. You are rewarded accordingly, as you will see come the Full Moon of the 16th. Remember that the Moon is your Money Planet and her phases are vital to your financial life. It waxes from the 1st to the 16th, giving you greater enthusiasm and ardour for financial affairs at that time. It becomes Full – at the maximum of its strength in your Money House – on the 16th, a good financial signal. You've got a big payday coming on that day.

This is a good month to get rid of undesirable things in your life. You are in the mood to eliminate and transform. Use this mood to your advantage. Get rid of old books, magazines and papers that you no longer need. Get rid of possessions that clutter up your house. Give what is useful to charity or to friends and keep only what you really need.

The major headline this month is your social life. Seldom have you experienced such rapture and social popularity. Romantic opportunities are not only abundant but happy as well. You'll find it difficult to choose amid such a wide selection. Singles will meet 'significant others' this month and marrieds will expand their social contacts. Fortunate business partnerships are also likely to come to pass. Your social life glitters. Romance is a beautiful combination of courtship, fantasy and physical intimacy. But remember to balance all this social activity with the demands of your career. Saturn in your (10th) Career House restrains you from losing yourself in the social merry-go-round. You've got work to do and responsibilities to handle. Don't neglect them, though you are sorely tempted to.

Mercury, your Ruling Planet, goes retrograde (backwards) towards the end of the month. Review your personal desires and personal appearance and make the necessary changes. This retrograde further reinforces your need to focus on other people's interests rather than your own. Though we should never neglect our own interests entirely, there are times when the needs of others come before our own – and this is one of those times, Gemini.

February

Best Days Overall: 8th, 9th, 10th, 18th, 19th, 26th, 27th, 28th

Most Stressful Days Overall: 1st, 2nd, 16th, 17th, 22nd, 23rd

Best Days for Love: 3rd, 4th, 5th, 6th, 7th, 13th, 14th, 15th, 16th, 17th, 22nd, 23rd, 24th, 25th

Best Days for Money: 3rd, 4th, 5th, 8th, 9th, 10th, 11th, 12th, 13th, 14th, 15th, 18th, 19th, 20th, 22nd, 23rd

The majority of planets – ranging from 60 to 80 per cent at different times – are in the Western and top halves of your Solar Horoscope this month, Gemini. Moreover, 80 per cent of the planets are moving forward this month, and after the

16th the total goes to 90 per cent moving direct. What does this tell us about your month ahead?

The forward motion of the celestial forces shows that this is a month of action and achievement. Your goals and projects are coming to pass. The dominance of your Western chart sector shows that the action is coming from others on to you. You are basically letting things happen and adjusting to situations and circumstances. The power at the top half of your chart shows that your interest lies in outward success and achievement, to the neglect of your home and family interests and to your own sense of personal harmony. This is not meant to be judgmental, only descriptive. It is natural that at certain times of life we focus on one thing over another, equally important thing. This is one of those times.

The Sun's entry into your (10th) Career House from the 19th onwards further reinforces your drive towards success.

The retrograde of your Ruling Planet Mercury until the 16th stresses further your own personal passivity regarding all the good things that are coming. There is a lesson here for you, Gemini. Sometimes we must make things happen and sometimes we must 'allow' things to happen, not by doing but by just letting go. Your goals and desires – hopefully you've kept them positive – are coming to pass through others and not through your own efforts. In fact – especially until the 16th – too much effort on your part could actually delay things.

Your skills as a communicator or marketeer are recognized by those in positions of authority after the 19th and could lead you to a career pinnacle. Your intellectual abilities bring you status and public recognition.

Your love life continues to shine, though this month you are more interested in the quality of your relationships rather than their quantity. You are also – especially after the 4th – more interested in physical intimacy than 'romance and courtship'. After the 19th you must do a real juggling act between your career and love life. Career drives threaten to upset your partner or lover, while your partner's demands on your time seem to interfere with your ambitions and work. Give to each its due. Your partner needs to recognize your legitimate career aspirations and you need to recognize your partner's need for your time and attention.

Rest and relax more this month. Let the cosmic waves carry you to your destination while you relax in peace.

March

Best Days Overall: 8th, 9th, 17th, 18th, 26th, 27th

Most Stressful Days Overall: 1st, 2nd, 15th, 16th, 21st, 22nd, 28th, 29th

Best Days for Love: 3rd, 4th, 8th, 9th, 13th, 14th, 17th, 18th, 21st, 22nd, 26th, 27th, 28th, 30th, 31st

Best Days for Money: 1st, 2nd, 3rd, 4th, 10th, 11th, 12th, 13th, 14th, 19th, 20th, 21st, 22nd, 30th, 31st

Like last month, the planets are still overwhelmingly concentrated in the top hemisphere of your Solar chart, showing the intensity of your ambition and drive for recognition and status in the world. This drive takes priority over everything – your family, personal desires or needs for emotional harmony. People are probably calling you 'career-driven', 'workaholic' and the like. You probably wonder about yourself as well. But this is only temporary. The planets are getting ready to shift to other parts of your Horoscope – though not yet. In the mean time, be career-driven and try to enjoy it!

This career energy is not all of your making. Elders, superiors – and later on this month even your family – are urging you onwards. They are exacting and demanding. They insist on work done well and real and true achievement. You do not shoot straight to the top right now; you attain your ends by degrees. Inch by inch you rise within the corporate structure or in your professional life. Intellectual ability is still the key to your success – as it was last month – and is being recognized now.

With Mercury, your Ruler, going speedily forward your health and confidence are better than last month, nevertheless rest and relax more until the 21st. Especially, conserve your mental and verbal resources now. These are carrying you to the heights and there is no need to waste energy thinking or talking needlessly. Talk by all means – your word is your fortune – but make your words count. This watching over your words becomes especially important now that you are assuming authority and responsibility. Your word carries more weight now and idle words are more difficult to retract.

Money is not a big priority this month yet you seem to be doing well. The Moon, your Money Planet, waxes as it moves through your Money House on the 10th, 11th and 12th. Expect extra earnings then. The Moon waxes from the 1st to the 17th, strengthening your earning power and your enthusiasm for financial matters. It wanes from the 17th to the 31st, diminishing your enthusiasm. Make investments in your savings accounts, funds or stock portfolios on the waxing Moon. Pay bills and debts – where possible – when the Moon wanes.

Your love life is stormy until the 21st. Have patience with a loved one until then. Love rockets with excitement after the 21st. You and your partner have a real case of spring fever!

April

Best Days Overall: 4th, 5th, 6th, 14th, 15th, 22nd, 23rd

Most Stressful Days Overall: 11th, 12th, 13th, 18th, 19th, 24th, 25th

Best Days for Love: 1st, 7th, 8th, 9th, 10th, 16th, 17th, 18th, 19th, 26th, 27th, 28th

Best Days for Money: 1st, 7th, 8th, 9th, 10th, 18th, 19th, 20th, 26th, 27th, 28th, 29th, 30th

The weight of the planetary power is still very much in the top half of your Solar Horoscope and the shift of planetary power to the East is becoming more established day by day. This means that your ambitions in the world continue to outweigh family and domestic urges, and your personal urges and interests come before those of others. Though others might see you as selfish and career-driven right now it is merely a shift of the pendulum and not a permanent character trait. You need to look after for yourself and do what you really want to do now. The time for catering to others will come and you will handle it then. Right now you are in charge of your life and in charge of your circumstances. What happens is up to you and you will enjoy the glory and the responsibilities of this.

This self-assertiveness and confidence (Mercury goes forward speedily this month) creates some short-term problems in your love life. Lovers or partners seem tentative, unsure of how things stand. They take a 'wait and see' attitude towards you – as if to see how far you will go in your ambitions and self-assertion. They feel you have put them on 'hold' while other things and interests take precedence. In a sense they are right. But in the long term the relationship will work out. They will get a chance to see what you really want to do and what your real needs are. Your social charisma is not yet what it should be or will be.

Your paths of greatest fulfilment this month are your career, platonic friendships and work.

There are two Eclipses this month. Steady readers of these reports already know that Eclipses are cosmic signals of long-term change. Cosmic announcements, if you will. The Lunar Eclipse of the 15th occurs in your 5th Solar House of Fun, Creativity, Speculations and Love Affairs, making favourable aspects to you. Thus, long-term changes in your creative life and with your children have favourable consequences for you. A new cycle of creativity begins. The Solar Eclipse of the 29th occurs in your 12th Solar House of Spiritual Wisdom and Charity, signifying a major change in your relationship with a charitable organization to which you belong. You could sever connections with this organization temporarily and begin relations with another one. The spiritual life in general is very important this month. Both the Sun and your Ruling Planet Mercury move through the 12th House during the latter part of the month. Thus, the Eclipse forces you to re-evaluate your charitable activities and the causes you support.

The Lunar Eclipse also brings some temporary financial upheaval. Any so-called losses are quickly recovered, however. Avoid speculating on or around the 15th. Otherwise, money seems not to be a big priority. The Cosmos grants you financial freedom this month, but you don't show too much interest in these matters.

Your health is excellent all month.

May

Best Days Overall: 1st, 2nd, 3rd, 11th, 12th, 19th, 20th, 29th, 30th

Most Stressful Days Overall: 9th, 10th, 15th, 16th, 21st, 22nd, 23rd

Best Days for Love: 6th, 7th, 8th, 15th, 16th, 17th, 24th, 25th, 26th, 27th, 28th

Best Days for Money: 4th, 5th, 6th, 7th, 8th, 9th, 10th, 15th, 16th, 17th, 18th, 24th, 25th, 29th, 30th, 31st

For most of the month the planetary power is still concentrated at the top half of your Solar chart, continuing to emphasize your ambitions and need for status. But this starts to change by the 21st as you start focusing more on personal happiness and feeling emotionally balanced. As far as personal freedom is concerned, there is a nice equilibrium right now. The planets are about evenly dispersed between the Eastern and Western hemispheres. You are not fawning over others but neither are you ignoring them.

Mercury, your Ruler, moves slowly this month and by the 24th actually starts going backwards. This shows that though you feel in good health and have plenty of energy you also feel a bit cautious and tentative in pursuing your goals. Your self-confidence and feelings of self-worth could be stronger. Caution is recommended, however, in domestic projects such as major home repairs, buying a home, redecorating and the like. A friend's efforts to help in these matters carry a hidden price-tag which you should look at. Domestic issues are not what they seem; investigate them more thoroughly.

Your love life – and especially a current, basically happy relationship – is at a standstill right now. It's as if neither you nor your lover knows where the relationship is going. The same is true with people you date. You have no idea where to take the relationship. All of this is, of course, temporary. Jupiter, your Love Planet, is retrograde all month, giving you and your lover the space to think things through. Your social confidence and charisma in general could be stronger. Still, there are many sensual and personal pleasures awaiting you during the latter part of the month – good food, lovely clothes, massages and the like.

Your (2nd) Money House is not that active this month so you have a lot of latitude where financial money are concerned. The Cosmos is not pushing you one way or the other. The Cosmos doesn't obstruct you in meeting financial goals but neither does it give you much interest in them. Nevertheless, your Money Planet, the Moon, will wax as it passes through your Money House on the 1st, 2nd and 3rd –

expect extra earnings then. Your financial peak occurs around the Full Moon of the 14th, which occurs in your 6th House of Health and Work. This shows that money comes through your work and that you have plenty of energy to achieve your work goals.

June

Best Days Overall: 7th, 8th, 9th, 16th, 17th, 25th, 26th

Most Stressful Days Overall: 5th, 6th, 12th, 13th, 18th, 19th

Best Days for Love: 3rd, 4th, 5th, 6th, 12th, 13th, 16th, 17th, 20th, 21st, 25th, 26th, 30th

Best Days for Money: 1st, 2nd, 3rd, 4th, 7th, 8th, 9th, 12th, 13th, 16th, 17th, 20th, 21st, 27th, 28th, 29th, 30th

There is good news and there is bad news for you this month, Gemini. The good news is that three powerful and helpful planets are in your own Sign, giving you energy, vitality and assistance. The bad news is that 60 per cent of the planets are involved in a Heavenly Grand Square aspect, showing a need for you to juggle conflicting and antagonistic elements in your life and to create something workable from this. This is not easy – and probably you will have a few failures – but ultimately you will be able to do it.

Where is this juggling act happening? In your case it is made up of your career, domestic life, social life and personal desires. Each area demands its due from you and each conflicts with the others. You must somehow find the centre – the point of balance – which will harmonize all these areas. Unfortunately there are no general rules on how to harmonize these things, as every personal situation is unique. Basically you must feel and sense your way through. Give each area its due – but no more than that. You must somehow rise above circumstances and see the situation from a grander perspective – see things the way your own higher mind sees things – and solutions will naturally reveal themselves. Also, remember that the harder it is to achieve something, the greater the fruits of success.

What further complicates the situation is that 50 per cent of the planets, including Mercury, your Ruler, and Jupiter, your Love Planet, are retrograde this month. The Grand Square always pushes action and change, whereas the retrograde planets work against action and change – a kind of temporary stalemate is the result. You know you must take action but you are prevented by various delays and fears. The arguments for and against action are equally powerful. The answer? Take whatever action it is possible to take, and only after due deliberation and study. When in doubt, do nothing.

In spite of all this you have a lot going for you and a lot of help around you. Your health and vitality are excellent. Your personal appearance shines. Also, the planets are pretty evenly spread out through the various sectors of your chart, giving you a greater sense of balance and perspective and fostering a spirit of compromise. This planetary spread is unlikely to push you into any 'extreme' or untenable position. Also, after the 17th Mercury, your Ruler, starts moving forward, giving you greater confidence and a better sense of what your own interests are. It will also reduce the sense of stoppage.

Your main problem in love is the same as it was last month – the need to balance your interests with those of your partner. You are being pulled in opposite directions.

July

Best Days Overall: 5th, 6th, 13th, 14th, 22nd, 23rd

Most Stressful Days Overall: 2nd, 3rd, 4th, 9th, 10th, 15th, 16th, 30th, 31st

Best Days for Love: 1st, 7th, 8th, 9th, 10th, 15th, 16th, 17th, 18th, 25th, 26th, 27th, 28th

Best Days for Money: 1st, 7th, 8th, 9th, 10th, 15th, 16th, 17th, 18th, 25th, 26th, 27th, 28th

Now that Mercury, your Ruler, is speedily moving forward, your personal confidence, charisma and influence are much stronger than they were last month. You make rapid progress towards your goals, to the amazement of others. Normally with this kind of planetary aspect you would be setting the pace, the trend and the policies in your life – but not so right now. You still need patience, not with yourself but with others. Fifty per cent of the planets are retrograde this month, causing a general impasse, a sense of inaction and delay. Therefore, even though you are confident and ready to act, others are not. Most of the delays going on this month are not your fault.

The planets are quite evenly dispersed between the Eastern and Western sectors of the Horoscope. This, combined with your Ruler's forward motion, shows a healthy sense of your own self-interest and no need to put others before yourself. On the other hand you are not walking all over other people, either. You've got the perspective just right.

The fast-moving, short-term planets are empowering the bottom half of your chart, showing an urge towards emotional harmony and security. Career issues can wait right now, for Saturn, your Career Planet, is retrograde. Focus on building a stable home base and getting the emotional support you need in order to further your career objectives. Work on your career behind the scenes. You will attain more by fostering and supporting other people's careers.

Your (2nd) Money House is active and powerful all month.

Money-making and acquiring of possessions are major priorities which you can't ignore. It looks like you will succeed where many others are floundering this month. The planets in your Money House are moving forward speedily. When you have more than two planets in your Money House – which is the case here – you earn money in a variety of ways. You have an ability to harness many different types of people and diverse personal skills towards one objective – the building of wealth. This month your sales ability, personal charm, pleasant appearance and uncanny intuition combine to increase your 'bottom line'. Your intuitions this month are not 'airy nothings' but practical, workable wealth ideas. Both men and women are eager to grant you financial favours.

Though you are personally healthy and magnetic this month, a cautious approach is still indicated in love. You have no problem attracting the opposite sex, but you are not sure how far you want to go with these relationships. You are stronger than your partner this period and tend to get your way. As the month progresses you and your partner begin to share more interests and the question of who gets his or her way becomes unimportant. Don't schedule either a marriage or divorce during this period.

August

Best Days Overall: 1st, 2nd, 9th, 10th, 19th, 20th, 28th, 29th

Most Stressful Days Overall: 5th, 6th, 12th, 26th, 27th

Best Days for Love: 5th, 6th, 14th, 15th, 24th, 25th, 26th, 27th

Best Days for Money: 5th, 6th, 14th, 15th, 21st, 22nd, 26th, 27th

As the month begins the planets are more or less evenly dispersed through the various sectors of your chart. While this gives you a balanced perspective on things, there is a possibility that you may spread yourself too thin now. Many diverse interests appeal to you and there is the danger that you will flit from one thing to another without finishing anything. With this kind of configuration it would be unreasonable to ask you to focus on one thing, because your need for change and variety would be thwarted. Undertake a few projects – but not too many – and focus on these.

After the 23rd of the month the planets shift to the Western half of your chart, making it the dominant sector of your Horoscope. Thus your social skills will get more exercise and you will have to be even more adaptable than usual to alien circumstances. Happily, adaptability is one of your main talents and you should have no problem with this.

Your paths of greatest fulfilment this month are your love life, your current relationship, the achievement of work goals (until the 12th), fun activities, personal creativity, children, intellectual interests and the home.

Always a lover of local, domestic travel, this month you get to indulge your whims. There are numerous jaunts around your immediate area and longer trips away from home, but not abroad. Your intellectual abilities – always quite keen – are even keener this month. Those attending summer school or summer classes will do well now.

An important shift of the Moon's North Node happens this month. This is a long-term trend and is worthy of mention. This Lunar Node – an abstract point in your chart where the Moon intersects the Sun's orbit – shows where good fortune and fulfilment can be found. It shifts from your 6th House of Work to your 5th House of Creativity, Fun and Children. The Stars are saying that you've done enough group work for a while and you now need to indulge in some personal activities.

After the 23rd the demands of your family are strong. You must socialize with them, entertain them or be entertained by them, and otherwise stabilize your home environment. This begins a short-term period of nostalgia for you. You are fascinated by the past, both intellectually and emotionally. History in general – but especially your personal history – is alluring. Friends, acquaintances and memories of times long gone come to you, to be reviewed from your current perspective. Family members are definitely reminiscing about your past exploits. This is good for your psychological health in that it allows you to digest these things from an adult perspective.

September

Best Days Overall: 6th, 7th, 15th, 16th, 24th, 25th

Most Stressful Days Overall: 2nd, 8th, 9th, 22nd, 23rd, 29th, 30th

Best Days for Love: 2nd, 4th, 5th, 10th, 11th, 12th, 13th, 14th, 20th, 21st, 24th, 25th, 29th, 30th

Best Days for Money: 2nd, 4th, 5th, 10th, 11th, 12th, 13th, 14th, 19th, 20th, 21st, 23rd, 24th, 25th, 29th, 30th

An unusually high percentage of the planets are now in the Western sector of your chart, making you less self-assertive, less able to go it alone and more dependent on the good graces of other people. With Mercury, your Ruler, moving slowly most of the month and then going retrograde by the 22nd, this lack of confidence and self-assurance is further reinforced. This is simply not the month for power struggles, independence or asserting yourself. This is not the month for creating your own conditions and circumstances. You'll succeed by adapting yourself harmoniously to existing conditions. Happily this is something you are well able to do, so personal success is likely.

The planets are still slightly weighted below the horizon of your chart, making you more family conscious and more interested in your emotional security. With your career in temporary limbo you are better off supporting other people's careers for a while - not in order to designate you for 'sainthood', but as a practical way to further your own career later on. The support you give now you will receive in the future, in the same quantity and of the same quality.

Your paths of greatest fulfilment this month are the family and family interests, the home, children, personal creativity, fun activities and your love life.

Your health could be better until the 23rd. This is not one of your peak health periods. Health can be enhanced by purifying your body through diet, exercise and colonics. Eat less until the 23rd. After the 23rd your normal vitality returns.

Handle all domestic chores and projects before the 23rd. Your urge now is for emotional and psychological purity. Your mood of nostalgia has its roots in the Cosmos. Old memories and experiences come back so that they can be resolved in a better way.

After the 23rd your personal creativity is at an all-time high. It is a kind of cosmic holiday for you. Go out, have fun and enjoy yourself. Children are happy to be with you - and you with them - after the 23rd.

Your love life is steadily improving and by the 23rd becomes really happy. A current relationship is progressing the way it should. New friends are made and romantic opportunities - both serious and not so serious - are plentiful. You are more in the mood for fun and games, while a romantic partner or prospect has deeper things in mind.

October

Best Days Overall: 3rd, 4th, 12th, 13th, 22nd, 23rd, 30th, 31st

Most Stressful Days Overall: 5th, 6th, 20th, 21st, 26th, 27th

Best Days for Love: 3rd, 4th, 7th, 8th, 9th, 15th, 16th, 17th, 18th, 24th, 25th, 26th, 27th

Best Days for Money: 3rd, 4th, 7th, 8th, 9th, 12th, 13th, 15th, 16th, 17th, 18th, 23rd, 24th, 25th, 26th, 27th

As with Aries and Taurus, the planetary power is focused in the Western sector of your chart right now, Gemini. Mercury, your Ruler, is among them. Thus you are still in an ever-increasing social circle. Your concerns lie with others rather than with yourself. You prefer partnerships and co-operative activities to doing things on your own. You are more dependent on others but also, because of this, you have the potential to achieve great things. This achievement hinges on the good grace and co-operation of others.

Mercury, your Ruler, is retrograde until the 14th, further weakening your sense of self. Laying down the law will not get you very far this month. You must seek consensus and the good opinion of others. What you lose in personal freedom – and this loss is considerable – you gain in social popularity. Your sense of self-esteem is even more mercurial. Much of it depends on how other people perceive you and on their approval and disapproval. The truth is that you are neither totally the way you define yourself nor completely the way others define you. You are a combination of both – and perhaps even more as well.

The planets are now more or less evenly balanced above and below the horizon of your chart. The momentum, however, is towards the upper sector, the sector above the horizon. Thus you are becoming ever more career conscious and worldly. You are not yet ignoring your family and family interests, but still finding the balance between the two.

Your paths of greatest fulfilment this month are parties, fun activities, personal creativity, the achievement of work goals and love and romance.

You are in one of the peak personal pleasure periods of your year. Your health and vitality are excellent; your personal creativity is at a yearly high. You are unusually popular with the opposite sex, a trend that is going to get stronger as the months go by. Your main desire for most of the month is to make the world happy. You are a lucky speculator until the 11th.

After the 14th you are in a period of action and achievement as 90 per cent of the planets are moving forward. A lot of action is finally taking place, but much of it is happening *to* you. When you do act, consult first with those involved.

November

Best Days Overall: 8th, 9th, 10th, 18th, 19th, 27th, 28th

Most Stressful Days Overall: 1st, 2nd, 3rd, 16th, 17th, 23rd, 29th, 30th

Best Days for Love: 2nd, 3rd, 4th, 5th, 14th, 15th, 23rd, 24th

Best Days for Money: 1st, 2nd, 3rd, 4th, 5th, 11th, 12th, 14th, 15th, 21st, 22nd, 23rd

The planets are now at their most westerly point of your Horoscope, making you very popular socially and almost totally involved with other people and their needs. You are in the most socially active period of a great social year. Until the 23rd it is best to clear up work goals so that you can handle the social blitz to come.

It's as if you forget about yourself completely during this period and give yourself over to the social scene. You go out of your way to fulfil the whims of lovers and friends. You seem caught up in various love affairs and the problem is whom to choose. A 'playmate' or someone involved in your creative life (perhaps a dance teacher) goes to great lengths to woo you into something deeper. Someone who has been a friend or a member on an organization to which you belong also goes to great and unusual lengths to court you. Very flattering stuff, indeed, but also very confusing. However, your true partner is neither of these. He or she is learned, cultured, wealthy (or someone who lives opulently) and perhaps foreign.

Your health is better before the 23rd than after. Your health can be enhanced now and for the long term by maintaining social harmony and balance in your love relationships. Problems in love have an undue impact on your health now. Before running to doctors make sure your relationship is OK. Chances are that if you clear that up your health problem will clear up as well. If you do need the services of a health professional, his or her work will be made much easier if you've sorted out any relationship worries first.

After the 21st all the planets are moving forward – very unusual – showing that you are in a month of action and achievement. But you are not really the one doing. It is all happening through others. The cosmic currents are pulling you towards love, marriage and social success.

Your paths of greatest fulfilment this month are children, personal creativity, parties and other fun activities, the achievement of work goals and, of course, love and romance.

Money-making seems one of your lowest priorities right now. You have great financial freedom but little interest in these matters.

December

Best Days Overall: 6th, 7th, 16th, 17th, 24th, 25th

Most Stressful Days Overall: 13th, 14th, 20th, 21st, 26th, 27th

Best Days for Love: 1st, 2nd, 3rd, 4th, 11th, 12th, 13th, 14th, 20th, 21st, 24th, 28th, 29th

Best Days for Money: 1st, 2nd, 8th, 9th, 11th, 12th, 20th, 21st, 28th, 29th, 30th, 31st

All the planets are moving forward this month, making this a period of action and achievement. You are making great progress towards all your goals, though you are not the one actually doing anything – your success is happening through others. The planets are now at the maximum Eastern point of your chart, making this one of your happiest social periods in a generally happy social year. Your popularity has never been greater. You give yourself to others almost totally. You are genuinely interested in them and they feel this. This is especially so in love. You go to unusual lengths to fulfil the whims, needs and desires of your partner or lover. Your dominant desire is to please your partner, to be the kind of partner that he or she needs you to be. The people you are meeting now – and the people that are currently in your social life – are more than capable of helping your goals and projects. It is the ideal social life.

Usually, this much power in the West requires effort to adapt to. But this month adaptation seems very simple, as the conditions you are involved with are better than any you would have created for yourself. There is much glitz, glitter and glamour in your social life now.

All the planets – with the exception of the Moon – are now firmly established above the horizon of your chart. They have not reached their peak at the top of your chart yet, but they are headed there. Thus you begin a cycle of career interest and advancement. Concerns about personal domestic bliss give way to concerns for the domestic bliss of others. Concerns about your career outweigh concerns about your emotional security. Concerns for the future dominate concerns of the past. Look forward to your goals and don't look back to 'the good old days'.

Your paths of greatest fulfilment now are your love life, parties and other fun activities, personal creativity, physical intimacy, religious studies and foreign travel.

Pluto, your Health Planet, has made a major move into your 7th House of Love and Marriage and will be there for many years to come. This shows that social harmony, harmony with your partner and friends and in a marriage or serious relationship have now become major factors in maintaining good health. Lack of harmony of any sort will always cause some physical ailment, but social 'dis-harmony' now has a more dramatic impact. This is a long-term trend. Before running to a health professional check to see whether your relationship is right; if it isn't, correct it. Chances are that the problem will fall away on its own. Rest and relax more until the 22nd.

Cancer

♋

THE CRAB

Birthdays from

21st June

to 20th July

Personality Profile

CANCER AT A GLANCE

Element – Water

Ruling planet – Moon
Career planet – Mars
Health planet – Jupiter
Love planet – Saturn
Money planet – Sun
Planet of fun and games – Pluto
Planet of home and family life – Venus

Colours – blue, puce, silver

Colours that promote love, romance and social harmony – black, indigo

Colours that promote earning power – gold, orange

Gems – moonstone, pearl

Metal – silver

Scents – jasmine, sandalwood

Quality – cardinal (= activity)

Quality most needed for balance – mood control

Strongest virtues – emotional sensitivity, tenacity, the urge to nurture

Deepest need – a harmonious home and family life

Characteristics to avoid – over-sensitivity, negative moods

Signs of greatest overall compatibility – Scorpio, Pisces

Signs of greatest overall incompatibility – Aries, Libra, Capricorn

Sign most helpful to career – Aries

Sign most helpful for emotional support – Libra

Sign most helpful financially – Leo

Sign best for marriage and/or partnerships – Capricorn

Sign most helpful for creative projects – Scorpio

Best Sign to have fun with – Scorpio

Signs most helpful in spiritual matters – Gemini, Pisces

Best day of the week – Monday

Understanding the Cancer Personality

In the Sign of Cancer the heavens are developing the feeling side of things. This is what a true Cancerian is all about – feelings. Where Aries will tend to err on the side of action, Taurus on the side of inaction and Gemini on the side of thought, Cancer will tend to err on the side of feeling.

The Cancerian tends to mistrust logic. Perhaps rightfully so. For them it is not enough for an argument or a project to be logical – it must *feel* right as well. If it doesn't feel right a Cancerian will reject it or chafe against it. The phrase 'follow your heart' could have been coined by a Cancerian, because it describes exactly the Cancerian attitude towards life.

The power to feel is a more direct – more immediate – method of knowing than thinking is. Thinking is indirect. Thinking about a thing never touches the thing itself. Feeling is a faculty that contacts the thing or issue in question directly. We actually touch and experience it. Emotional feeling is almost like another sense that humans possess, a psychic sense. Since the realities that we come in contact with during our lifetime are often painful and even destructive, it is not surprising that the Cancerian chooses to erect barriers of defence – a shell – to protect his or her vulnerable, sensitive nature. To Cancerians this is only common sense.

If Cancerians are in the presence of people they don't know or in a hostile environment, up goes the shell and they feel protected. Other people often complain about this, but one must question their motives. Why does this shell disturb them? Is it perhaps because they would like to sting and feel frustrated that they can't? If your intentions are honourable and you are patient, have no fear. The shell will go down and you will be accepted as part of the Cancerian's circle of family and friends.

Thought-processes are generally analytic and separative. In order to think clearly we must make distinctions, separations, comparisons and the like. But feeling is unifying and integrative. To think clearly about something you have to distance yourself from it. But to feel something you must get close to it. Once a Cancerian has accepted you as a friend he or she will hang on. You will have to be really bad to lose the friendship of a Cancerian. If you are related to Cancerians they will never let you go no matter what you do. They will always try to maintain some kind of connection even in the most extreme circumstances.

Finance

The Cancer-born has a deep sense of what other people feel about things and why they feel as they do. This faculty is a great asset in the workplace and in the business world. Of course it is also indispensable in raising a family and building a home, but it also has its uses in business. Cancerians often attain great wealth in a family type of business. Even if the business is not a family operation, they will treat it as one. If the Cancerian works for somebody else then the boss is the parent figure and the fellow employees are brothers and sisters. If a Cancerian is him- or herself the boss, then all the workers are the children. Cancerians like the feeling of being providers for others. They enjoy knowing that others derive their sustenance because of what they do. It is another form of nurturing.

With Leo on their Solar 2nd House (of Money) cusp, Cancerians are often lucky speculators, especially with residential property or hotels and restaurants. Resort hotels and nightclubs are also profitable for the Cancerian. Waterside properties allure them. Though they are basically conventional people they sometimes like to earn their livelihood in glamorous ways.

The Sun, Cancer's Money Planet, represents an important financial message: in financial matters Cancerians need to be less moody, more stable and fixed. They cannot allow their moods – which are here today and gone tomorrow – to get in the way of their business life. They need to develop their self-esteem and feelings of self-worth if they are to realize their greatest financial potential.

Career and Public Image

Aries rules the 10th Solar House (of Career) cusp of Cancer, which indicates that Cancerians long to start their own business, to be more active publicly and politically and to be more independent. Family responsibilities and a fear of hurting other people's feelings – or getting hurt themselves – often inhibit them from attaining these goals. However, this is what they want and long to do.

Cancerians like their bosses and leaders to act freely and to be a bit self-willed. They can deal with that in a superior. Cancerians expect their leaders to be warriors in their defence.

When the Cancerian is in the position of boss or superior he or she behaves very much like a 'warlord'. Of course the wars they wage are not egocentric but in defence of those under their care. If they lack some of this fighting instinct – independence and pioneering spirit – Cancerians will have extreme difficulty in attaining their highest career goals. They will be hampered in their attempts to lead others.

Since they are so parental, Cancerians like to work with children and they make great educators and teachers.

Love and Relationships

Like Taurus, Cancer likes committed relationships. Cancerians function best when the relationship is clearly defined and everyone knows his or her role. When they marry it's usually for life. They are extremely loyal to their beloved. But there is a deep little secret that most Cancerians will never admit to: commitment or partnership is really a chore and a duty to them. They enter into it because they know of no other way to create the family that they desire. Union is just a way – a means to an end – rather than an end in itself. The family is the ultimate end for them.

If you are in love with a Cancerian you must tread lightly on his or her feelings. It will take you a good deal of time to realize how deep and sensitive Cancerians can be. The smallest negativity upsets them. Your tone of voice, your irritation, a look in your eye or an expression on your face can cause great distress for the Cancerian. Your slightest gesture is registered by them and reacted to. This can be hard to get used to, but stick by your love – Cancerians make great partners once you learn how to deal with them. Your Cancerian lover will react not so much to what you say but to the way you are actually feeling at the moment.

Home and Domestic Life

This is where Cancerians really excel. The home environment and the family that they create are their personal works of art. They strive to make things of beauty that will outlast them. Very often they succeed.

Cancerians feel very close to their family, their relatives and especially their mothers. These bonds last throughout their lives and mature as they grow older. They are very fond of those members of their family who become successful and they are also quite attached to family heirlooms and mementos. Cancerians also love children and like to provide them with all the things they need and want. With their nurturing, feeling nature Cancerians make very good parents – especially the Cancerian woman, who is the mother *par excellence* of the Zodiac.

As a parent the Cancerian's attitude is 'my children right or wrong.' Unconditional devotion is the order of the day. No matter what a family member does, the Cancerian will eventually forgive him or her, because 'you are, after all, family.' The preservation of the institution – the tradition – of the family is one of the Cancerian's main reasons for living. They have many lessons to teach others about this.

Being so family-orientated, the Cancerian's home is

always clean, orderly and comfortable. They like old-fashioned furnishings but they also like to have all the modern comforts available. Cancerians love to have family and friends over, to organize parties and to entertain at home – they make great hosts.

Horoscope for 1995

Major Trends

1994 was basically a holiday year, a year for the much-needed rest and recuperation that you so richly deserved. Though 1995 is very much a happy year – the overall trends keep getting better – it is more of a work-orientated year. In 1994 money came to you through luck, creativity and speculations. In 1995 it comes through work and service. Productivity is the key word this year.

In 1994 many of you were deluged with creative ideas. When inspiration comes it is one of the great thrills in your life. When you get inspired it is both important and fun. In 1995 you need to work out these new ideas – in all their details and ramifications – and put them into practice. This is less fun, for after the inspiration comes the perspiration. But if you do everything right the financial rewards will be great. Don't get the idea that this is going to be all work and no play. If you ignore the fun aspect of life this year you will be making a mistake. Work, but have fun as well.

In 1994 your partner was rather mean with you – not for lack of love but because he or she felt financially strapped. This changes in 1995 for the better.

Your love life is still active and exciting in 1995, but this year you lean more towards committed relationships than towards fun and games. Love was so easy in 1994 that many of you saw no need for marriage. (More on this later.)

In 1994 many of you travelled a lot, either for profit or

pleasure. This year you need to stick closer to home and be much more selective and discriminating about travel. Your partner is going to have a lot to say about where you go or don't go and even whether or not you go at all.

Health

1994 brought you a big improvement in health compared with 1993. This trend of good health continues. Most of the major planets are making harmonious aspects to you, and Jupiter, the planet of luck and benevolence, will be in your (6th) House of Health for an unusually long time this year. Thus your House of Health is prominent in 1995 in a positive way.

Besides being the planet of luck and benevolence, Jupiter also happens to be your personal Lord of Health. And Jupiter will be in its own domain – the Sign of Sagittarius where it is unusually powerful – for all of 1995. This is good news. If you are coming into the new year with a health problem, you can expect it to clear up by the time 1995 is over. Not only is the problem going to be healed but its deeper causes will be understood so that you never need be bothered by it again. The causes can be traced to many areas – improper nutrition, negative emotions or an unsuitable career or lifestyle. Whatever the causes, they will be revealed and corrected.

Your understanding of the laws of health is becoming greatly expanded this year, which will enable you to take preventive measures against future problems. Your health, nutrition and exercise become interesting fields of study for you this year. You have a special attraction to courses, books and seminars on these subjects. The philosophy of health and disease is just as interesting to you – and just as important – as the technicalities of the subject. Visits to health spas become likely holiday spots.

Many of you looking for careers will choose work in the health field this year. When other influences in your

Horoscope favour this you can be very successful. Those of you already in health professions will discover that your healing abilities are greatly enhanced. You have a special healing touch right now. This will certainly come in handy as the health of a parent and that of a sibling are delicate; you can be a special force for healing here.

Your interest in health matters is going to increase as the year goes on. This will be a long-term trend here, as Pluto moves into your Health House on 10th November and will stay there for the next 10 to 15 years.

The Moon is your Ruling Planet, Cancer. It has most to do with your physical body, energy and appearance. It is not your Health Planet *per se*, but it affects your body's vitality. You will tend to feel more energetic and enthusiastic (as well as to look better physically) when the Moon is waxing than when it is waning. This is just the rhythm of your nature. If you feel lacklustre or low in energy on some days, check the phase of the Moon. Chances are that it is waning and that your fatigue is just temporary. When the Moon begins its waxing phase or comes under more harmonious aspects you will feel much better.

Home and Domestic Life

Though your home and family are always interesting and important to you, Cancer, this year they are slightly less important than usual. Your 4th House of Home and Family is not prominent this year. This means that the Cosmos is neither helping nor obstructing your family relations or domestic projects. You have more freedom within the home and the family, freedom to pursue your real interests. The most notable change for the better this year is that your family or some family members drop their opposition to your partner or lover.

Family and domestic interests become prominent from 22nd June to 8th September and from 16th September to 24th October. Family members bring you financial opportunities and friends come to visit or stay in your home. Your parents also come to visit or stay, as do bosses or superiors from work. Many career issues will be determined and defined by entertaining done at home. Work from the home done during this period brings profits and happiness.

Many of you are going to acquire a second home this year – the grandeur of which depends on other things. For some this might mean a simple summer home or a 'time-share' in a holiday home. For others it might mean a second palace. It all depends on your personal circumstances. The opportunity, money and inclination will come for this and you should make the most of them for this will be a happy and fortuitous event. This second home is likely to preoccupy you more than your first – your primary – home.

A sibling (if you have one) moves into a larger residence this year, or remodels and expands his or her present one. If you have a sibling of child-bearing age, he or she is also likely to become a parent – this could be the reason for the move. A second sibling (if you have more than one) is moving around like a gypsy from place to place. Your parents are also changing their residence.

Love and Social Life

Your 7th House of Love and Marriage is still very prominent -- as it has been for many years now – in your 1995 Horoscope. Happily this area of life is getting progressively easier and more joyful. True, it is not as happy as it will be in 1996, but it is improved over 1994. The changes, the turbulence, the romantic roller-coasters, the experimentation continues in this area just as it has for the past few years. You are getting much better at adapting to change in your relationships. You are also getting better at exploring the new, the innovative and the experimental. Experiments in love and in romantic overtures are more likely to succeed this year. You are less intimidated by unconventional friends than you have been in the past. You can love them precisely because they are unconventional.

Though you are more serious about love this year and you want to go beyond fun and games, your relationships are still unstable. Your affections remain fickle, subject to sudden changes. You are in love one minute and out of love the next. The transiting planets have much to do with these 'changes of heart'.

Those of you who are single might be better off not marrying this year and just playing the field. Real love will come next year and it might be wiser to sow your wild oats now while you can. All your trial-and-error efforts at love are preparing you for the real thing, which looms on the horizon. If you are involved in a serious relationship this year, living together some kind of informal 'trial marriage' might be the way to go. By the end of the year you'll know whether this relationship can work or not.

Marriages that are weak to begin with have little chance of weathering the year. Of course, do whatever you can to make your present relationship happy and harmonious. But if after you've done your best things still don't work out, let go. Definitely do not hang on to something out of fear.

This year, marrieds will find that their partner's interests have shifted from mere money-making – though this is still important – to more intellectual pursuits. Your partner is taking courses and doing an unusual amount of reading this year. He or she is also deriving great satisfaction from charitable ventures and ministering to others this year. A selfless, spiritual quality – along with great interest in ESP, dreams and mysticism – has entered his or her life.

Singles will find themselves more attracted to educated, intellectual people. You like a partner who can teach you things and guide you into the unknown. In general, you are becoming ever more popular socially, and romantic opportunities are becoming increasingly abundant.

A sibling's marriage is in trouble, though on the outside all seems picture-perfect.

Career and Finance

Your 2nd House of Money and Possessions is not very prominent in this year's Horoscope, Cancer. Neither is your 10th House of Career and Ambition. Of course this doesn't mean that you won't earn money nor that you won't pursue your career, only that these things are less important than other things. In fact, you might even feel a greater sense of financial freedom precisely because money is less important to you. You are not in a position to be coerced or pinched financially.

As mentioned earlier, your partner alternates this year between wild generosity towards you and outrageous meanness. This is not moodiness or irrationality but a reflection of the state of your partner's earning power. It is experimental and changing. At times earnings are wildly high – at which times he or she is more generous with you. At other times money is very tight – these are the times he or she seems mean. Your partner's experimentation is going to lead him or her to complete economic freedom, but in slow stages. It is necessary for him or her to see what doesn't work before what does can be seen clearly. Like you, your partner seems less career-driven than in recent years.

You have the potential for large earnings from your creative ideas and projects. Sports, athletics and companies that deal in these things seem a possible source of wealth. Child care, entertainment and the industries that deal with these callings are also profit-making for you. Your partner can earn money through new inventions and high technology. Your parents profit from a lucky investment.

The Sun is your financial guide, Cancer. The Sun has phases just as the Moon does; you can utilize this information for your financial benefit. The Sun is considered to be waxing – growing – as the days get longer. This occurs from 21st December, the shortest day of the year, to 21st June, the longest. This is the waxing, growing Sun force. The Sun wanes as the days get shorter from 21st June to 21st

December. Thus your earning potential is stronger from 21st December to 21st June, when the Sun is waxing. This is the time for you to start new projects and make investments. On the waning Sun you are better off clearing debts and selling possessions at a profit. The Aspects to the Sun, detailed in the month-by-month forecasts below, are also important factors.

Self-improvement

As mentioned, you are going to make big improvements in your health and in your understanding of health this year. Opportunities for courses, seminars and the like are coming to you and you should take them. You are also going to enlarge your domestic sphere by adding a new home to the one you already have.

You are going to become a more productive and valuable employee. This is a valid way to increase your earnings, though not necessarily in the short term. By being more productive you become worth more on the 'subtle levels of existence', and this is bound – sooner or later – to reflect on your 'bottom line'. You are learning one of the great keys to success this year, to enjoy the work that you do. The joy of the work itself – not necessarily the rewards you get – should motivate you. Your workplace will become more pleasurable almost by itself, but you can help make it even better. Get involved in your work with your whole being and attention. Feel the joy of a job well done, not because some supervisor is watching you but for your own sake. If you can't find joy in the work you are currently doing, look for work that you can find joy in. The opportunities will certainly come.

Month-by-month Forecasts

January

Best Days Overall: 5th, 6th, 15th, 16th, 24th, 25th

Most Stressful Days Overall: 1st, 2nd, 7th, 8th, 22nd, 23rd, 28th, 29th

Best Days for Love: 1st, 2nd, 5th, 7th, 8th, 15th, 16th, 17th, 18th, 19th, 24th, 25th, 26th, 27th, 28th, 29th

Best Days for Money: 1st, 2nd, 7th, 8th, 10th, 11th, 17th, 18th, 22nd, 23rd, 26th, 27th, 30th, 31st

Most of the planets are in the Western sector of your Solar Horoscope this month, Cancer, showing that you are socially active and attaining your goals through the grace of others. You are in situations not of your making and must make the best of it. Your own interests take a back seat to other people's this month. Yet there are many compensations here. First off you get a chance to develop and refine your social skills. Secondly, you become a much more valuable worker and employee this month. Your ability to provide service – your productivity – increases to such an extent that you are any employer's dream come true. You really enjoy your work this month. You love it totally. The work itself is the reward as far as you are concerned – and though the monetary benefits do inevitably follow these are just 'icing on the cake' for you.

Your workplace has suddenly become very sociable, tightly knit and family-like. There are parties there. Gatherings. Fun. Pleasures. Singles are likely to find romance at work.

Though this is not your best health month – you should rest and relax more until the 20th – you are going to hear good news on the health front. A long-standing health problem is harmoniously and happily resolved during this period. Your own personal healing abilities – and this is important for those of you who are health professionals – are strengthened. Health professionals have the magic touch now and gain great satisfaction from it.

Your love life is active and exciting; money comes to you through your social contacts and through your partner's contacts. Marrieds are very experimental in their courtship with each other. Singles are experimental in their choice of partners. There is an emphasis on the fulfilment of romantic fantasies now. As long as you keep the fantasies non-destructive you are fine.

Venus, the Lord of your Home and Family interests, goes conjunct with Jupiter from the 14th to the 16th. Many of you will have opportunities to move or enlarge your house during this time. Others will merely beautify or buy new accessories for the home. Still others will perhaps redecorate. The stars show some definite improvement in daily living conditions. Women Cancerians will be at their most fertile.

Earnings are strong during this period. Until the 20th money and earning opportunities come through social contacts. After the 20th benefits come through making money for others and through the generosity of your partner. You are not overly enthusiastic about wealth during this period, however. Other things are more interesting.

February

Best Days Overall: 1st, 2nd, 11th, 12th, 20th, 21st

Most Stressful Days Overall: 3rd, 4th, 5th, 18th, 19th, 24th, 25th

Best Days for Love: 1st, 2nd, 4th, 5th, 6th, 7th, 11th, 12th, 16th, 17th, 20th, 21st, 24th, 25th

Best Days for Money: 3rd, 4th, 5th, 8th, 9th, 10th, 13th, 14th, 15th, 18th, 19th, 22nd, 23rd, 26th, 27th, 28th

The majority of planets are congregated in both the top and the Western hemispheres of your Solar chart this month, Cancer. By the end of the month 90 per cent of the planets will be in forward motion. There is no doubt that you are in a period of achievement and action. Your life is moving forward on most fronts, yet you feel that you are being 'pulled' by events rather than in control of them. The forward motion of your plans and projects is definitely positive, but you sense that things are happening *to* you and not coming *from* you. This is a strange feeling, but quite normal under the circumstances.

You are outwardly-orientated this month, which is again a bit strange for someone who is a natural introvert like yourself. Yet at times it is healthy to go outside oneself and join in other people's realities.

The workplace is still pleasurable, though some of the rapture of last month is beginning to die down. Your social life is exciting and harmonious after the 4th as Venus moves into your (7th) Marriage House and stays there for the rest of the month. Your partner is romantic but unpredictable, which adds to the fun. Singles find love at parties and through introductions made by friends. Seminars and group activities – perhaps of political or professional organizations – are likely to lead to romance. A casual friend wants to be more than that this month – and shows his or her interest very unexpectedly. This doesn't seem like a long-term thing but rather a short-term infatuation. Handle it accordingly. Married people find more romance with their partners.

In your financial life there are all kinds of cosmic signals that suggest caution and restraint. Mars, your Career Planet is retrograde (travelling backwards) all month in your (2nd) Money House. Your Money Planet, the Sun, travels with conservative Saturn after the 19th. And, until the 16th, Mercury is retrograde. Think through all financial deals – especially long-term commitments – very carefully. If you take risks – and sometimes we must – calculate them very carefully and try to hedge against them. A financial partnership is brewing, but get all the details before you commit yourself. Singles find great pressure to spend money on social activities – going out, dating and the like – but Saturn suggests not going over your budget for these activities.

Your Money Planet in the intuitive Sign of Pisces after the 19th shows that your financial intuition is sharp. But you must test these intuitions as to their practicality and applicability. Staying within your budget is perhaps your toughest financial challenge this month.

Your health is excellent all month.

March

Best Days Overall: 1st, 2nd, 10th, 11th, 12th, 19th, 20th, 28th, 29th

Most Stressful Days Overall: 3rd, 4th, 17th, 18th, 24th, 25th, 30th, 31st

Best Days for Love: 1st, 2nd, 8th, 9th, 10th, 17th, 18th, 19th, 20th, 24th, 25th, 26th, 27th, 28th, 29th

Best Days for Money: 1st, 2nd, 3rd, 4th, 10th, 11th, 12th, 13th, 14th, 19th, 20th, 21st, 22nd, 30th, 31st

Like last month, the overwhelming planetary power is at the top of your Solar Horoscope this month. Thus your career urges continue to be powerful. These urges become even stronger in the spring as the Sun moves in and illuminates your (10th) Career House. It's OK for you to be career-driven now as you tend to spend too much time on domestic issues by nature. Understand that if you are successful and have an honoured place in your business and profession your family will benefit. Don't think of this career push as neglecting your family, think of it as something you owe them.

You are very much concerned with foreign countries and foreign affairs this month. A trip abroad seems likely but it should be planned meticulously. Better a few delays at the beginning than to suffer even greater inconvenience because of poor planning and inadequate preparation.

Though the workplace is still a fundamentally happy place for you, this month you feel edgy there. You want to be out in the wild blue yonder, exploring exotic lands and cultures. You find it hard to focus on the job at hand.

Opportunities for higher education come to you now, but don't think that this will be a lark or some kind of escape from responsibility. On the contrary, there's a lot of work and discipline involved. Don't take these things on unless you are willing to pay the price.

Your health is excellent until the 21st; after that rest and relax more. Focus on your career and let go of lesser priorities. If you do take it easier you will hear some good news about a health problem. The Moon, your Planetary Ruler, waxes from the 1st to the 17th and wanes from the 17th onwards. You will feel more energetic and confident – and even look better – when it waxes than when it wanes. Luckily, the Moon waxes as it moves through your (2nd) Money House on the 13th and 14th. Expect a windfall then.

Finances are a priority this month. A pending deal has been delayed and delayed, and this is causing you some concern. By the 24th it will go forward again. Career success comes after the 21st and dramatically improves your 'bottom line'. Career doubts and confusions are cleared up when Mars, your Career Planet, moves forward on the 24th, and by the New Moon of the 31st. Your financial acumen and acuteness are recognized by elders and superiors; this boosts your status further.

Until the 21st you seem tentative and cautious in money matters. After this, though, your confidence is great. A new courage and aggressiveness enter your attitudes towards money. You have real financial fearlessness. You see your goal and go after it regardless of obstacles and blockages. You are unstoppable as you sweep the opposition off their feet.

April

Best Days Overall: 7th, 8th, 16th, 17th, 24th, 25th

Most Stressful Days Overall: 1st, 14th, 15th, 20th, 21st, 26th, 27th, 28th

Best Days for Love: 7th, 8th, 16th, 17th, 20th, 21st, 24th, 25th, 26th, 27th, 28th

Best Days for Money: 1st, 9th, 10th, 18th, 19th, 20th, 26th, 27th, 28th, 29th, 30th

This is a tumultuous, active month full of important changes for you. Try to roll with the punches and rest and relax as much as possible. You need to be very discerning in your use of energy now. Act only when you think you can be effective, otherwise take a 'wait and see' attitude. Chances are that time itself will reveal your next steps. When in doubt, do nothing.

The planets are still very much concentrated at the top half of your Horoscope, energizing your worldly and career ambitions. Good career progress is being made now. You shine in your profession or business. You shine before the world.

There is a shift of the planetary power towards the Eastern sector of your Horoscope this month as well. Thus the recent dominance of your Western sector on your social life and concern with others is very much lessened. The planets are now evenly dispersed in the Western and Eastern sectors of your chart. This shows that there is more self-assertiveness and personal freedom than you've had recently. You still need other people to attain your ends but you are no longer *totally* at their mercy. A greater measure of personal control is yours.

There are two Eclipses this month, Cancer. Eclipses are always cosmic signals of long-term change regardless of your Sign. But for a Cancer Eclipses are even more dramatic, for the Moon is your Personal Ruler and the Sun is your Financial Ruler. Therefore, Eclipses of these two heavenly bodies always show long-term change in your personal image and appearance and in your financial life. In the case of the Lunar Eclipse of the 15th, definitely take a reduced schedule and avoid gruelling, demanding or risky activities. Your physical energy and vitality will tend to be 'eclipsed' on this day. The Solar Eclipse of the 29th shows a need to avoid risky financial ventures or investments for a few days before and after. In other words, your financial judgement will tend to be 'eclipsed' either by personal ego or by emotional concerns. Let this Eclipse pass before making any important financial decisions.

In addition, the Lunar Eclipse occurs in your 4th House of Home and Family, revealing some important change in the home and in your dealings with family members. The Solar Eclipse of the 29th occurs in your 11th House of Friends, showing a long-term change in your friendships (this House also affects scientific interests). The nature of your 'fondest hopes and wishes', another 11th House area, also undergoes temporary upheaval.

Rest and relax more this month.

May

Best Days Overall: 4th, 5th, 13th, 14th, 21st, 22nd, 23rd, 31st

Most Stressful Days Overall: 11th, 12th, 17th, 18th, 24th, 25th

Best Days for Love: 4th, 5th, 6th, 7th, 8th, 14th, 15th, 16th, 17th, 18th, 21st, 22nd, 23rd, 26th, 27th, 28th, 31st

Best Days for Money: 6th, 7th, 8th, 9th, 10th, 15th, 16th, 17th, 18th, 24th, 25th, 29th, 30th

The fact that more of the planets have shifted over to the Eastern half of the Horoscope gives you a greater sense of balance and perspective this month, Cancer. You have a better idea of your own interests and are not completely at the mercy of other people. The good graces of others are still important, but you are no longer neglecting yourself and what you want to do.

Most of the planets are still above the horizon in your chart, emphasizing your ambitions and outward success – but this is slowly starting to change. You are definitely less career-driven this month than you were last month, and next month you will be less career-driven still.

Career activities are still favourable and a modest pay rise or promotion is likely around the 12th. You are popular with elders and superiors at work and with the public in general. Your current status has a kind of glamour to it that others like.

Your paths of greatest fulfilment this month involve the career, personal creativity, relating to children, fun activities, platonic friendships and work.

The pace at work has slowed considerably now and the need is to plan more and do less, at least for the moment.

On the social front you are enjoying friends more than actual romance. Singles find that friendship is the seed from which romance blossoms. A conflict with a current lover seems to centre around financial issues. Compromise will resolve this conflict, as it's not long term. Your lover or partner is taking bold steps towards economic freedom – radical steps. He or she wants total freedom in the ways that money is earned and the ways it is spent. Your lover doesn't want to have to answer to anybody. You are, in the mean time, more interested in physical intimacy than in courtship.

On the health front your vitality and constitution continue to be sound. But an unconventional health regime, diet or exercise plan that you are considering needs more thought and study.

Finances are exceptionally good now and your fondest financial hopes and dreams are coming to pass this month – only to be supplanted, of course, by new hopes and wishes. A sudden financial windfall comes around the 21st, either through a friend or your partner.

June

Best Days Overall: 1st, 2nd, 10th, 11th, 18th, 19th, 27th, 28th, 29th

Most Stressful Days Overall: 7th, 8th, 9th, 14th, 15th, 20th, 21st

Best Days for Love: 1st, 2nd, 5th, 6th, 10th, 11th, 14th, 15th, 16th, 17th, 18th, 19th, 25th, 26th

Best Days for Money: 3rd, 4th, 7th, 8th, 9th, 12th, 13th, 16th, 17th, 20th, 21st, 27th, 28th, 29th, 30th

The planets are more or less evenly distributed through the various sectors of your chart this month. They are not exactly evenly balanced, but there are no terrible imbalances. Thus you have a balanced perspective on life and are unlikely to take extreme positions on anything. This will help you to deal with some major conflicts going on now – for this is a unique and unusual month.

First off there is a Heavenly Grand Square aspect occurring all month. It is most intense before the 22nd, but it is in effect even after that. The Grand Square requires you to do a juggling act between interests and people – two concerns that are essentially antagonistic. Each is important in your life and demands attention. In your case, the 'tugs of war' involve your work goals versus your partner's work goals; your personal spiritual revelations versus the teachings of your church or religious upbringing; the urge to travel locally versus the urge to travel abroad; mundane pursuits versus the urge for higher education.

The Grand Square reveals the need for action and change – something new must be built. A new form or lifestyle must be created that will encompass all these concerns harmoniously. Yet with 50 per cent of the planets retrograde there is a stress on caution and inaction. And here you are, stuck between two equally powerful urges.

This situation will start to ease up after the 17th when Mercury starts going direct. And, after the 22nd when the Sun moves into your own Sign, you should notice a greater sense of self-confidence and will once again be able to recognize what's best for you. Constructive actions will become less difficult then. Not easy by any means, but less difficult.

Finances are bit sticky before the 22nd. You have to work harder to maintain your usual level of earnings. But after then there is great improvement. You tend to be overly sacrificing with your money before the 22nd, giving more than your share to charities and to those in need. In business ventures, too, there is a sense of sentiment overruling good business sense. But this will change after the 22nd.

Your love life is stormy before the 22nd. This has to do with personal travails that your partner or lover is going through and not with the basic relationship. By the 22nd the relationship stabilizes.

Your health is good all month.

July

Best Days Overall: 7th, 8th, 15th, 16th, 25th, 26th

Most Stressful Days Overall: 5th, 6th, 11th, 12th, 17th, 18th

Best Days for Love: 7th, 8th, 11th, 12th, 15th, 16th, 25th, 26th

Best Days for Money: 1st, 7th, 8th, 9th, 10th, 15th, 16th, 17th, 18th, 27th, 28th

In spite of all the hurdles and delay – 50 per cent of the planets are retrograde – this is one of the best months of your year, Cancer. You make great personal progress and sail towards your financial and personal goals without obstruction. You are a marvel to friend and foe alike. Your health is excellent, your vitality superabundant and your personal charisma strong.

With so many planets moving through your own Sign you are more influential this month and tend to get your way. Yet you are not stepping on other people or pushing them around. You get your way with charm and grace and others seem happy to yield to you. With both the Eastern and Western sectors of your chart more or less evenly balanced you have a balanced perspective between your needs and other people's, and others sense this.

This is a month of physical activity, personal pleasure and sensual delights. You excel in sports and exercise programmes. You enjoy keeping active and fit.

Your (2nd) Money House also gets a lot of stimulation from the planets this month. Three planets move into this area after the 23rd and the New Moon of the 27th occurs there. Anything you need to know about your present financial situation – investments, purchases or deals – will be revealed to you towards the end of the month. You can expect a net increase in your 'bottom line' by the time the month is over. You shine as a financial wheeler-dealer. Both women and men are eager to help you achieve financial goals. Speculations are favourable and you tend to be generous when giving to worthy causes. Your financial dreams are quite practical after the 26th. New scientific and technological knowledge leads you to profits and otherwise increases your earning power.

Your Career Planet, Mars, is in your 3rd House of Communication until the 22nd, showing that you can boost your career by getting more knowledge through studies and intellectual pursuits. Self-promotion pays. After the 22nd you seem more ambitious for your family or family members than you are for yourself. There is a wisdom in this. As you promote other people's careers your own gets promoted as well. Mars in your 4th House of Family also reinforces what was said earlier about building a stable home and emotional base. The higher you would go in the world, the deeper must be your emotional foundations.

Your partner or lover seems to be pursuing intellectual interests during this period; you are supportive about this. Communication seems particularly good between you as your intellectual interests harmonize. Singles are attracting the opposite sex, but marriage or a serious commitment should not be scheduled this month. Singles find love at universities, church socials and in foreign lands.

August

Best Days Overall: 3rd, 4th, 12th, 21st, 22nd, 31st

Most Stressful Days Overall: 1st, 2nd, 7th, 8th, 14th, 15th, 28th, 29th

Best Days for Love: 3rd, 4th, 5th, 6th, 7th, 8th, 12th, 13th, 14th, 15th, 21st, 22nd, 26th, 27th, 31st

Best Days for Money: 5th, 6th, 14th, 15th, 24th, 25th, 26th, 27th

Amazingly, many of the frustrations of the past few months have fallen away of their own accord. Many of the delays are easing as two important planets start moving forward again. The planetary power is still increasing in your Western hemisphere though, showing that you need patience and are not yet ready to do things on your own. Adapt yourself to situations and put other people first. If you do this, your own needs will be fulfilled quite naturally.

Mars, your Career Planet, occupies the lowest point of your chart, showing that it is your 'lowest priority' at the moment. Your family comes before your career. Personal happiness and emotional security still take precedence. Even other people's careers come before your own. This is a period during which you continue to be more ambitious for others than you are for yourself. Your family as a whole – or perhaps individual family members – are enjoying career success. Your role is supportive for the moment.

Your paths of greatest fulfilment are the achievement of work goals, dietary regimes, body detoxification, personal creativity, children, fun activities, money-making and the home.

Your health and vitality are excellent all month. If you have had a nagging health problem of late, this month you hear good news about it. Jupiter, your Health Planet, finally starts to go forward again. You make progress in personal health. Floundering dietary regimes can now be made to work.

Your (2nd) Money House is very powerful this month and the planets in this House are favourably aspected. Earnings begin to zoom after the 2nd. Financial opportunities come through friends and neighbours; all the wealth you need is close to home. Your financial judgement and intuition are sound and your generosity to the underprivileged is great. The more you give the more you get. Your ability to go beyond your normal work quota also adds to your bank balance. You are a very productive worker this month.

Don't think that the pursuit of knowledge is impractical. It has important financial results after the 23rd. Sales activities go well and enhance your net worth.

Your love life is still at something of an impasse. This fosters the status quo. Marrieds tend to stay married and singles tend to stay single. New relationships are entered into very cautiously. New friends are looked over carefully. You don't accept others straight away. Your social judgement is not as sound as it usually is.

September

Best Days Overall: 8th, 9th, 17th, 18th, 19th, 27th, 28th

Most Stressful Days Overall: 4th, 5th, 10th, 11th, 25th

Best Days for Love: 4th, 5th, 8th, 9th, 12th, 13th, 14th, 17th, 18th, 19th, 24th, 25th, 27th, 28th

Best Days for Money: 2nd, 4th, 5th, 10th, 11th, 12th, 13th, 14th, 20th, 21st, 23rd, 24th, 25th, 29th, 30th

The unusually high percentage of the planets in the Western sector of your Horoscope – after the 23rd it will be 100 per cent – signals your ever-increasing social activity and feeling dependent on others. You tend to lose your own centre temporarily, to forget who you are and to see the world as other people see it. There is nothing wrong with this *per se*, but it is quite dangerous to lose your own perspective on things. You run the risk of letting yourself be defined by others and of seeking yourself in other people.

You are so aware of others now that decision-making is more difficult. You see every side of every argument. Very much like a Libra now, you put every position on your 'inner scale' and weigh it. This is the cause for your lack of decisiveness. You so much want to please everyone that you run the risk of pleasing no one. Finding a way forward is the challenge you must face this month.

There is a positive side to all of this. You have genuine empathy for others. You are more socially charismatic than usual. You are a gifted politician now and get things done by consensus. It's as if, temporarily at least, you exist for other people.

Your paths of greatest happiness this month are intellectual pursuits, local travel, the home, domestic projects, family interests and the achievement of health and work goals.

Your health is excellent until the 23rd, but after that you should rest and relax more. Your health is enhanced by eating the right foods, having a sense of being useful to others and fostering a sound philosophy of health and disease.

Financial matters go reasonably well until the 23rd, though you do have to resolve a financial conflict with your partner or lover around the 14th. Money comes through sales and marketing projects and you tend to spend on computers and communication equipment. After the 23rd you see how psychological understanding – always your strong point – translates into earning power. Your ability to discern moods and trends helps you to prosper. You tend to earn money through family connections, family businesses and real estate. You also tend to spend more on your family. Be patient with your partner for his or her affairs still seem deadlocked temporarily. Apparently your partner is working on big things, and these take more time.

Though you are more socially popular than you've been in a long while, a current love affair needs time. It seems to go backwards instead of forward. It would not be wise to plan a marriage or begin divorce proceedings at this time.

October

Best Days Overall: 5th, 6th, 15th, 16th, 24th, 25th

Most Stressful Days Overall: 1st, 2nd, 7th, 8th, 9th, 22nd, 23rd, 28th, 29th

Best Days for Love: 1st, 2nd, 3rd, 4th, 5th, 6th, 15th, 16th, 24th, 25th, 28th, 29th

Best Days for Money: 3rd, 4th, 7th, 8th, 9th, 12th, 13th, 17th, 18th, 23rd, 24th, 25th, 26th, 27th

This is a highly unusual but happy month. First off, the Western sector of your Horoscope is very prominent, with 90 to 100 per cent of all the planets positioned there now. Secondly there are two Eclipses – cosmic announcements – this month. One of these involves your Ruler, the Moon, the other involves your Money Planet, the Sun. Thirdly, after the 14th, 90 per cent of the planets will be in forward motion, ending, almost completely, the general sense of stalemate of recent months.

What does this all mean for you? Well, the focus in the Western sector shows a greater dependence on others, an urge to form partnerships and to associate with others, and the need to obtain consensus before doing anything. You continually need to adapt to situations not of your creation and make the best of them. Your self-esteem is very much tied up with how others see you – which at times can lead you to being hurt. Yet this sensitivity makes for social popularity and an increasing circle of friends. Your good comes to you through others, with little personal effort. You tend to see yourself as other people see you.

The Lunar Eclipse of the 8th is the more important of the two Eclipses as it involves your Ruler. It occurs in your 10th House of Career, heralding long-term changes in the career and in the corporate hierarchy in which you are involved. Expect shifts of power within your company. Some superiors leave or are removed. New ones come in. Your public persona gets re-defined now. Take a reduced schedule on this day.

The Solar Eclipse of the 24th occurs in your 5th Solar House of Fun, Speculations and Love Affairs. This indicates that a lucky speculation or financial windfall will get temporarily Eclipsed. The returns will either be temporarily lessened or come in much later than expected. There will be upheavals with children as well, but these upheavals will lead to a healthier relationship later on. Repressed grievances come to the surface to be dealt with. Your personal creativity undergoes long-term change. A love affair outside of marriage is thrown into turmoil and is likely to end.

Rest and relax more until the 24th. Your health and vitality return to above normal levels after then.

November

Best Days Overall: 6th, 7th, 16th, 17th, 25th

Most Stressful Days Overall: 4th, 5th, 18th, 19th, 25th

Best Days for Love: 1st, 2nd, 3rd, 4th, 11th, 12th, 14th, 15th, 21st, 22nd, 23rd, 24th, 25th, 26th, 29th, 30th

Best Days for Money: 1st, 2nd, 3rd, 4th, 5th, 11th, 12th, 14th, 15th, 21st, 22nd, 23rd

Ninety to 100 per cent of the planets continue to energize the Western sector of your chart this month, and their Western swing has not yet peaked. Thus you are called to adapt yourself to situations that are alien to you, to put others ahead of yourself, and to allow things to happen rather than making them happen. You need the good opinion and the good graces of other people now.

The majority of the planets are still below the horizon of your chart, making your need for emotional security stronger than your need for career success.

Your paths of greatest fulfilment are personal creativity, the achievement of work goals, dietary regimes and love.

Emotional harmony and domestic happiness are fostered

this month by creativity around the home, having more fun at home, taking part in activities with children and being of practical service to family members and those who are part of your emotional support system.

You can prepare for future career expansion by becoming a more productive worker now. Master the details, dot the 'I's and cross the 'T's – and enjoy yourself as you do so. Make it a game, make it fun. This will attract the positive attention of superiors. The interesting thing is that though you are relatively unambitious during this period, a career promotion – in harmony with your family needs – is likely during right now.

Pluto, your Planet of Fun and Games, makes a major, long-term move into your 6th House of Work this month, and it will stay there for many years to come. Since this only happens every 15 to 30 years (Pluto's orbit is very erratic) it is worth mentioning. You need to achieve work goals in creative ways. Bring fun and originality into your work for the long term. This shift also shows that your personal creativity – the expression of repressed artistic feelings in constructive ways – is now a factor in your general health. Repressed creativity can negatively affect your health.

Finances are excellent this month and you are a lucky speculator. You earn money pleasurably and through personal creativity; you don't take the money-making game too seriously. You are lighthearted and loose, thus you probably earn more. After the 23rd money comes through your work. Windfalls come through overtime, greater productivity and the like.

December

Best Days Overall: 8th, 9th, 18th, 19th, 26th, 27th

Most Stressful Days Overall: 1st, 2nd, 16th, 17th, 22nd, 23rd, 28th, 29th

Best Days for Love: 3rd, 4th, 8th, 9th, 13th, 14th, 18th, 19th, 22nd, 23rd, 24th, 26th, 27th

Best Days for Money: 1st, 2nd, 11th, 12th, 20th, 21st, 28th, 29th, 30th, 31st

With the exception of the Moon, all the planets are in the Western sector of your chart, as they were last month. This month is different in that the planets are now at the most westerly point of the Horoscope. This will be a peak period socially.

You are still unusually 'other-orientated', putting others ahead of yourself and gaining your good through the goodness of others. Other people are like mirrors to you now, in which you see yourself. You are in a position – and this has been going on for the past few months – where you need others to form favourable judgements about you. You cannot afford for them to have erroneous or slanted opinions about you. This is perhaps the most burdensome part of this kind of stellar configuration. You need constantly to explain yourself and what you mean in order to fend off negative judgements. This is tiresome and difficult, but necessary.

After the 22nd your social life becomes even more active than ever and others seem more favourably disposed and less likely to form negative judgements about you.

The planets are moving upwards in your chart, and by the 22nd 70 to 80 per cent of them will be there. Thus you are becoming ever more ambitious, ever more concerned with the future and with your status in society and in your profession. You are spending more and more time with administrators, government officials and 'power people', and less time with your family. However, with the Moon's North Node in your 4th House of Family it would be very unwise for you to ignore them completely. Give them their due.

Your paths of greatest fulfilment are the home and family,

keeping fit, the achievement of work goals, your love life and physical intimacy.

There is no question that your social life is the dominant interest this month. Marriage and romance are very much on your mind. Singles are likely to find that special someone now; marrieds become more romantic with each other. Love is a real roller-coaster ride, but this is all part of the excitement. Your lover will not allow you to take him or her for granted. Passionate break-ups are followed by equally passionate make-ups. Old friends leave and new ones are made. Social surprise follows social surprise in endless progression.

Your health is good until the 22nd, but after that rest and relax more.

Leo

♌

THE LION

Birthdays from
21st July
to 21st August

Personality Profile

LEO AT A GLANCE

Element – Fire

Ruling planet – Sun
Career planet – Venus
Health planet – Saturn
Love planet – Uranus
Money planet – Mercury

Colours – gold, orange, red

Colours that promote love, romance and social harmony – black, indigo, ultramarine blue

Colours that promote earning power – yellow, yellow-orange

Gems – amber, chrysolite, yellow diamond

Metal – gold

Scents – bergamot, frankincense, musk, neroli

Quality – fixed (= stability)

Quality most needed for balance – humility

Strongest virtues – leadership ability, self-esteem and confidence, generosity, creativity, love of joy

Deepest needs – fun, elation, the need to shine

Characteristics to avoid – arrogance, vanity, bossiness

Signs of greatest overall compatibility – Aries, Sagittarius

Signs of greatest overall incompatibility – Taurus, Scorpio, Aquarius

Sign most helpful to career – Taurus

Sign most helpful for emotional support – Scorpio

Sign most helpful financially – Virgo

Sign best for marriage and/or partnerships – Aquarius

Sign most helpful for creative projects – Sagittarius

Best Sign to have fun with – Sagittarius

Signs most helpful in spiritual matters – Aries, Cancer

Best day of the week – Sunday

Understanding the Leo Personality

When you think of Leo, think of royalty – that way you'll get an idea of what the Leo character is all about and why Leos are the way they are. It is true that for various reasons some Leo-born are not always expressing this quality, but even if they are not they should like to do so.

A monarch rules not by example (as does Aries) nor by consensus (as do Capricorn and Aquarius) but by personal will. Will is law. Personal taste becomes the style that is imitated by all subjects. A monarch is somehow larger than life. This is how a Leo desires to be.

When you dispute the personal will of a Leo it is serious business. He or she takes it as a personal affront, an insult. Leos will let you know that their will carries authority and that to disobey is demeaning and disrespectful.

A Leo is king (or queen) of his or her personal domain. Subordinates, friends and family are the loyal and trusted subjects. Leos rule with benevolent grace and in the best interests of others. They have a powerful presence; indeed, they are powerful people. They seem to attract attention in any social gathering. They stand out because they are stars in their domain. Leos feel that, like the Sun, they are made to shine and rule. Leos feel that they were born to special privilege and royal prerogatives – and most of them attain this status, at least to some degree.

The Sun is the Ruler of this Sign, and when you think of sunshine it is very difficult to feel unhealthy or depressed. Somehow the light of the Sun is the very antithesis of illness and apathy. Leos love life. They also love to have fun; they love drama, music, the theatre and amusements of all sorts. These are the things that give joy to life. If – even in their best interest – you try to deprive Leos of their pleasures, good food, drink and entertainment, you run the serious risk of depriving them of the will to live. To them life without joy is no life at all.

Leos epitomize humanity's will to power. But power in and

of itself – regardless of what some people say – is neither good nor evil. Only when power is abused does it becomes evil. Without power even good things can't come to pass. Leos realize this and are uniquely qualified to wield power. Of all the Signs, they do it most naturally. Capricorn, the other power Sign of the Zodiac, is a better manager and administrator than Leo – much better. But Leo outshines Capricorn in personal grace and presence. Leo loves power where Capricorn assumes power out of a sense of duty.

Finance

Leos are great leaders but not necessarily good managers. They are better at handling the overall picture than the nitty-gritty details of business. If they have good managers working for them they can become exceptional executives. They have vision and a lot of creativity.

Leos love wealth for the pleasures it can bring. They love an opulent lifestyle, pomp and glamour. Even when they are not wealthy they live as if they are. This is why many fall into debt, from which it is sometimes difficult to emerge.

Leos, like Pisceans, are generous to a fault. Very often they want to acquire wealth solely so that they can help others economically. Wealth to Leo buys services and managerial ability. It creates jobs for others and improves the general well-being of those around them. Therefore – to a Leo – wealth is good. Wealth is to be enjoyed to the fullest. Money is not to be left to gather dust in a mouldy bank vault but to be enjoyed, spread around, used. So Leos can be quite reckless in their spending.

With the Sign of Virgo on Leo's 2nd House (of Money) cusp, Leo needs to develop some of Virgo's traits of analysis, discrimination and purity when it comes to money matters. They must learn to be more careful with the details of finance (or to hire people to do this for them). They have to be more cost-conscious in their spending habits. Basically, they need to manage their money better. Leos tend to chafe under financial constraints, yet these constraints can help Leos reach their highest financial potential.

Leos like it when their friends and family know that they can depend on them for financial support. They don't mind – even enjoy – lending money, but they are careful that they are not being taken advantage of. From their 'regal throne' Leos like to bestow gifts upon their family and friends and then enjoy the good feelings these gifts bring to everybody. Leos love financial speculations and – when the celestial influences are right – are often lucky.

Career and Public Image

Leos like to be perceived as wealthy, for in today's world wealth often equals power. When they attain wealth they love having a large house with lots of land and animals.

At their jobs Leos excel in positions of authority and power. They are good at making decisions – on a grand level – but they prefer to leave the small details for others to take care of. Leos are well respected by their colleagues and subordinates, mainly because they have a knack for understanding and relating to those around them. Leos usually strive for the top positions even if they have to start at the bottom and work hard to get there. As might be expected of such a charismatic Sign, Leos are always trying to improve their work situation. They do so in order to have a better chance of advancing to the top.

On the other hand, Leos do not like to be bossed around or told what to do. Perhaps this is why they aspire so for the top – where they can be the decision-makers and needn't take orders from others.

Leos never doubt their success and focus all their attention and efforts on achieving it. Another great Leo characteristic is that – just like good monarchs – they do not attempt to abuse the power or the success they achieve. If they do so this is not wilful or intentional. Usually they like to share their wealth and try to make everyone around them join in their success.

Leos are – and like to be perceived as – hard-working, well-established individuals. It is definitely true that they are capable of hard work and often manage great things. But don't forget that, deep down inside, Leos really are fun-lovers.

Love and Relationships

Generally, Leos are not the marrying kind. To them relationships are good while they are pleasurable. When the relationship ceases to be pleasurable a true Leo will want out. They always want to have the freedom to leave. That is why Leos excel at love affairs rather than commitment. Once married, however, Leo is faithful – even if some Leos have a tendency to marry more than once in their lifetime. If you are in love with a Leo, just show him or her a good time. Travel, go to casinos and clubs, the theatre and discos. Wine and dine your Leo love – it's expensive but worth it and you'll have fun.

Leos generally have an active love life and are demonstrative in their affections. They love to be with other optimistic and fun-loving types like themselves, but wind up settling with someone more serious, intellectual and unconventional. The partner of a Leo tends to be more political and socially conscious than he or she is and more libertarian. When you marry a Leo, mastering the freedom-loving tendencies of your partner will definitely become a life-long challenge – but be careful that Leo doesn't master you.

Aquarius sits on Leo's 7th House (of Love) cusp. Thus if Leos want to realize their highest love and social potential they need to develop a more egalitarian, Aquarian perspective on others. This is not easy for Leo, for 'the king' finds his equals only among other 'kings'. But perhaps this is the solution to Leo's social challenge – to be 'a king among kings'. It's all right to be royal, but recognize the nobility in others.

Home and Domestic Life

Although Leos are great entertainers and love having people over, sometimes this is all show. Only very few close friends will get to see the real side of a Leo's day-to-day life. To a Leo the home is a place of comfort, recreation and transformation; a secret, private retreat – a castle. Leos like to spend money, show off a bit, entertain and have fun. They enjoy the latest furnishings, clothes and gadgets – all things fit for kings.

Leos are fiercely loyal to their family and of course expect the same from them. They love their children almost to a fault; they have to be careful they don't spoil them too much. They also must try to avoid attempting to make individual family members over in their own image. Leos should keep in mind that others also have the need to be their own people. That is why Leos have to be extra careful about being over-bossy or over-domineering in the home.

Horoscope for 1995

Major Trends

1994 was a family, psychological, 'behind the scenes' type of year. You were building the emotional support system necessary to pursue your career goals in the future. It was a serious, work-orientated year with little outlet for your flamboyant fun-loving nature. The truth is you were not really yourself. You were forced to develop other, perhaps weaker, attributes of your nature for future success later on. Your health and self-esteem were not what they should have been.

Happily all this is changing. Saturn, which for two years or so was opposing you in the Sign of Aquarius, is now firmly positioned in Pisces, moving away from its stressful aspect to you. Jupiter, which was also making stressful aspects to you, will be in the Sign of Sagittarius – in harmonious relations with you – all year. Pluto has been making stressful aspects to you for many, many years now. This year Pluto is getting ready to leave Scorpio and move into the more compatible Sagittarius. There it will remain for many years to come, strengthening and supporting you. The long-term trends are positive indeed. 1995 is like a new birth for you. You are born into yourself, into a universe that loves and supports you for who you are. The sense of blockage, frustration, resistance and struggle which you have felt for so many years is finally leaving. You achieve goals and express yourself with ease. Genuine happiness comes into your life in various ways. 1995 is a fun year, and no one knows how to have fun better than you. Enjoy.

Health

Your 6th House of Health has been prominent in your Solar Horoscope for many years now, Leo. It continues to be prominent in 1995. All your experimenting these past few years has probably shown you how many different approaches to health there are. Irrespective of all the health fads that you've been involved in – perhaps in spite of them – your health improves dramatically. Was it that new health food that did it? Was it the new diet or exercise regime that helped you to feel vital and glowingly alive? Perhaps. The Horoscope shows that your health improves almost by itself.

The Celestial Forces are pouring their Life-Force into you and this is stronger than any medicine. Life-Force – called by various names in different cultures – is the Ultimate Health Tonic. The planets have always been pouring their Life-Force into you, but because they were in stressful aspect you had trouble receiving and assimilating it. Now they are filling you with life and power in ways that are comfortable and harmonious to you. Towards the end of the year – 10th

November – when Pluto leaves the Sign of Scorpio you will again feel your natural superabundant vitality. Few Signs have this kind of vitality.

In spite of these improvements, however, there still is a trend of experimentation going on. Perhaps you are experimenting with other people's health, trying out different techniques to heal others. Perhaps you want to enhance your vitality further, to break records for endurance and the like. If this is so, you will certainly succeed. You have a lot going for you this year. A sibling could use your knowledge and expertise about health in 1995.

Home and Domestic Life

Though your 4th Solar House of Home and Family continues to be prominent in your 1995 Horoscope it is not as prominent as it was last year. Whatever remodelling or expansion that needed to be made has by now been made. The emotional support that you needed is now in place. This year you just perfect what was done last year, adding the finishing touches. By the time Pluto leaves your 4th House on 10th November you will have acquired all the domestic comforts and psychological insights that you need.

You still need to get rid of old possessions in the home and old emotional baggage from your childhood. This has been a long-term trend and it continues for most of the year. By now you should be quite good at this sort of thing.

You are less involved with family members this year and more involved with children – an activity you love by your nature. Many Leo women have given birth in the past year. Others are involved with their grandchildren more. Still others are involved with the children of lovers or partners. This is a source of great pleasure to you. You have a special knack with them – especially after the psychological expansions that you've had in 1994. Children teach you things that you can't learn from any book.

Though your primary residence seems in ship-shape order,

those of you who have second or even third homes are having some problems with them. All kinds of repair work needs to be done and the value of the home – especially the third one – has gone down. It will be difficult to sell, if selling is what you have in mind.

Those of you looking to acquire a second home don't seem to be clear as to what exactly you want. You are not sure whether it should be in the mountains or near water. Should it be 'high-tech' or 'artsy'? You see something that you think is your dream house and a week later you see something better. You are learning your true desire through trial and error.

Love and Social Life

Your 7th House of Love and Marriage continues to be prominent and important in your 1995 Solar Horoscope. It is a lot happier and fulfilling than it has been in the past two years. The sense of idealism and experimentation in relationships continues – as this is a long-term trend – but experiments are more likely to bring happiness than disappointment this year.

For the past two years or so you've had the need to be more selective in your romantic adventures. You couldn't let yourself go romantically. You felt inhibited – very unlike you – in giving and receiving love. Much of this had to do with health concerns. But now these health concerns are gone, and you are more free and uninhibited.

Your partner's attitude towards you has also changed for the better. For the past two years your partner has tended to be overbearing, controlling, and probably exacting with you, criticizing every little thing. This year your partner has shifted the focus to money matters, leaving you alone. This is the situation with marrieds. Singles will find that, whereas they were once attracted to older, more stable 'parental' figures, they are now attracted to freer unconventional types.

Singles are being led – through trial and error,

experimentation and bold new paths – to their ideal love. Ideal love is certainly worth the price of a few failures.

Jupiter will be in your 5th House of Love Affairs and Fun and Games all year. This is going to increase the romantic opportunities available to you. Whether you are single or married there are many people out there who want to show you a good time, without getting too serious. You are more receptive to this right now. This is heady stuff for the self-esteem, but also confusing. A big part of you wants a serious, committed relationship while another part wants fun and games. If you can find both of these qualities in one person this year you'll have found the ideal relationship. Those of you involved with Leos take note. Show them a good time and be willing to be experimental in love.

Mars makes an unusually long four-month transit in your own Sign this year, from 23rd January to 26th May. When this happens you are going to become more forceful, more self-centred – but not in a malicious way – more argumentative and self-willed. True, your self-confidence will be strong, but you run the risk of seeming arrogant and overbearing to your partner. Be careful. Know your own strength.

As has been the trend for many years now, you find love at the workplace or in hospitals and health clinics. Co-workers or those involved in your health care are particularly attractive. This is not too surprising, because health and work have been important interests for you and you tend to spend a lot of time in these pursuits. This increases the likelihood of romantic opportunity there.

But it goes deeper than that. You long for a person who not only shows you a good time and who is innovative and experimental, but who wants to serve your needs in practical ways. You want to serve and be served. You want someone who cares about your physical well-being and the details of your everyday life. Bosses will tend to fall in love with their secretaries, patients with their doctors, nurses or therapists and vice versa, workers with co-workers.

Career and Finance

Money and career are not priorities this year, Leo. Work is important, but not in terms of your career as much as your self-esteem and social standing. You are not working hard in order to attain career goals – power and position and the like – but to feel productive, of service and to be worthy of love. You don't mind helping others to prosper so long as these others allow you the freedom to enjoy life this year. Those who have Leos in their employ should take note. Don't be upset if a Leo you know is not that serious at the workplace. This is a year in which Leos want to have some fun. Make the workplace fun for them and you will have a happy and productive employee. Give Leo some scope for experimenting with different ways to get the job done and you might get some brilliant, profitable ideas.

The workplace is more like a school for you Leo than a job. Here you are learning valuable skills, social graces and the ability to build consensus. You are making social contacts here that you will have for the rest of your life. Many of the people you meet through your work are not only going to be romantic partners but also potential investors in your projects and plans. Love the workplace and respect it for what it is.

This is a year in which you make money by helping others to prosper. Debts are repaid with sudden, lightning-like rapidity. Be careful that you don't get into debt just as suddenly. If you are looking for investors, these too will come when you least expect it and probably in the shape of the most unlikely of people. Ideas that you get at the workplace can lead to new inventions and royalties.

Those of you looking for work are likely to find it through your partner or through people involved in your partner's financial life.

Your partner is much more involved in money matters than you are. This has become a long-term priority. The earnings of your partner fluctuate wildly, and he or she is working hard to get things on an even, more controllable keel. Your partner needs to become more businesslike about finances – to make better buying decisions and to get the most out of existing resources. He or she is working hard to eliminate waste and unnecessary expense. This is why your partner seems less generous with you. Over the long haul though, your partner will be fair and just. You will get what you deserve, but no more.

Emotional and psychological insights can bring you money in all sorts of ways this year, by enhancing your creativity and by releasing creative ideas that were submerged in the psychic quagmire or the past. Whether you lived in a palace or not, in 1994 you transformed your home more into the image of your ideal. It has become your personal showcase, on whatever economic level you happen to be. Thus your home can be a source of profit as well as the place where you live.

Self-improvement

Your major area of improvement this year – and this will happen quite naturally and with little effort on your part – is in your creativity and the fun aspect of your life. The creative ideas are there in superabundance, you just need to work out the practical details.

You can improve your social life – as well as economic affairs – by co-operating with your partner's financial goals. Don't become part of his or her problem. Help your partner create the solution.

Saturn, the great tester, will be in your 8th House of Transformation and Elimination for the next two years. This suggests that you are going to be taught major life lessons about letting go of the old and the outworn, releasing yourself from vain attachments and recognizing the need to re-invent yourself as you will. Most of us – until we learn the lessons of the 8th House – are really creations of our parents, society and culture. We are not really ourselves. Saturn in the

8th House will teach you to develop yourself along the lines of your true heart's desire. Be patient and co-operate with the process. The rewards are great.

Month-by-month Forecasts

January

Best Days Overall: 7th, 8th, 17th, 18th, 26th, 27th

Most Stressful Days Overall: 3rd, 4th, 10th, 11th, 24th, 25th, 30th, 31st

Best Days for Love: 1st, 3rd, 4th, 7th, 8th, 11th, 17th, 18th, 19th, 20th, 26th, 27th, 28th, 29th, 30th, 31st

Best Days for Money: 1st, 2nd, 7th, 8th, 12th, 13th, 17th, 18th, 19th, 20th, 21st, 23rd, 27th, 30th, 31st

Though 80 to 90 per cent of the planets are in the Western segment of your Horoscope – and you know that your good comes from the grace of others – you don't give in easily to others. Partly this is due to your kingly Leo nature and partly due to having Mars in your own Sign. Yes, you are dependent on others but self-assertive as well. It would be best to tame this over-assertiveness as it doesn't dignify you but rather reveals inherent weaknesses. Use the Mars force for sports, body-building and exercise rather than getting involved in power struggles that will get you nowhere.

Don't be dismayed by your career plans being delayed. Authorities who have been favouring you will continue to favour you, only they need time to review things. There are many secret issues that have to be resolved before your career can go forward again – and it will, and favourably to boot. Be patient. If you feel you have been overlooked for some promotion or job, Mars being retrograde (moving backwards) all month is going to give the powers that be time to correct their errors.

In the mean time, have fun this month. This is a kind of holiday month for you. Jupiter, Venus and Pluto will all be in your 5th House of Fun and Creativity for most of the month. Go to the theatre, the disco or cinema. Attend parties, or throw some. Speculations are favourable and your personal creativity is at an all-time high. Spend time with children. If you have your own, spend more time with them. If you haven't have any children, volunteer to help other people with theirs. There's a lot of joy and fulfilment here for you.

Romantic opportunities are abundant this month, Leo, only none of them seem too serious. But you of all people know how to enjoy any relationship just for what it is. Enjoy the opportunities as they arise without putting too many expectations on them. Romance has the potential to become serious after the 20th.

On the financial front you are working for your earnings and you go way beyond the call of duty in order to earn your money. Curiously, you might make more from a lucky speculation – or from your creativity – than from all of this hard work! Yet work you must and let the chips fall where they may. Your Money Planet, Mercury, goes retrograde on the 26th, so be more cautious about financial commitments then. Don't sign any contracts or make any major purchases during this retrograde period. Financial ventures need more careful review.

Your health is excellent this month, but after the 20th rest and relax more.

February

Best Days Overall: 3rd, 4th, 5th, 13th, 14th, 15th, 22nd, 23rd

Most Stressful Days Overall: 6th, 7th, 20th, 21st, 26th, 27th, 28th

Best Days for Love: 4th, 5th, 6th, 7th, 16th, 17th, 24th, 25th, 26th, 27th, 28th

Best Days for Money: 3rd, 4th, 5th, 9th, 10th, 13th, 14th, 15th, 16th, 18th, 19th, 22nd, 23rd, 26th, 27th, 28th

Though the planets are quite evenly dispersed between the top and bottom halves of your Solar Horoscope, 80 to 90 per cent of them are still in the Western sector. This shows that you are mostly focused on other people and their needs; you are not creating and shaping events so much as reacting to them; you tend to – or perhaps are forced to – overlook your own interests in favour of other people's. There is no need to tell a Leo how uncomfortable this can be, yet no other Sign can derive as much benefit from this as Leo. Yes, you are a king or queen, but so are others. They too are royal and worthy of having their way. By all means affirm your royal prerogatives, but affirm theirs as well. Your social skills are getting sharpened and if you handle this right you'll find that your own interests get taken care of quite naturally.

Mercury, your Money Planet, is still retrograde until the 16th. Though you feel that you are going backwards financially – some deals and payments due you are probably delayed – the actuality here is otherwise. If you cannot apply caution to your financial dealings, the Cosmos will supply the caution. Deals, investments and major purchases need further review. The retrograde of your Money Planet shows that your financial judgement is not as sound as it should be. This could lead to losses – thus the need for caution. Your earning power is still very strong, however, and you will see this when Mercury starts going forward after the 16th. A literal flood of earning opportunities comes to you – through your social contacts and through your partner. Your partner or lover is expecting financial support from you this month as well. Support him or her, but within reason. Don't let your Royal Generosity – usually larger than life – get the better of you. Give but give with measure.

Your love life is still wonderful and is getting better and better over the long term. Your Love Planet, Uranus, is poised to move into your (7th) Marriage House – signifying happy changes and more control over your social life. Singles still find romance with therapists, healers and health professionals. Many of you are working to become worthy of that Great Love to which you aspire. For, unless you find yourself worthy – and you are the only judge – the ideal mate and the ideal love can only lead to disappointing pain.

Though overall your health is good, rest and relax more until the 19th.

March

Best Days Overall: 3rd, 4th, 5th, 13th, 14th, 21st, 22nd, 30th, 31st

Most Stressful Days Overall: 5th, 6th, 7th, 19th, 20th, 26th, 27th

Best Days for Love: 5th, 6th, 8th, 9th, 15th, 16th, 17th, 18th, 24th, 25th, 26th, 27th, 28th

Best Days for Money: 3rd, 4th, 8th, 9th, 13th, 14th, 15th, 16th, 19th, 20th, 21st, 22nd, 30th, 31st

Though like last month, the planetary power is congregated in the Western hemisphere of your chart there is a shift of power now to the top half of your chart. You are becoming ever more ambitious and ever more concerned with your place in the world and society. This need to adapt yourself to other people and to put others ahead of yourself is still not comfortable for you. It is good for you, but not comfortable.

It can be good for you – one of the most powerful Signs of the Zodiac – to experience some feeling of 'powerlessness', even if it is temporary. You will see that 'powerlessness' has some good points. You get to develop your social skills, for one, and secondly you are liberated from any sense of guilt or responsibility. Enjoy your guilt-free existence while you can.

Though you are feeling personally powerless your career is blossoming, thanks to the help of partners and friends. So long as you put others before yourself this month you will rise.

This feeling of powerlessness is going to leave you this spring, when the Sun, your Ruling Planet, moves into a powerful and happy Grand Formation in Fire Signs. Tremendous new energy and vitality come to you. And, though you must still adapt yourself to others, you feel good nevertheless. Your health and vitality surge boundlessly. Your spirits are high. You look exceptionally good. And you have superabundant creativity.

Your love life is important and happy this month. There is a beautiful blend of idealism and romance with your partner. There is almost an artistic quality to the relationship – as if it were a work of art that you were both creating. And, though there is great emphasis on courtship and the romantic pleasantries, there is plenty of passion and physical intimacy.

On the financial front it is again a question of putting other people's financial interests ahead of your own. You need to help others to prosper right now, receiving your own good as a natural by-product of this. Debts are easily paid and easily made. Your credit rating is good – but not boundless. Don't try to raise your limit now. Your financial goals are achieved through the grace of other people and not so much by your own efforts. Sharpen and hone your social skills.

Finances are better this month than last month, however. Mercury, your Money Planet, moves forward all month. Your financial confidence and judgement are stronger now than they were last month. Delayed financial deals now start moving, but caution and good business sense are still needed.

April

Best Days Overall: 1st, 9th, 10th, 18th, 19th, 26th, 27th, 28th

Most Stressful Days Overall: 2nd, 3rd, 16th, 17th, 22nd, 23rd, 29th, 30th

Best Days for Love: 4th, 7th, 8th, 14th, 15th, 16th, 17th, 21st, 22nd, 23rd, 26th, 27th, 28th

Best Days for Money: 1st, 9th, 10th, 11th, 12th, 13th, 18th, 19th, 20th, 21st, 26th, 27th, 28th, 29th, 30th

This is a fiery, passionate month full of changes, but you have more than enough energy to cope. There are important adjustments in your career, social life and personal image.

Most of the planets are still concentrated in the Western and upper halves of your chart. Your ambitions in the world are more important to you than emotional harmony and family interests. Also, the need to cater to others and to adapt to existing circumstances and conditions is still quite strong. You must play out the hand that is dealt to you now – and play it as skilfully as possible.

The changes that are coming about – caused by two Eclipses and by Uranus' major move into your (7th) House of Love – seem to be initiated by others and not by you. This is what makes it all a bit difficult to handle. But with so much power in Fire Signs this month – and with your planetary Lord, the Sun, involved in a happy Grand Triangle – the results are fortuitous and you don't seem unduly perturbed. The changes are lucky, though they may not appear so.

Uranus' move in your Marriage House signifies major changes and upheavals in your current relationship and in your social life in general. And, though Uranus is not in your Marriage House permanently – it will retrograde out of there in June – it is still putting a current relationship in crisis. Whether this relationship can survive depends on how healthy it was to begin with. This is a time when hidden motives, dissatisfactions and conflicts of interest will surface. Philosophical and religious differences – and issues of personal freedom – are also highlighted. The time you spend on your career and ambitions – and it is considerable this month – is another bone of contention. So your relationship is under pressure. If you can withstand the pressure your current 'lump of coal' will become a diamond.

Your health is excellent until the 20th – super, in fact. But after then it would be best to rest and relax more. Conserve energy by focusing on essentials and letting lesser things go. Stress on your vitality comes from trying to balance the demands of your career with those of your partner.

The Lunar Eclipse takes place on the 15th, the Solar Eclipse on the 29th. Though both Eclipses are important it is the Solar Eclipse of the 29th that has the biggest impact on you, for the Sun (the planet being eclipsed) is your Planetary Ruler. Definitely take a reduced schedule on that day.

May

Best Days Overall: 6th, 7th, 8th, 15th, 16th, 24th, 25th

Most Stressful Days Overall: 13th, 14th, 19th, 20th, 26th, 27th, 28th

Best Days for Love: 1st, 2nd, 3rd, 6th, 7th, 8th, 11th, 12th, 16th, 17th, 19th, 20th, 26th, 27th, 28th, 29th, 30th

Best Days for Money: 6th, 7th, 8th, 9th, 10th, 11th, 12th, 15th, 16th, 19th, 20th, 24th, 25th, 29th, 30th

Some of the fast-moving, short-term planets are shifting over to the Eastern sector of your Horoscope now, Leo. This brings more comfort to you. You are in a better position to create your own conditions and circumstances. You are less dependent on the good graces of others and have a greater feeling of personal freedom. Understand, now, you haven't complete personal freedom yet, but you have more than you've had recently. You needn't put other people first right now but can balance your desires with theirs. You can't ignore others, nor can you over-assert yourself. But things are coming more into balance this month.

Your paths of greatest fulfilment this month lie in religious studies, foreign travel, the home and family, children, personal creativity and – after the 17th – your career.

Your 10th House of Career is very active this month. In spite of the fact that a high percentage of the planets are going retrograde, you are making excellent career progress now. While most people around you (unless they too happen to be Leos) are experiencing delays, reviews, re-evaluations and doubts, you sail on without obstructions. Career success is especially great after the 17th, when Venus, your Career Planet, moves into your Career House – her own domain. There it acts especially powerfully on your behalf, giving you charm with elders and authorities, lending glamour to your efforts and ambitions and making you popular with the public in general. You are in one of the peak career periods of your year, so enjoy. Promote yourself with charm and grace rather than with brashness.

Your health will be much better after the 21st than before. Until then rest and relax more and otherwise conserve your energy. Think of your energy the way a businessperson thinks of money in the bank. It is not meant to be hoarded, but to be used effectively and towards practical ends. Use it, but don't waste it.

The recent crisis in your love life – with your marriage partner or lover – is going to ease off a bit this month. Your partner is reconsidering some rash actions. You are still going to have to deal with the issue of personal freedom in the future if the relationship is going to work out. Romantic opportunities are abundant though you are not sure how serious they are. Don't leap into either a marriage or divorce after the 5th.

June

Best Days Overall: 3rd, 4th, 12th, 13th, 20th, 21st, 30th

Most Stressful Days Overall: 10th, 11th, 16th, 17th, 22nd, 23rd, 24th

Best Days for Love: 5th, 6th, 7th, 15th, 16th, 17th, 24th, 25th, 26th

Best Days for Money: 3rd, 4th, 5th, 6th, 7th, 8th, 9th, 12th, 13th, 16th, 17th, 20th, 21st, 25th, 26th, 30th

This is a highly unusual month for you, Leo. You will need a lot of patience and stamina to handle things. The Sun, your Ruling Planet, and Mercury, your Money Planet, are involved in a rare Grand Square aspect denoting stress, difficulty, crisis and the need to build something from conflicting and antagonistic elements. Happily this is not a long-term aspect and the situation eases up as the month progresses.

Though your health is basically good, there are great challenges to your self-esteem and feelings of self-worth now. You want to shine in a group or professional organization to which you belong, but you are perhaps forced to take a lesser position. There is conflict between your personal creativity and the need to co-operate with others. There is also conflict between spending your money on group interests or on fun things, between spending on helping friends or on personal pleasure. This is not a good month to speculate. There is also more conflict between the financial interests of others – most notably your partner – and your own. At present these interests seem divergent, though they need not be.

The Grand Square is pushing you to action and your fiery, impulsive nature also pushes you to action. But 50 per cent of the planets being retrograde creates a compulsion to inaction. You are locked between these two opposing forces. An impossible situation, you say – and you are right. The Celestial Powers are fond of creating 'impossible situations' so that we can grow. As the month progresses you will see that there are some actions you *can* take, and that the situation is not as impossible as it seems.

Mercury, your Financial Planet, is not only besieged this month it is also retrograde until the 17th. This is going to be a bit stressful financially. You have to work harder to maintain your normal income level and there are many delays involved with payments due you and with the consummation of deals. Watch your spending and walk the extra mile for your employer or customers. Things will straighten out next month.

Your romantic life seems to be 'on hold' this month as well. Your social confidence is not what it should be and a current relationship is cool. Not cold, but cool. There is a feeling of going backwards to where you started. Platonic friendships seem more interesting to you than romance right now. Neither a marriage nor a divorce is recommended this month. More thought and study are needed before you make either move. Your social judgement is not what it should be and will be.

July

Best Days Overall: 1st, 9th, 10th, 17th, 18th, 27th, 28th

Most Stressful Days Overall: 7th, 8th, 13th, 14th, 20th, 21st

Best Days for Love: 3rd, 4th, 7th, 8th, 12th, 13th, 14th, 15th, 16th, 21st, 25th, 26th

Best Days for Money: 1st, 2nd, 3rd, 4th, 5th, 6th, 9th, 10th, 15th, 16th, 17th, 18th, 25th, 26th, 27th, 28th, 30th, 31st

Though 50 per cent of the planets are still retrograde this month, you are less affected by this than other people are. Most of your important Planetary Rulers are going forward. Thus, where others are experiencing stalemate and delays you glide forward without obstacles. Of course you still need to have patience this month, for we are always affected in some degree by what's happening around us. But it may help you to know that the delays going on are not your fault.

With the planets evenly balanced between the Eastern and Western sectors of your Horoscope, your self-confidence and sense of self-worth are much stronger now than they have been in recent months. Yet you are not overly assertive nor overly aggressive (except perhaps in financial matters). You have a good sense of what other people need as well as of what you need. You also have more options than you've had of late: you can attain your ends through social grace and through others or on your own if you need to. You are no longer totally dependent on others.

As the month goes on, the planetary power becomes increasingly weighted at the bottom half of your chart, making you less ambitious for yourself and more ambitious for others. You prefer personal happiness and pleasure to outward career success right now. This will change later on in the year, but for now this is how you feel. Yes, you've got summer fever – and then some!

Until the 23rd you are in a spiritual, introverted period. You feel a subconscious need for spiritual atonement and expiation. You want to put things right with whatever deity you worship. Of itself this is wonderful, for it is usually not safe to venture into a new cycle of activity without getting the go-ahead from your personal divinity first.

Very often the urge to atonement expresses itself in good works, charitable activities, philanthropy, volunteer work, helping those in need and more prayer and meditation. The dream life becomes more active and subconsciously there is more receptivity to dreams, intuitions and subtle energies. Others may consider you unrealistic, idealistic and perhaps impractical. But you will have the last laugh. When your new cycle of activity begins after the 23rd you will be sure and confident. Receptivity to your own true intuition is always the short-cut to success.

Your health is excellent all month, but gets exceptionally good after the 23rd. Your personal magnetism and charisma are strong, making you influential with others and exceptionally appealing to the opposite sex. If only your Love Planet, Uranus, were moving forward, the prediction would be for rapturous love. But Uranus' retrograde shows that lovers or potential lovers are a bit timid and hesitant with you, perhaps intimidated by your excessive magnetism. Go slow in love this month.

Finances are super all month.

August

Best Days Overall: 5th, 6th, 14th, 15th, 24th, 25th

Most Stressful Days Overall: 3rd, 4th, 9th, 10th, 16th, 17th, 31st

Best Days for Love: 1st, 2nd, 5th, 6th, 7th, 8th, 9th, 10th, 14th, 15th, 16th, 17th, 26th, 27th

Best Days for Money: 5th, 6th, 14th, 15th, 16th, 17th, 26th, 27th

Much of the general standstill of recent months is easing up. You will feel this most dramatically in your educational interests, religious studies, domestic projects, personal creativity and travel plans. The delays in these areas are now past history.

Most of the planets are very much below the horizon of your Solar chart, showing that happiness and emotional fulfilment and security come before your career and ambitions. Those wishing to employ a Leo should understand this. They must present their career offers in a way that allows the Leo to find time for family interests and emotional harmony.

There is still more power in the Western sector of your chart than in the Eastern sector, but this is not as great a problem as it would be at other times. There is so much power in your own Sign right now that you are unlikely to overlook your own interests. There is a healthy balance between self-interest and other people's interests.

Your paths of greatest fulfilment this month are foreign travel, the study of foreign cultures, personal creativity, money-making, intellectual interests, the family and enhancing your personal image.

This is one of the happiest months of your year. Most of the planets are kind to you now. It is a month of excellent health, a shining personal appearance, self-confidence, personal charisma and *lots* of personal pleasure. In spite of the fact that so many planets are in the Western sector you still manage to get your way this month. Your personal charm melts away all opposition.

Your appeal to the opposite sex is also unusually strong now; you are attracting romantic prospects by the droves. You probably have to fight them off with a stick! Yet, with your Love Planet still retrograde much of this popularity is neither serious nor long term. Play, but don't commit to anything. You can have things your way in love this month.

Finances, too, are unusually good. Mercury, your Money Planet, moves forward speedily and is in its own House, your

Money House, for a good part of the month. Earning power is strong. Your financial judgement and aptitude are sound. Most importantly you possess financial confidence and fearlessness. Very often this is enough to carry the day when things get rough. Speculations are very favourable now. Follow your intuitions.

September

Best Days Overall: 2nd, 10th, 11th, 20th, 21st, 29th, 30th

Most Stressful Days Overall: 6th, 7th, 12th, 13th, 14th, 27th, 28th

Best Days for Love: 4th, 5th, 6th, 7th, 12th, 13th, 14th, 22nd, 23rd, 24th, 25th

Best Days for Money: 2nd, 6th, 7th, 10th, 11th, 15th, 16th, 20th, 21st, 22nd, 23rd, 24th, 25th, 29th, 30th

The planetary trend continues in a westerly direction, though the percentage is not as a high as for some of the other Signs. You are increasingly called upon to rely on other people for your good. More and more you need to adapt to situations not of your making. Your ability to adapt – not one of your strong points – will determine your success this month.

Others will attempt to define your personality; weaker Signs than you would succumb to this. Happily your own sense of self is so strong that these others are unlikely to succeed.

The planetary power is overwhelmingly concentrated below the horizon of your chart this month, showing your interest in family and family values. Your attempts of late to marshal family support for your career goals and projects will bear fruit in the coming months. Domestic projects are moving forward nicely after some months of delay. Your role in the world now is supportive rather than centre-stage. Make other people look good, make others shine and you will eventually become the star that you are meant to be.

Your paths of greatest fulfilment now are money-making, intellectual interests, personal creativity and fun activities.

Your love life is still rather thwarted, but there is a difference between a pleasant and unpleasant impasse. Until the 23rd the impasse is pleasant and you rather enjoy the status quo. After the 23rd there is more conflict with the beloved, which will force some kind of resolution. Singles need to be more socially active than usual if they are to find romantic opportunities. You need to go out and create romantic possibilities after the 23rd. Don't schedule either a marriage or divorce during this period.

Earning power is strong until the 22nd. You are an astute shopper and investor right now, on top of all the details (unusual for a Leo). After the 22nd, however, Mercury (your Money Planet) goes retrograde, slowing down your earning power and making your financial judgment unrealistic. Avoid making major purchases or investments after the 22nd. Take the time to study things more carefully. Be patient with financial delays or late payments. This is not a financial disaster, just a breather. Use the time to perfect your projects, plans and products.

October

Best Days Overall: 7th, 8th, 9th, 17th, 18th, 26th, 27th

Most Stressful Days Overall: 3rd, 4th, 10th, 11th, 24th, 25th, 30th, 31st

Best Days for Love: 1st, 2nd, 3rd, 4th, 11th, 15th, 16th, 21st, 24th, 25th, 28th, 29th, 30th, 31st

Best Days for Money: 3rd, 4th, 7th, 8th, 9th, 12th, 13th, 17th, 18th, 20th, 21st, 22nd, 23rd, 26th, 27th, 30th, 31st

The planetary power is mostly in the Western sector of your Horoscope this month. It has been there for quite a while, but this month it is even more so. This means that although it is in your nature to rule, you must do so by consensus. You must also exercise authority with other people's interests ahead of your own. Your life is inextricably bound up with other people's and you are not really your own person. Adaptation – something difficult for you, Leo – is the key to harmony and success.

By the 14th 90 per cent of the planets are moving forward, ending the general climate of stalemate of past months. You are in a month of achievement and action, but you are not really the cause. Events happen of themselves; you mostly react to them. Both the good and the bad that happen are not really of your making so there is no need for guilt or feelings of responsibility. The way in which you react to them, however, is your responsibility.

The overwhelming majority of planets are in the lower hemisphere of your chart this month, fostering the need for emotional harmony and security. You shine as a nurturer and supporter this month. You are the outstanding supporter of other people's careers rather than your own. Your dominant wish right now is to feel emotionally at ease – if you can have that and a career too, all is well and good. But if pressed you will choose emotional ease.

Your paths of greatest fulfilment are intellectual interests, communication, the home, domestic projects, family interests, personal creativity and fun activities.

Sales and communication projects foster your 'bottom line', but you will probably see the result only after the 14th when Mercury goes forward. A very pleasurable foreign trip is on the cards after the 21st.

There are two Eclipses this month: a Lunar Eclipse on the

8th and a Solar Eclipse on the 24th. Of the two, the Solar Eclipse of the 24th is the more significant for you. It involves your Ruling Planet (the Sun) and occurs in your 4th House of Family and Domestic Affairs. This Eclipse announces major, long-term changes in the home and in your family pattern. Your will in the home is temporarily 'eclipsed', causing a short-lived upheaval. As the dust settles you will find the new pattern more in keeping with your heart's desire than the old pattern was. Repressed feelings and grievances were actually holding you back. Now that they've come up you can resolve them. Take a reduced schedule on this day.

November

Best Days Overall: 4th, 5th, 14th, 15th, 23rd

Most Stressful Days Overall: 6th, 7th, 21st, 22nd, 27th, 28th

Best Days for Love: 2nd, 3rd, 4th, 7th, 14th, 15th, 17th, 23rd, 24th, 25th, 27th, 28th

Best Days for Money: 4th, 5th, 11th, 12th, 14th, 15th, 16th, 17th, 21st, 22nd, 23rd

After the 4th, 90 to 100 per cent of the planets – an incredible percentage – are in the Western sector of your chart, making this a month in which you give yourself over to others almost completely. You lose yourself in order to find yourself. What other people want to do is the right thing for you to do. Their interests come before your own. You are like a beautiful sunset, beautiful in your sacrifice, surrendering your ego for the sake of others. Love is all that matters now. Your sunrise will come in due course; that will be the time for self-assertiveness and personal creation.

Eighty to 90 per cent of the planets are below the horizon

of your chart, favouring domestic and family issues over career interests. The shifting planets suggest that you are finishing with an old domestic lifestyle, or with a move or refurbishment of the home. You seem to be at the point where you've just about got things where you want them and are ready to move on to other things. You advance in your career by nurturing the careers of others.

Your paths of greatest fulfilment are your home and family life, children, personal creativity, fun activities and intellectual interests.

After the 23rd you enter one of the happiest and most successful periods of your year. Many wonderful things happen, much progress is made towards your goals, your creativity is at an all-time high and all sorts of entertainments are offered to you. Yet all these things come mostly through others and not by your personal efforts. You receive what you have given out.

Early in the month you earn money through communication and sales efforts. After the 4th financial opportunity comes through the sale of your home or home furnishings and through family connections. After the 23rd money comes via your personal creativity and personal charisma. The way you look brings customers or the right earnings opportunities to you. After the 23rd you become a very lucky speculator, though please don't bet more than you can afford to lose. Money is earned easily and by doing things you enjoy. Your special talent with children translates into cash.

Your health and vitality are much better after the 23rd than before. Rest and relax more before the 23rd.

December

Best Days Overall: 1st, 2nd, 11th, 12th, 20th, 21st, 28th, 29th

Most Stressful Days Overall: 3rd, 4th, 18th, 19th, 24th, 25th, 31st

Best Days for Love: 3rd, 4th, 13th, 14th, 22nd, 23rd, 24th, 25th, 31st

Best Days for Money: 1st, 2nd, 11th, 12th, 13th, 14th, 20th, 21st, 22nd, 23rd, 28th, 29th, 31st

All the planets – with the exception of the Moon – are firmly established in the Western sector of your chart, although they have not yet reached their most westerly point. You are becoming ever more socially conscious and 'other-orientated'. It is not enough for you now to shine with your own light. You want to be loved and appreciated by others. And you are succeeding at this.

Right now you are in one of the happiest periods of your year – and perhaps your life. The month seems like one long party. The nightlife is intense. Your personal creativity is strong. Always a bit of a show-off, this month you are more so as your urge to be centre-stage is unusually strong. Romantic opportunities abound, but the more serious ones come after the 22nd. Speculations are favourable and you enjoy the way you earn your money this month, especially before the 12th. You are the king or queen of all the nightspots in town.

With most of the planets still below the horizon of your chart the emphasis is still very much on emotional harmony and security. You are more concerned with being emotionally at ease than with being at ease with the public at large. You are still looking to the past and trying to come to terms with that rather than looking ahead to your future. Psychological studies prosper.

Your health is excellent all month. Seldom have you felt so much sheer energy and vitality. However, health problems could arise from personal over-indulgence – with food, physical intimacy and liquor. Indulge by all means, but don't overdo it.

After the 22nd the demands of the workplace call to you. The pace at work becomes hectic, yet it is not without its pleasures. The workplace is still the likely meeting place for romantic trysts. Singles will tend to find that special someone there – suddenly and unexpectedly. A serious romance is brewing now.

Finances are unusually good all month. Before the 12th, money is earned through creativity and speculations. Your financial optimism is sky-high and you tend to overspend. After the 22nd you become more prudent. Money is earned through your work and you have a better sense of the value of a pound. Though you will earn more before the 12th you will be a better, more discriminating shopper after the 12th. Postpone purchases until then.

Virgo

♍

THE VIRGIN

Birthdays from

22nd August

to 22nd September

Personality Profile

VIRGO AT A GLANCE

Element – Earth

Ruling planet – Mercury
Career planet – Mercury
Health planet – Uranus
Money planet – Venus
Planet of family and home life – Jupiter

Colours – earth tones, ochre, orange, yellow

Colour that promotes love, romance and social harmony – aqua blue

Colour that promotes earning power – jade green

Gems – agate, hyacinth

Metal – quicksilver

Scents – lavender, lilac, lily of the valley, storax

Quality – mutable (= flexibility)

Quality most needed for balance – seeing the big picture

Strongest virtues – mental agility, analytical skills, ability to pay attention to detail, healing powers

Deepest needs – to be useful and productive

Characteristic to avoid – destructive criticism

Signs of greatest overall compatibility – Taurus, Capricorn

Signs of greatest overall incompatibility – Gemini, Sagittarius, Pisces

Sign most helpful to career – Gemini

Sign most helpful for emotional support – Sagittarius

Sign most helpful financially – Libra

Sign best for marriage and/or partnerships – Pisces

Sign most helpful for creative projects – Capricorn

Best Sign to have fun with – Capricorn

Signs most helpful in spiritual matters – Taurus, Leo

Best day of the week – Wednesday

Understanding the Virgo Personality

The virgin is a particularly fitting symbol for those people born under the Sign of Virgo. If you meditate on the image of the virgin you will get a good understanding of the essence of the Virgo type. The virgin, of course, is a symbol of purity and innocence – not naïve, but pure. A virginal object has not been touched. A virgin field is land that is true to itself, the way it has always been. The same is true of virgin forest: it is pristine, unaltered.

Apply the idea of purity to the thought processes, emotional life, physical body and activities and projects of the everyday world, and you can see how Virgos approach life. Virgos desire the pure expression of the ideal in their mind, body and affairs. If they find impurities they will attempt to clear them away.

Impurities are the beginning of disorder, unhappiness and uneasiness. The job of the Virgo is to eject all impurities and keep only that which the body and mind can use and assimilate.

The secrets of good health are here revealed: 90 per cent of the art of staying well is maintaining a pure mind, a pure body and pure emotions. When you introduce more impurities than your mind and body can deal with, you will have what is known as 'dis-ease'. It is no wonder that Virgos make great doctors, nurses, healers and dietitians. They have an innate understanding of good health and they realize that good health is more than just physical. In all aspects of life, if you want a project to be successful it must be kept as pure as possible. It must be protected against the adverse elements that will try to undermine it. This is the secret behind Virgo's awesome technical proficiency.

One could talk about Virgo's analytical powers – which are substantial. One could talk about their perfectionism and their almost superhuman attention to detail. But this would be to miss the point. All of these virtues are manifestations of a Virgo's desire for purity and perfection – a world without Virgos would have ruined itself long ago.

A vice is nothing more than a virtue turned inside out, a virtue that is misapplied or used in the wrong context. Virgos' apparent vices come from their inherent virtue. Their analytical powers, which should be used for healing, helping or perfecting a project in the world sometimes get misapplied and turned against people. Their critical faculties, which should be used constructively to perfect a strategy or proposal, can sometimes be used destructively to harm or wound. Their urge to perfection can become worry and lack of confidence; their natural humility can become self-denial and self-abasement. When Virgos turn negative they are apt to turn their devastating criticism on themselves, sowing the seeds of self-destruction.

Finance

Virgos have all the attitudes that create wealth. They are hard-working, industrious, efficient, organized, thrifty, productive and eager to serve. A developed Virgo is every employer's dream. But until Virgos master some of the social graces of Libra they won't even come close to fulfilling their financial potential. Purity and perfectionism, if not handled correctly or gracefully, can be very trying to others. Friction in human relationships can be devastating not only to your pet projects but – indirectly – to your wallet as well.

Virgos are quite interested in their financial security. Being hard-working, they know the true value of money. They don't like to take risks with their money, preferring to save for their retirement or for a rainy day. Virgos usually make prudent, calculated investments that involve a minimum of risk. These investments and savings usually work out well, helping Virgos achieve the financial security they seek. The rich or even not so rich Virgos also like to help their friends in need.

Career and Public Image

Virgos reach their full potential when they can communicate their knowledge in such a way that others can understand it. In order to get their ideas across better, Virgos need to develop greater verbal skills and more non-judgemental ways of expressing themselves. Virgos look up to teachers and communicators; they like their bosses to be good communicators. Virgos will probably not respect a superior who is not their intellectual equal – no matter how much money or power that superior has. Virgos themselves like to be perceived by others as being educated and intellectual.

The natural humility of Virgos often inhibits them from fulfilling their great ambitions, from acquiring name and fame. Virgos should indulge in a little more self-promotion if they are going to reach their career goals. They need to push themselves with the same ardour that they would use to foster others.

At work Virgos like to stay active. They are willing to learn any type of job as long as it serves their ultimate goal of financial security. Virgos may change several occupations during their professional lives, until they find the one they really enjoy. Virgos work well with other people, are not afraid to work hard and always fulfil their responsibilities.

Love and Relationships

If you are an analyser or a critic you must, out of necessity, narrow your scope. You have to focus on a part and not the whole; this can create a temporary narrow-mindedness. Virgos don't like this kind of person. They like their partners to be broad-minded, with depth and vision. Virgos seek to get this broad-minded quality from their partners since they sometimes lack it themselves.

Virgos are perfectionists in love just as they are in other areas of life. They need partners who are tolerant, open-minded and easy-going. If you are in love with a Virgo don't waste time on impractical romantic gestures. Do practical and useful things for him or her – this is what will be appreciated and what will be done for you.

Virgos express their love through pragmatic and useful gestures, so don't be put off because your Virgo partner doesn't say 'I love you' day-in and day-out. Virgos are not that type. If they love you, they will demonstrate it in practical ways. They will always be there for you; they will show an interest in your health and finances; they will fix your sink or repair your radio. Virgos deem these actions to be superior to sending flowers, chocolates or St Valentine's Day cards.

In love affairs Virgos are not particularly passionate or spontaneous. If you are in love with a Virgo, don't take this personally. It doesn't mean that you are not alluring enough or that your Virgo partner doesn't love or like you. It's just the way Virgos are. What they lack in passion they make up for in dedication and loyalty.

Home and Domestic Life

It goes without saying that the home of a Virgo will be spotless, sanitized and orderly. Everything will be in its right place – and don't you dare move anything around! For Virgos to find domestic bliss, however, they need to ease up a bit in the home, to allow their partner and kids more freedom and to be more generous and open-minded. Family members are not to be analysed under a microscope, they are individuals with their own virtues to express.

With these small difficulties resolved, Virgos like to stay in and entertain at home. They make good hosts and they like to keep their friends and families happy and entertained at family and social gatherings. Virgos love children, but they are strict with them – at times – since they want to make sure their children are brought up with the right sense of family and values.

Horoscope for 1995

Major Trends

1994 was a year of great creativity and intellectual expansion. Not only did your intellectual capacities grow but the material tools for creativity and communication also came to you – new telephones, fax machines, computers, modems, audio and video equipment and the like. Many of you also bought new cars in 1994.

1995 will be the year in which you expand your emotional capacities and psychological insights. 1995 is a year in which you see the limits of intellectual brilliance – awesome though this is. For, unless brilliant thought is accompanied by the 'right feeling', it is sterile, lifeless and devoid of real power. Getting your emotional life in order is not the most comfortable activity for you Virgo, because you are by nature an intellectual. But when you do this the end result will be an enhancement of the intellect and an even greater outburst of creativity. The impact on your overall health and well-being will also be considerable. Saturn, now in a stressful alignment with you for the next few years, is another argument for emotional cleansing and refinement.

There are many changes in your love and social life this year as well, Virgo, for Saturn in your 7th House of Marriage all year is changing your fundamental attitudes to love and partnerships. You need to limit your social activities and be more selective about whom you take into your heart. Your heart is like your home, it cannot be open to all comers. Love everyone, but be selective about who comes in.

Health

Uranus, your Health Lord, is still very much stimulated by the other planets this year – most notably by Neptune – making your health an important priority. Further, as mentioned earlier, Saturn has now come into a stressful alignment with you. Your vitality is not what you have been accustomed to for the past few years. There are no health disasters here, mind you, just a lessening of your physical energy – and probably of your self-esteem. Your body, your ego and self-concept are now undergoing testing and trials. For example, if you think you can work 20 hours a day and party the rest of the time, Saturn is now going to test this. If you think that you can lift 800 pounds and run 40 miles a day, Saturn (through the people and events that this planet controls) is going to put you to the test. It will confront you with your limits. This kind of thing is often misunderstood by people and considered a form of 'punishment' or disaster. Really it is nothing more than the revelation of inherent human weakness and limitation. Rejoice in it, for it will help you to redesign your activities more realistically. Knowledge of your infinite potential is essential to health and success. But knowledge of your limits – which are always changing – is equally important.

Physical fitness is built through pressure. We force the body to overcome resistance. Pressure applied properly actually makes the body stronger, though while you are undergoing it the sensation is not pleasant! Saturn is going to apply the exactly measured pressure that your body needs to make it fit. Thus by the time Saturn leaves its stressful alignment, your body will be stronger and healthier than before. Saturn also fosters dietary discrimination and weight loss. 1995 is a good year to shed those pounds. Mystics assert that the keys to physical longevity and endurance are in the keeping of Saturn. Thus you can expect to learn techniques and lifestyle choices that will prolong your life. Don't think that these secrets are replays of what you read in the popular press. They will be very specific to you and your life situation.

There is no question that you should be more measured with your physical energy now. Maximize your energy by not wasting it frivolously on unnecessary activity. Plan more and achieve more with less effort. Rest when you are tired.

Talk less and listen more. Think less and perceive more. Eat foods that are less difficult to digest. All of these things will liberate energy for your true goals and help you to resist ailments.

Home and Domestic Life

Your 4th House of Home and Family becomes very prominent this year and for many years to come for you, Virgo. Jupiter, the Lord of your 4th House of Home and Family Interests, spends an unusual amount of time in his own domain this year. And, towards the end of the year – 10th November – Pluto will move into this House and stay there for many years. Many of you are going to move to larger and better quarters this year. If you have been contemplating a move, this is the year to do it. Think big. Think lavishly and opulently. Have no fear, for Jupiter wants more for you than you want for yourself. Some of you might not physically move but renovate and expand your existing home. The net effect will be the same. By the time the year is out you will be in a larger, happier residence.

Women of childbearing age are especially fertile this year. Pregnancies are likely. Men are also more fertile. Your family as a whole expands in various ways by the time 1995 ends. Your family circle extends through marriages and new births and through meeting people who will become like family to you – people who are naturally part of your 'emotional support system'.

Family life has its positive and negative side; this year you see its positive side. Your family supports you and your goals. Your family helps you to prosper financially. Your family lavishes gifts for the home upon you.

Not only are you getting a new home but you are also getting flash items for the home this year. Furniture, beds and the like. If you are a man it is your mother who is unusually generous and supportive. If you are a woman it is your father.

Those of you who invested in real estate in years past will find that your property is worth more this year, though there might be delays in actually reaping the profits.

Perhaps more important than everything mentioned so far is the psychological consequences of Jupiter's transit. Though your physical vitality is not what you are used to there is a great, rock-bottom optimism in you. Your ability to give and receive emotional support is greatly expanded. You are more able to express love and good feeling this year. You are much more the nurturer than the critic.

Love and Social Life

Both the 7th House of Marriage and the 5th House of Love Affairs are prominent in your Horoscope in 1995, Virgo. This is both good and bad. On the negative side, it creates confusion in your love live. You are not sure whether you just want good times or a serious, committed relationship. Both are available to you this year, but probably with different people. On the positive side, there are abundant romantic opportunities, many fish in the sea. Lovers come and go. You call the shots in the relationship, as you are the one with the options.

To further confuse things, Neptune, Lord of your Marriage House, has been travelling with Uranus, the Great Innovator and Experimenter. This makes you idealistic and experimental in love. You have been in a process of learning what you don't want rather than learning what you do want. Because of this some people are accusing you of fickleness and instability, but really you are just exploring. Every time you think you have found your ideal you see a higher and better ideal. Singles are especially prone to this kind of feeling. Marrieds who are in a good relationship are being experimental within that relationship – trying out different lifestyles and playing out different fantasies.

Saturn, the Great Tester, is firmly positioned in your House of Marriage. This shows many things. First off, your current marriage or relationship is being tested. Its true nature will be unmasked over the next few years. You will not be able to hide behind illusions about your partner. The naked truth will be revealed. Hidden motives will be exposed. Though this sounds grim, it need not be. If the relationship is good and based on love, neither of you has anything to fear. The relationship will get stronger. If the relationship was weak to begin with its inherent shortcomings will emerge and you will be forced to see things as they are. Truth and reality are always the best medicine. You can build on reality; you can't build on illusion or delusion.

For singles, Saturn is going to make you cautious about too much experimentation. Saturn will give you a longing for something more stable and enduring in your love life, something that could lead to marriage. Young people will be attracted to someone older, more stable and more established. Older people will be attracted to someone younger. This is because younger people will secretly enjoy being 'managed and controlled', while older people will want to do the managing and the controlling.

Saturn forces you to be more selective – not only on the romantic front but on the social front as well. You have to make hard choices. You can't socialize with everyone who wants to be your friend. You have to limit your focus. A few good friends are better than myriads of lukewarm ones. Look for the few good ones.

Career and Finance

Neither your 2nd House of Money nor your 10th House of Career and Ambitions are prominent this year, Virgo. You've got bigger fish to fry. Of course you will work and earn money this year, but it comes rather easily and you are not overly compulsive about it. The Cosmos is granting you the freedom to shape your career and financial life as you see fit. You will work because it is your nature to work. It is your character. An unemployed Virgo is a miserable creature.

Basically you are preparing your home base and psychological support system for career advancement later on. Don't neglect this secret preparation. Without a solid foundation a building cannot stand. The taller the building the deeper its foundations must be. The higher your aspirations, the deeper your psychological insight and emotional stability must be.

Still there are financial opportunities for you this year. Real estate investments are favourable. Family connections and parents provide substantial earning opportunities. Industries that deal with the home, child care, home furnishings or decorating are lucrative. The restaurant, hotel or travel businesses are also good. You might find work in one of these industries or you might profit by investing in them.

Speculations are favourable in general, but be prepared to ride a roller-coaster. Both winnings and losses can be wildly high. If you have strong nerves, ultimate success is likely. Trust your intuition.

Your partner also seems unconcerned about money. The first four months of the year he or she is almost sacrificial about it – giving generously and impulsively to the needy and to charitable organizations. From 26th May to 8th September your partner is especially supportive and generous with you, probably because of certain help you've provided. Money is likely to come to you during this period through law suits, insurance companies and investments as well. Many of the ideas you developed in 1994 can be profitable this year – especially those that have to do with writing, sales and marketing skills. Journalism articles are likely to be sold.

Self-improvement

The improvements taking place in your home and domestic situation have already been described. They are going to happen almost by themselves. All you need to do is cooperate and go along with the flow of events. The area of relationships will be improved as well, but through hard work on your part. You are likely to be disappointed with friends and perhaps lovers this year. Saturn is very good at revealing reality and unmasking motives. You cannot let yourself become embittered by these disappointments. You must learn and practise the art of forgiveness – not just verbal, intellectual forgiveness, but forgiveness from the heart. This will lift you to a higher plane of romance and friendship and bring those who are truly for you into your life. You must learn to praise all the people in your life – a difficult feat for you, Virgo, as you are such a critic and perfectionist. Praise the good in them. If you are around people about whom you have nothing to praise, it is best to let them pass out of your life.

Month-by-month Forecasts

January

Best Days Overall: 1st, 2nd, 10th, 11th, 19th, 20th, 21st, 28th, 29th

Most Stressful Days Overall: 5th, 6th, 12th, 13th, 26th, 27th

Best Days for Love: 1st, 2nd, 6th, 7th, 8th, 10th, 11th, 17th, 18th, 19th, 20th, 21st, 26th, 27th, 28th, 29th

Best Days for Money: 5th, 6th, 7th, 8th, 17th, 18th, 22nd, 23rd, 26th, 27th

The overwhelming majority of planets are clustered in the Western and bottom halves of your Solar Horoscope this month. Thus you are socially active and dependent on the grace of others for your good. You must put the interests of others over your own in order to attain your goals this month.

The preponderance of power in the bottom half of your chart shows that you are more concerned with personal, emotional harmony than with outward, career success. You would choose happiness over glory and status right now. There's nothing wrong with that, for without a solid emotional base – a harmonious emotional base – career success is a shaky thing indeed.

There is much pleasure in simple things this month. Family gatherings and relations with your family are happy. This is a good month to move or redecorate the home. It is also a good time to entertain in and from the home. Family support is strong, generous and pleasant. You can expect increased earnings through your family or family connections from the 14th to the 16th. This can come in the form of money or as some luxurious item for the home. Your general mood is happy and optimistic. Women are overly fertile this month.

If you have children they are more rebellious this month and your challenge is to find just the right balance between offering them freedom and showing them discipline. You cannot go too far either way. Happily the New Moon of the 1st is going to clarify your confusion.

A similar conflict exists in your current relationship or marriage. Too much order, limitation and control is stifling; too much freedom can destroy the relationship. Find the balance. Give freedom but within firm limits.

Mercury, your Ruling Planet and the Lord of your Career, goes retrograde (backwards) towards the end of the month (on the 26th). You will find it more difficult to assert yourself during this period and you seem to lack confidence. Use this period to review your personal and career goals. Once these are more clearly defined it will be easier to assert yourself in these areas.

Your health is excellent all month but especially until the 20th. After the 20th your health interests seem to depend on your partner. Help your partner's health problems and your own (if there are any) will just melt away.

February

Best Days Overall: 6th, 7th, 16th, 17th, 24th, 25th

Most Stressful Days Overall: 1st, 2nd, 8th, 9th, 10th, 22nd, 23rd

Best Days for Love: 1st, 2nd, 4th, 5th, 6th, 7th, 16th, 17th, 24th, 25th

Best Days for Money: 3rd, 4th, 5th, 6th, 7th, 13th, 14th, 15th, 16th, 17th, 18th, 19th, 22nd, 23rd, 24th, 25th

Eighty to 90 per cent of the planets are still in the Western and bottom hemispheres of your Solar chart this month. This shows that you continue to be much more interested in emotional harmony and family issues than in your career and outward status. You are also much more involved with others – interacting with them and dealing with situations that they create for you rather than creating your own.

Your lack of ambition is reinforced by the retrograde of Mercury, which rules not only your personal interests but also your Career House. You are reviewing – and rightfully so – your ambitions in the world and where your priorities lie. The retrograde of Mercury shows your lack of self-assertion and influence right now as well. Your good comes to you through others and through their grace. When clarity comes about your personal interests – and it will in the coming months – you will once again be in a position to assert yourself more strongly. Avoid power struggles now and play the cards dealt you as skilfully as possible. There is no special distinction in getting a good hand if you are the dealer. It takes more skill – and wisdom – to play a hand that you had nothing to do with. The ideal is to play every hand well.

Rest and relax more this month. Don't waste energy railing against circumstances. Do your best and relax in the hands of a higher and loving power. Enjoy putting other people ahead of yourself – temporarily. Next month your health improves considerably.

Your social life is excellent this month. Singles find abundant romantic opportunities but are exceedingly 'picky and choosy'. Those getting involved with a Virgo this month are apt to find themselves scrutinized and analysed like they've never been analysed before. You don't know what perfectionism is until you've had a Virgo check you over. Virgos need to be careful not to overdo this nit-picking. Perfection is relative here on Earth. Only in Heaven is it absolute. Don't drive love away by being obsessively careful.

Earnings this month are excellent, though perhaps not as big as they were last month. Money comes through creativity and creative projects and through speculative ventures that have been carefully thought out. The sale of a home or of home furnishings yields profits. Inspired financial ideas come towards the end of the month and they involve old or new partners.

March

Best Days Overall: 5th, 6th, 15th, 16th, 24th, 25th

Most Stressful Days Overall: 1st, 2nd, 8th, 9th, 21st, 22nd, 28th, 29th

Best Days for Love: 1st, 2nd, 5th, 6th, 8th, 9th, 15th, 16th, 17th, 18th, 24th, 25th, 26th, 27th, 28th, 29th

Best Days for Money: 3rd, 4th, 8th, 9th, 13th, 14th, 17th, 18th, 21st, 22nd, 26th, 27th, 28th, 30th, 31st

Like last month, most of the planets are still congregated in the Western hemisphere of your Solar chart, showing that you are involved in situations not of your making and are being forced to adapt yourself to them. You are forced to put other people's interests ahead of your own. Your good comes to you through the grace of others. This kind of configuration also shows that your social life comes first.

The importance of your social life this month is further reinforced by the power in your 7th House of Marriage. Saturn is there all year, the Sun is there until the 21st and, on the 15th, Mercury, your Ruler, moves into it. No question about it, you are caught up in the social whirl and it seems that you rather enjoy it. Your partner or lover definitely enjoys your attention. How can he or she dislike it? You are catering to his or her every whim and putting your partner's interests and desires above your own. Anyone in love with a Virgo this month is getting a rather good deal.

A lot of this behaviour stems from a special need to polish your social skills. Part of it comes from your need to feel worthy of love, and nothing makes you feel worthier than service. It is your highest ideal. Yet there is a lot of fun and physical intimacy involved here as well. Though you are a workhorse you are willing to have fun in order to foster true romance. There are a lot of evenings out – to sporting events, operas, concerts, dramas, nightclubs and the like. There is a lot of hand-holding and watching of sunsets. Your Horoscope shows a nice combination of courtship and physical intimacy this month.

Your vitality is not what it should be or even will be right now. Rest and relax more. Recognize your physical limits. Though it is OK and very noble to put other people before yourself, it is not noble if this affects your health. If you are not well you can't serve anybody. Let the law of your constitution guide you now.

Finances are strong all month though they are not a big priority. Money comes through your work and the supply is adequate. If you need more you are able to work more and thus get more. During the latter part of the month a windfall comes from your partner. An investment proves profitable.

An investor is interested in your ideas. An insurance payment comes to you. This is money that has nothing really to do with your personal earning power.

The earnings of your partner are slow early in the month but pick up after the 21st and really skyrocket after the 24th, when your partner's Money Planet starts moving forward again.

April

Best Days Overall: 2nd, 3rd, 11th, 12th, 13th, 20th, 21st, 29th, 30th

Most Stressful Days Overall: 4th, 5th, 6th, 18th, 19th, 24th, 25th

Best Days for Love: 2nd, 3rd, 7th, 8th, 12th, 13th, 16th, 17th, 20th, 21st, 24th, 25th, 26th, 28th, 29th, 30th

Best Days for Money: 1st, 7th, 8th, 9th, 10th, 14th, 15th, 16th, 17th, 18th, 19th, 26th, 27th, 28th

The planets continue their shift to the upper half of your Solar Horoscope this month, emphasizing worldly ambitions and the urge to raise your status and position in society. Moreover, most of the planets are still in the Western hemisphere, suggesting that you need to adapt to conditions and cultivate the good graces of others so that your own good can come to pass.

Your health and work interests are most interesting this month. The power in your Solar 8th House of Elimination and Transformation shows that you are involved in getting rid of things in your life: detoxifying your body, losing weight and the like. Uranus, Lord of your 6th House (of Health and Work) makes a major move into the Sign of Aquarius this month, highlighting a break with old, traditional diets and health regimes. Your experimental urges in health matters are really set free. You want nothing less than absolute physical fitness and will not compromise in any way. This attitude permeates your work interests as well. You want a kind of total freedom to work in your own way and at your own pace. New technology might satisfy your sense of freedom in that it liberates your time, but a change at work might be the real solution.

Your love life is active and happy this month. There is still a lot of courtship but the passionate side is strong as well. You are serving your partner by enhancing his or her income, by fulfilling sensual fantasies and by re-inventing yourself in his or her image. This is fun for a while but you can't keep this up for too long. Re-invention is wonderful but you must stay true to yourself.

Singles are attracted to people of high social status this month. It's as if you are enamoured more of a person's position than by the person him- or herself. You are looking for a lover who can help your career.

Religion and philosophy are also important this month. After the 17th your 9th House of Travel, Education, Religion and Philosophy becomes powerful. Moreover, both Eclipses, the Lunar Eclipse of the 15th and the Solar Eclipse of the 29th, are causing even further spiritual activity and much-needed long-term change. Present methods of prayer and meditation get discarded as inadequate. Current philosophies are put to the test and probably found wanting. Old concepts about reality get uprooted so that new and better ones can take their place. There is nothing to fear in this.

The Lunar Eclipse of the 15th shows long-term financial changes as well. This probably relates to your change in jobs. Be patient with a friend around this time. The upheaval is short lived.

May

Best Days Overall: 9th, 10th, 17th, 18th, 26th, 27th, 28th

Most Stressful Days Overall: 1st, 2nd, 3rd, 15th, 16th, 21st, 22nd, 23rd, 29th, 30th

Best Days for Love: 6th, 7th, 8th, 9th, 10th, 15th, 16th, 17th, 18th, 21st, 22nd, 23rd, 26th, 27th, 28th

Best Days for Money: 6th, 7th, 8th, 11th, 12th, 15th, 16th, 17th, 24th, 25th, 26th, 27th, 28th

Though the Western sector of your Horoscope is still the dominant one this month, its percentage of dominance is beginning to lessen – especially after the 21st. In the mean time, put others ahead of yourself, hone your social skills and play the hand that the Cosmos has dealt you as skilfully as possible. When the Western sector of the Horoscope dominates you are not judged on conditions and circumstances *per se*, but on how well you adapt to alien conditions and on how well you play the game.

All this is further reinforced by the slowness and tentativeness of Mercury's motion this month. Though your health is good – especially until the 21st – you seem to lack personal confidence and direction. You are not quite sure where your personal interests lie and especially seem doubtful about where your career is going. This is good, for it will spur you to review and to chart a new and better course.

This is not a month for asserting yourself too strongly, nor for insisting on too much personal freedom. Avoid power struggles – especially after the 21st – at all costs.

Your paths of greatest fulfilment are intellectual pursuits, studies, sales and marketing projects, the home and family, physical intimacy and getting rid of useless baggage in your life. After the 21st religious studies and foreign travel bring you happiness and fulfilment.

Forty per cent of the planets are retrograde this month, creating a general feeling of impasse and inaction. Be patient with yourself and with others. The delays that you experience this month are not targeted solely at you – others are also experiencing these things. After the 24th, Mercury (your Ruling Planet) also goes retrograde, putting the grand total of planetary retrogrades at 50 per cent. Tread softly. Do whatever constructive things you can do and let the universe handle the rest according to its own marvellous timing.

Your career is going to become active after the 21st. Study all proposed job shifts, promotions and other propositions very carefully. Delay giving an answer (either positive or negative) until you have studied the ramifications of and motives behind these things thoroughly. You are not being told everything.

Rest and relax more after the 21st.

June

Best Days Overall: 5th, 6th, 14th, 15th, 22nd, 23rd, 24th

Most Stressful Days Overall: 12th, 13th, 18th, 19th, 25th, 26th

Best Days for Love: 5th, 6th, 14th, 15th, 16th, 17th, 18th, 19th, 23rd, 24th, 25th, 26th

Best Days for Money: 3rd, 4th, 5th, 6th, 7th, 8th, 9th, 12th, 13th, 16th, 17th, 20th, 21st, 25th, 26th, 30th

Mercury, your Ruling Planet, is not only retrograde most of the month but is part of a stressful Grand Square aspect all month. Moreover, the unusual planetary power in the Sign of Gemini makes stressful aspects to your own Sun Sign. You need to lay low this month, avoid power struggles where you can – though it is doubtful that you will able to avoid all of them – and conserve your energies for your priorities. You need to tread the delicate path that winds between hyperactivity and complete stasis. The arguments and pressures for both these positions are equally powerful, but neither course will succeed by itself. You need to act – not out of panic or pressure – but because you know that the action will be effective. And you need to be able to stand still – not to act – when your actions would be futile. When in doubt, do nothing.

Your paths of greatest fulfilment this month involve intellectual interests, dealings with neighbours and siblings, the home and family, religious studies, higher education and your career.

With Mercury retrograde your self-confidence is not strong. This is understandable since you are not yet completely clear on what your personal and career interests are. On the other hand, Mars sits in your own Sign of Virgo all month. This creates a tendency to overcompensate for personal insecurities. Virgos can be overly belligerent this month – too combative for the wrong reasons. In addition, the feeling of being under siege could make you overly aggressive in the wrong ways and at the wrong times. Watch your motives now. On the positive side, the Cosmos has supplied you with superabundant courage and valour to deal with the trials and changes of the month.

Your career is active this month – and will wind up being successful – but you will work unusually hard for your success and be thrown into situations that you haven't been trained for. What is particularly difficult here is that your domestic and family interests pull you in opposite directions to the demands of your career. All people always have to balance their career and home life – but right now the conflict is particularly acute as the demands of each are diametrically opposed. The same is true with your social life, marriage and personal interests. All of these are conflicting with each other and you must somehow create a harmony from these discordant and antagonistic forces. Give to each its due and be prepared for a few failures. You won't strike the balance overnight. This is not a time to be overly idealistic. Focus on what works.

Though you probably won't heed this advice, you should rest and relax more until the 21st.

July

Best Days Overall: 2nd, 3rd, 4th, 11th, 12th, 20th, 21st, 30th, 31st

Most Stressful Days Overall: 9th, 10th, 15th, 16th, 22nd, 23rd

Best Days for Love: 2nd, 3rd, 4th, 7th, 8th, 11th, 12th, 15th, 16th, 20th, 21st, 25th, 26th, 30th, 31st

Best Days for Money: 1st, 5th, 6th, 7th, 8th, 9th, 10th, 15th, 16th, 17th, 18th, 25th, 26th, 27th, 28th

Though 50 per cent of the planets are still retrograde this is a much easier month than last month. Yes, the sense of stalemate still persists, but the stresses and conflicts of last month are gradually diminishing by their own weight and by the 11th most of them will be gone.

You are much more in charge of things this month than you were last month. First off, Mercury, your Ruler, moves forward speedily and confidently. Secondly, the dominance of planetary power is in the Eastern sector of your chart. You are more of a free agent now. You call the shots and you create conditions and circumstances. If others get obstinate or try to block your will you have all the power to go it on your own now.

Mercury moves through three Signs and Houses this

month, showing your dominant interests. Until the 11th it moves through your (10th) Career House, demonstrating that although you face career conflicts you are overcoming them and moving forward with confidence. Keep pursuing your career interests. After the 11th Mercury moves through your (11th) House of Friends and Group Activities. Thus you are more active with professional or political organizations. Platonic friendships are happy and interesting. Your fondest dreams and desires are coming true, with the help of your friends. After the 26th Mercury moves into your 12th House of Spiritual Wisdom and Charity, joining the Sun there. This gives you urges to make peace with your divinity, whichever divinity you worship. It makes you more idealistic, charitable and more giving of yourself for humanitarian purposes.

Your health is excellent all month and will get progressively better as the month moves on. There seem to be some health problems affecting your partner and you are actively involved in the healing process. Success is likely.

Your paths of fulfilment this month involve the home, family interests, family relationships, intellectual interests, friendship and philanthropic activities.

Though you are personally magnetic and attractive to the opposite sex, your love life is not what it should be. Your lover seems hesitant, tentative and confused about the relationship. Issues of physical intimacy seem a stumbling block between you. Perhaps you are too involved in your partner's finances – helping your partner to prosper and the like – and not involved enough in romantic issues. Your partner is dutiful and does the right thing but the passion is lacking. Be patient.

August

Best Days Overall: 7th, 8th, 16th, 17th, 26th, 27th

Most Stressful Days Overall: 5th, 6th, 12th, 19th, 20th

Best Days for Love: 3rd, 4th, 5th, 6th, 7th, 8th, 12th, 14th, 15th, 21st, 22nd, 26th, 27th, 31st

Best Days for Money: 1st, 2nd, 5th, 6th, 14th, 15th, 26th, 27th, 28th, 29th

The fast-moving, short-term planets are moving ever more eastward in your Solar chart and will reach their maximum Eastern position after the 23rd. Thus you are increasingly self-assertive, aware of your self-interest and actually pursuing your own needs. Happily you are neither going to be riding roughshod over others nor completely ignoring their interests in the process.

Much of the hold-up of recent months is easing off now. You will feel this most dramatically in your intellectual interests, schooling and domestic projects. A new sense of movement and progress comes in all these areas.

The planets are still very much concentrated at the bottom half of your chart, below the horizon. Thus you are still more interested in personal happiness, emotional harmony and family values than in your career and 'outer' life. As the months progress the power below the horizon will increase, showing a need to build your emotional and family base and set the stage for future career success. In terms of career your role is more supportive now. You get further by fostering other people's careers – especially those of family members or those who are like family to you – than by cultivating your own.

Your paths of greatest fulfilment this month are charity and philanthropy, enhancing your personal image, personal pleasures and good times, money-making, the home and family.

You are in an excellent financial period. Your financial judgement is sound and your confidence strong. In spite of all your recent aggressiveness in money matters – you have been avidly pursuing financial goals and perhaps getting into conflicts over money – money seems to come to you not from your aggressiveness but through a 'back door', almost supernaturally. Mysterious, secret financial doors open to you this month, showing that your supply comes by grace and not by 'force'. Your generosity to the poor and those in need is probably what has unlocked these secret doors, for in truth – especially early in the month – you are very generous.

Your financial intuition is exceptional before the 23rd. After then you become more pragmatic and practical about money matters. You are definitely a better shopper – likely to get better deals – after the 23rd than before. But you will make more money before the 23rd.

Your health is excellent all month but especially after the 23rd. Romantic opportunities are abundant, but be patient in love. Your Love Planet still retrogrades and much of the opportunities you are attracting are not serious or long term.

September

Best Days Overall: 4th, 5th, 12th, 13th, 14th, 22nd, 23rd

Most Stressful Days Overall: 2nd, 8th, 9th, 15th, 16th, 29th, 30th

Best Days for Love: 4th, 5th, 8th, 9th, 12th, 13th, 14th, 22nd, 23rd, 24th, 25th

Best Days for Money: 2nd, 4th, 5th, 10th, 11th, 12th, 13th, 14th, 20th, 21st, 24th, 25th, 29th, 30th

The power in the Eastern sector of your chart favours independence, self-assertion and personal dominion over your own life. You have the power to create what you will and others will be forced to adapt to it. Only remember that with Mercury, your Ruler, moving cautiously and slowly this month, so should you. You don't want to create anything that you will rue later on. After the 22nd, when Mercury goes retrograde, you will have the opportunity to rethink and perfect your personal goals and desires.

Eighty to 90 per cent of the planets are in the bottom half of your chart this month. This further emphasizes the 'me first' attitude you've adopted of late. You want emotional security and family harmony and will sacrifice glory and public acclaim for it. In career matters your role is supportive. You would rather see others attain outward success than yourself. The price that people pay for career success seems like a punishment to you.

Your paths of greatest happiness this month are personal pleasures, the enhancement of your personal image, money-making, your family and domestic projects.

Earnings are bittersweet this month. On the one hand your (2nd) Money House sees a lot of action. There are many earning opportunities open to you and much support for your financial goals. Money is earned easily and pleasurably. Yet, Mercury's retrograde happens in your Money House. This shows not a lack of earning power *per se* but a lack of focus or lack of clarity about financial goals. It also shows a need for caution in all financial dealings. Do more homework before buying or investing. Avoid signing contracts after the 22nd; wait until next month when Mercury goes direct again.

Your health is excellent all month, your vitality unusually great.

Your love life is still rather stalemated this month. On the one hand you want to have fun with the opposite sex, on the other you want an enduring, true relationship that will stand the test of time. There is no easy solution to this. Only time and more thought will resolve it.

October

Best Days Overall: 1st, 2nd, 10th, 11th, 20th, 21st, 28th, 29th

Most Stressful Days Overall: 5th, 6th, 12th, 13th, 26th, 27th

Best Days for Love: 1st, 2nd, 3rd, 4th, 5th, 6th, 11th, 15th, 16th, 20th, 21st, 24th, 25th, 29th

Best Days for Money: 3rd, 4th, 7th, 8th, 9th, 15th, 16th, 17th, 18th, 22nd, 23rd, 24th, 25th, 26th, 27th

The planets are now equally balanced between the Eastern and Western sectors of your Horoscope. This is by far the best configuration. It gives you a balanced perspective between your personal desires and interests and those of others. It offers you the option of either getting the co-operation of others or going it alone if need be. You have the power to do either. You are neither pushily assertive nor overly dependent on others. You get on with other people but they don't define your personality. Your self-esteem is not tied up with the good opinion of others.

Eighty to 90 per cent of the planets are below the horizon of your chart, showing an almost compulsive urge for emotional security and ease. You need to feel good about yourself at all costs and, unless you do, pursuing your ventures in the world will not bring happiness. You need to get at your emotional roots and find out why and how you tick. You need to learn more about yourself than about gaining experience in the outside world. And, with Jupiter moving forward through your 4th House, you are succeeding at this.

Your paths of greatest fulfilment now involve your family, domestic interests, psychological studies, money-making and intellectual pursuits.

There are two eclipses this month. The first is a Lunar Eclipse on the 8th which occurs in your 8th House of Shared Resources. This signals a temporary falling out with a partner over finances, short-lived setbacks to your partner's income and a brief lack of generosity from your partner. All of these will lead to a more stable pattern after the dust settles. The Solar Eclipse takes place on the 24th in your 3rd House of Intellectual Interests. This will affect those of you who are students, causing long-term changes in your education. You may change schools, or switch to a different degree course. Faulty communication equipment will tend to flare up over the next six months.

November

Best Days Overall: 6th, 7th, 16th, 17th, 25th

Most Stressful Days Overall: 1st, 2nd, 3rd, 8th, 9th, 10th, 23rd, 29th, 30th

Best Days for Love: 1st, 2nd, 3rd, 4th, 7th, 14th, 15th, 17th, 23rd, 24th, 25th, 26th, 29th, 30th

Best Days for Money: 2nd, 3rd, 4th, 5th, 14th, 15th, 18th, 19th, 23rd, 24th

All the planets are moving forward this month, Virgo, making this a month of action and achievement. With Mercury, your Ruler, moving ahead speedily, your progress is rapid.

The planets are shifting from the Eastern sector of your chart, where they have been for many months now, into the Western sector. This signals a shift in your attitude and orientation. Whereas for many months you could afford to be self-assertive, independent and 'doing your own thing', now you can't. Your social urges are becoming stronger. You are becoming more 'other'-orientated. Whereas for many months you haven't needed the good opinion of others, now you do. You have reached a stage in your creation of circumstances where others make things happen. Tone the self down and start thinking about others.

The trend towards emotional security is still strong, as 80 to 90 per cent of the planets are below the horizon of your chart. Though you will make good career progress this month it will happen in spite of your lack of interest. Nurture other people's careers now (and you have no problem with this) and your own will be furthered very naturally. Your role is supportive this month, both in family issues and in career matters.

Your paths of greatest fulfilment are money-making, domestic issues, family relationships and psychological studies.

Earnings are unusually strong after the 3rd. A lucky sale brings a substantial financial windfall. Neighbours help manifest your financial goals. You are going way out of your usual orbit in the pursuit of both earnings and 'big-ticket' (large, expensive) items.

The impasse in your love life is over, as Saturn is finally moving forward in your (7th) House of Marriage. A current relationship moves forward again. And, because of your ever-growing involvement and concern for others, your social popularity increases. Parties – especially of a corporate type – and entertainment venues continue to be the most likely places where you'll meet potential romantic partners.

December

Best Days Overall: 3rd, 4th, 13th, 14th, 22nd, 23rd, 31st

Most Stressful Days Overall: 6th, 7th, 20th, 21st, 26th, 27th

Best Days for Love: 3rd, 4th, 13th, 14th, 22nd, 23rd, 24th, 26th, 27th, 31st

Best Days for Money: 1st, 2nd, 3rd, 4th, 11th, 12th, 13th, 14th, 16th, 17th, 20th, 21st, 24th, 28th, 29th

The planets are now firmly established in the Western sector of your chart, making you more socially conscious and 'other-orientated', more dependent and less self-assertive. The 'me first' attitude which you've had for so many months is no longer useful or desirable for you. It is counter-productive now. This is not a time for you go it alone or to try to change conditions and circumstances. Your need now is to adapt to outside conditions and to love and be loved. Social success is your main goal and you will achieve it now.

Most of the planets continue to be at the bottom half of your chart, making you more nostalgic. You are looking towards the past. You are also more inclined to choose emotional harmony and security over career success. In truth, with so much power in your (4th) House of Family this month, domestic pursuits and delving into your past are unusually pleasurable activities. There is a joy in reminiscing about the past. Pleasant memories of the good old days reappear and put you in a good mood. Family activities and relationships are unusually pleasurable and profitable as well. A move or enlargement of your residence is occurring.

Psychological studies prosper. Prominent people – helpful ones – from your childhood reappear to recall old times. The past is digested and understood. A part of you wants to emulate the past.

Your urge to nurture is very active this month and brings you great pleasure. Profitable real estate deals are coming your way. Those of you looking to sell your home at a good price are likely to do so this month.

Aside from all the family activity, this month in general is one of personal pleasure and indulgence. Romance is in the air. Singles are likely to find their ideal mate this month. Emotions of love go sky-high and ultra-low. Affections tend to be extreme one way or the other. Personal creativity is strong and will translate into cash and added prestige. Speculations are favourable all month.

Your health is much improved after the 22nd. Before then try to rest and relax more.

Libra

♎

THE SCALES

Birthdays from

23rd September

to 22nd October

Personality Profile

LIBRA AT A GLANCE

Element – Air

Ruling planet – Venus
Career planet – Moon
Health planet – Neptune
Love planet – Mars
Money planet – Pluto
Planet of home and family life – Saturn

Colours – blue, jade green

Colours that promote love, romance and social harmony – carmine, red, scarlet

Colours that promote earning power – burgundy, red-violet, violet

Gems – carnelian, chrysolite, coral, emerald, jade, opal, quartz, white marble

Metal – copper

Scents – almond, rose, vanilla, violet

Quality – cardinal (= activity)

Qualities most needed for balance – a sense of self, self-reliance, independence

Strongest virtues – social grace, charm, tact, diplomacy

Deepest needs – love, romance, social harmony

Characteristic to avoid – violating what is right in order to be socially accepted

Signs of greatest overall compatibility – Gemini, Aquarius

Signs of greatest overall incompatibility – Aries, Cancer, Capricorn

Sign most helpful to career – Cancer

Sign most helpful for emotional support – Capricorn

Sign most helpful financially – Scorpio

Sign best for marriage and/or partnerships – Aries

Sign most helpful for creative projects – Aquarius

Best Sign to have fun with – Aquarius

Signs most helpful in spiritual matters – Gemini, Virgo

Best day of the week – Friday

Understanding the Libra Personality

In the Sign of Libra the universal mind – the soul – expresses its genius of relationship, that is, its power to harmonize diverse elements in a unified, organic way. Libra is the soul's power to express beauty in all of its forms. And where is beauty if not within relationships? Beauty doesn't exist in isolation. Beauty arises out of comparison – out of the just relationship of different parts. Without a fair and harmonious relationship there is no beauty, whether it be in art, manners, ideas or the social or political forum.

There are two faculties humans have that exalt them above the animal kingdom. The first is their rational faculty, as expressed in the Signs of Gemini and Aquarius. The second is their aesthetic faculty, exemplified by Libra. Without an aesthetic sense we would be little more than intelligent barbarians. Libra is the civilizing instinct or urge of the soul.

Beauty is the essence of what Librans are all about. They are here to beautify the world. One could discuss Librans' social grace, their sense of balance and fair play, their ability to see and love another person's point of view – but this would be to miss their central asset: their desire for beauty.

No one – no matter how alone he or she seems to be – exists in isolation. The universe is one vast collaboration of beings. Librans, more than most, understand this and understand the spiritual laws that make relationships bearable and enjoyable.

A Libra is always the unconscious (and in some cases conscious) civilizer, harmonizer and artist. This is a Libra's deepest urge and greatest genius. Librans love instinctively to bring people together, and they are uniquely qualified to do so. They have a knack for seeing what unites people – the things that attract and bind rather than separate individuals.

Finance

In financial matters Librans can seem frivolous and illogical to others. This is because Librans appear to be more concerned with earning money for others than for themselves. But there is a logic to this financial attitude. Librans know that everything and everyone is connected and that it is impossible to help another to prosper without also prospering yourself. Since enhancing their partner's income and position tends to strengthen their relationship, Librans choose to do so. What could be more fun than building a relationship? You will rarely find a Libra enriching him- or herself at someone else's expense.

Scorpio is the Ruler of Libra's Solar 2nd House of Money, giving Libra unusual insight into financial matters and the power to focus on these matters in a way that disguises a seeming indifference. In fact, many other Signs come to Librans for financial advice and guidance.

Given their social graces, Librans often spend great sums of money on entertaining and organizing social events. They also like to help others when they are in need. Librans would go out of their way to help a friend in dire straits, even if they have to borrow from others to do so. However, Librans are also very careful to pay back any debts they owe and like to make sure they never have to be reminded to do so.

Career and Public Image

Publicly, Librans like to appear as nurturers. Their friends and acquaintances are their family and they wield political power in parental ways. They also like bosses who are paternal or maternal.

The Sign of Cancer is on Libra's 10th House (of Career) cusp; the Moon is Libra's Career Planet. The Moon is by far the speediest, most changeable planet in the Horoscope. It alone among all the planets travels through the entire Zodiac – all 12 Signs and Houses – every month. This is an important key to the way in which Librans approach their careers and also to some of the things they need to do to maximize their career potential. The Moon is the planet of moods and feelings – and Librans need a career in which they have free expression for their emotions. This is why so many Librans are involved in the creative arts. Libra's ambitions wax and wane like the Moon. They tend to wield power according to their mood.

The Moon 'rules' the masses – and that is why Libra's highest goal is to achieve a mass kind of acclaim and popularity. Librans who achieve fame cultivate the public as other people cultivate a lover or friend. Librans can be very flexible – and often fickle – in their career and ambitions. On the other hand, they can achieve their ends in a great variety of ways. They are not stuck in one attitude or one way of doing things.

Love and Relationships

Librans express their true genius in love. In love you could not find a partner more romantic, more seductive or more fair. If there is one thing that is sure to destroy a relationship – sure to block the love force from flowing – it is injustice or imbalance between the lover and the beloved. If one party is giving too much or taking too much, resentment is sure to surface at some time or other. Librans are careful about this. If anything, Librans might err on the side of giving more, but never of giving less.

If you are in love with a Libra make sure you keep the aura of romance alive. Do all the little things. Have candlelit dinners, travel to exotic places. Bring flowers and little gifts. Give things that are beautiful although not necessarily expensive. Send cards. Ring regularly even if you have nothing particular to say. The niceties are very important. Your relationship is a work of art: make it beautiful and your Libra lover will appreciate it. If you are creative about it, he or she will appreciate it even more; for this is how your Libra will behave towards you.

Librans like their partners to be aggressive and even a bit self-willed. They know that these are qualities they sometimes lack and so they like their partners to have them. In relationships, however, Librans can be very aggressive – but always in a subtle and charming way! Gorbachev's 'charm offensive' and openness of the late 1980s (which revolutionized the then-Soviet Union) is typical of a Libra.

Librans are determined in their efforts to charm the object of their desire – and this determination can be very pleasant if you're on the receiving end.

Home and Domestic Life

Since Librans are such social creatures, they don't particularly like mundane domestic duties. They like a well-organized home – clean and neat with everything needful present – but housework is a chore and a burden, one of the unpleasant tasks in life that must be done, the quicker the better. If a Libra has enough money – and sometimes even if not – he or she will prefer to pay someone else to take care of the daily household chores. However, Librans like to do some gardening and they love to have flowers and plants in the home.

A Libra's home is modern and furnished in excellent taste. You will find many paintings and sculptures there. Since Librans like to be with friends and family, they enjoy entertaining at home and they make great hosts.

Capricorn is on the cusp of Libra's 4th Solar House of Home and Family. Saturn, the planet of law, order, limits and discipline, rules Libra's domestic affairs. If Librans want their home life to be supportive and happy, they need to develop some of the virtues of Saturn – order, organization and discipline. Librans, being so creative and so intensely in need of harmony, can tend to be too lax in the home and too permissive with their children. Too much of this is not always good; children do need freedom, but they also need limits.

Horoscope for 1995

Major Trends

1994 was a year of great financial expansion and controlled, disciplined creativity. This year you seem sated financially. You are where you want to be and you are ready to reap the rewards of financial success – that is, being able to expand your mind and intellectual interests. Money buys you the freedom to take courses, study and develop your mind. By the time Pluto, which has been in your 2nd House of Money for many years, leaves Scorpio and moves into Sagittarius this year, the financial transformations that you've been working on will have been completed. On to higher, less materialistic pursuits!

Family and domestic issues will continue to be important this year, as they have been for many years now. 1996 will be more active and happier on this front than 1995. The emotional support that you're trying to build for the future is up, down and subject to sudden, unexpected changes. But keep working on it, for in 1996 it will come.

Health

Your health and vitality have been steadily improving year by year. 1995 is better than 1994, just as 1994 was better than 1993. Still your vitality is not what it should be and will be. This is because Uranus and Neptune have been making stressful aspects to you for many years now. They have been making you stronger through shocking, surprising events and powerful physical changes. Your body is being tempered – as fine steel is – through the interplay of opposite and radical forces.

Though your health is improved this year, your 6th House of Health has become very prominent. Saturn is there for the next two years. This suggests that you have to work at physical fitness and maintaining your health. You have to restrict and purify your diet, do exercise that is good for you if perhaps a bit unpleasant and otherwise undergo some health regime. When Saturn is through with you its gift will be enduring health.

Saturn is the Lord of your 4th House of Home and Family, which suggests that your family and particularly your emotional harmony are vital factors in maintaining good health this year. Mood control and the avoidance of depressive thoughts and feelings will significantly improve any health problem you might have.

For many years you have been experimental with your health – with health regimes and different approaches to health. Perhaps you have even been faddish, flitting from one 'miracle' system to the next. There's nothing wrong with this trial-and-error approach as it generally leads to the right answers. But some people indulge in these things to avoid doing what really needs to be done, because what is needed is sometimes unpleasant. This year you need to take one regime, one system and apply it faithfully. Healing efforts have a cumulative impact which you will lose if you move quickly from one thing to another. Your family and children, though unstable in many other ways, are unusually supportive of your health regimes and practices. Creative expression will also alleviate any health problems this year.

Home and Domestic Life

As mentioned, the 4th House of Home and Family interests is still very prominent in 1995. Again – as has been the case for many years now – your family situation and relationships are unstable, turbulent and difficult to predict. Family members feud one day and make up the next. There are serious break-ups that happen suddenly, and equally sudden comings together. Your residence is continually changing. A series of moves are on the horizon. Once moved in you find you need to make renovations and changes to the home. All of this is giving you expertise and experience in home-building. All of this is leading you to your ideal and perfect home. Though outsiders who don't know you would be daunted by all of this hyperactivity, for you it is not as stressful as it seems. You have plenty of help available to ease you through these changes. When there is a family feud, a co-worker or therapist is there to get you through. When you need to move there is help. When you need to renovate there is help. Saturn and Neptune, the Lords of the Home and the Workplace respectively, are in 'mutual reception' – unusually co-operative on your behalf.

Though you are moving around a lot this year the really happy move will come next year.

Part of your role this year is to bring healing to the warring factions in your family. This will be hard work and will tax even your diplomatic skills. If you persist you will succeed, but more importantly you will gain great knowledge of human nature and people's feelings.

Your eldest sibling prospers and travels a lot this year. There is a great rise in status for him or her. Your second eldest sibling is as yet unstable and unsettled, still looking to find him- or herself and involved in all kinds of experimentation. The income of a parent is very volatile this year, going wildly up one day and wildly down the next. This parent is involved in something new and unique, and he or she hasn't yet mastered all the details and intricacies. The other parent seems unconcerned with earnings and is focused on health – and with good results. Good news will come about his or her health problem. This parent is also focused on work, especially on becoming a more productive worker.

Love and Social Life

Though love and romance will always be important to you, Libra, this year they are less so. Your 7th House of Love and Marriage is just not prominent this year. For singles, uncommitted, fun-type love affairs are more likely than marriage. Whether you are married or single, the status quo is unlikely to change. The Cosmos is not pushing you one way or another. You have much social freedom this year, but less interest in this area of your life.

There will be periods during which romance does become important – on a monthly basis. The Moon visits your House of Marriage two days every month and you should follow these short-term trends in the month-by-month forecasts, below. Looking at the year as a whole, romance becomes important and unusually active from 21st March to 17th May and from 22nd July to 8th September. Significant relationships are likely to be formed at these times

Mars, your Lord of Love, makes an unusually long transit (four months) through the Sign of Leo, your 11th Solar House of Friends, Group Activities and Fondest Wishes. This occurs from 23rd January to 26th May. This reinforces what was said earlier about fun-and-games types of relationship, because Leo likes to play and is not especially fond of marriage. There are other ways this scenario can play itself out, however. A friend could become a hot romantic partner. Or your lover could become more like a friend. Many of you are going to experience your 'fondest hopes and wishes' in love this period – albeit briefly. Once you attain one fondest wish, another, perhaps higher 'fondest wish' will come your way. During this period you will want friendship from your lover. Hot romance will not be enough for you. You will find romance through organizations you belong to.

Your parents' marriage (and those of your superiors at work) are undergoing great changes and turbulence. They are working out their relationships through trial and error and a few upheavals.

Career and Finance

Your 2nd House of Money and Possessions continues to be prominent this year, though not as prominent as it was last year. The 10th House of Career is pretty inactive as you are much more focused on getting your home and family life in order than in outward, objective success. Money, too, is more important to you right now than status or prestige. As the year goes by money becomes less and less important, however. Jupiter, which helped you expand tremendously in 1994, has left your Money House. Pluto will also leave by the end of the year. This is a signal that you have attained your financial goals and are now free to work on other things.

Pluto in your Money House – he is also the Lord of the House – still shows that you need to pare down your expenses and get rid of unnecessary investments and possessions. You prosper – as you did in 1994 – by pruning, cutting and trimming. You become a leaner, trimmer economic force this year; reduced somewhat, but more profitable. After so many years in your Money House, Pluto has given you the ability to transform losses into profits and financial pain into success. You have a knack for taking a losing proposition and making it profitable, of taking a dying company and giving it new life.

You take a low profile on wealth this year by preferring not to flaunt your possessions. You keep your assets well hidden. You are much richer than others believe you to be.

Though you always love to enhance your partner's income, you are still concentrating on your own earning power – this has been a healthy long-term trend. The investments that you have left over – after your pruning – will be profitable this year. Interest and dividend income is up. Money will come to you, even though you put less emphasis upon it.

This is a year in which you increase and upgrade your communication equipment – your phone systems, computers, modems, fax machines and the like. All kinds of new equipment are coming to you. Many of you are also going to buy new cars this year.

Journalistic, sales and marketing ideas are profitable this year and will become even more profitable next year. That is, you will reap the rewards of your sales, marketing and public relations efforts. These areas represent a good long-term investment.

Your partner seems unconcerned about money this year. He or she is much more interested in status and prestige than money. Your partner's career is undergoing a lot of changes – as it has for many years now – but the trial-and-error experiments are beginning to pay off. His or her career is successful this year. The changes happen smoothly and pleasurably.

The income of a parent and your eldest sibling is a roller-coaster ride. Scary at times, happy at times, but never dull. There is such a sense of tension and uncertainty there that they might be better off relaxing so that they do not block earnings because of their anxieties. The income of your second eldest sibling is stressful this year. There is a need for budgeting and better management of existing income. You might be called upon to help out.

Self-improvement

Jupiter moving though your 3rd Solar House of Intellectual Interests is going to improve your communication abilities with almost no effort on your part. The opportunities come, the money is there, all you need to do is go along with it. You will be taking courses and seminars – perhaps in religious or philosophical studies – reading more and writing more. Many of you will also get more involved in teaching others these things. The 3rd Solar House deals with teaching as well as learning. Your education is expanding through travel this year as well. Though there is not much foreign travel in your future, you will be making long trips domestically. One likely scenario is that you attend courses or seminars in other cities. The things you learn through your travels are part of your education. Your concept of community widens beyond just the immediate neighbourhood. The country as a whole will become part of your community.

As discussed earlier, you need to adopt a strict dietary and health regime. This won't be easy – you like the finer things in life, especially sweets. This dietary regime is necessary not only for health reasons but for your personal image and self-esteem. With the North Lunar Node making a major move into your 1st House of the Body and Personal Image in August, you derive long-term happiness and satisfaction from enhancing, perfecting and beautifying your image.

Month-by-month Forecasts

January

Best Days Overall: 3rd, 4th, 12th, 13th, 22nd, 23rd, 30th, 31st

Most Stressful Days Overall: 1st, 2nd, 7th, 8th, 15th, 16th, 28th, 29th

Best Days for Love: 1st, 2nd, 5th, 6th, 7th, 8th, 17th, 18th, 19th, 20th, 26th, 27th

Best Days for Money: 5th, 6th, 7th, 8th, 15th, 16th, 17th, 18th, 24th, 25th, 26th, 27th

The planetary forces are overwhelmingly clustered in the bottom half of your Solar Horoscope this month, Libra. This shows that you are more interested in personal harmony and happiness – emotional fulfilment – than in career success. You want a stable home base and a strong emotional support system. You will probably turn down any career opportunity – no matter how lucrative – that threatens this emotional stability. Besides, you've got enough action at home and with your family to keep you very busy this month. Not only are friends – perhaps groups of them –

visiting you, there are also visitors from foreign lands.

Hectic and busy though your family life may be, the place of real fulfilment this month is in your intellectual interests. Sales and marketing projects are very successful. If you are student you do very well in your studies now. Learning is both a joy and profitable as well. Journalists make more money at their craft. Writers sell manuscripts profitably. Neighbours and siblings are generous with you. A new car and new communication equipment come to you. Your power to 'network' and communicate is greatly expanded.

If you are not a full-time student you might think about enrolling in some course – and your Solar Horoscope suggests various possibilities. Courses on money management, law, investing, personal beauty and glamour and religious studies are the most favourable.

Your love life is a bit rocky right now. This refers to your current serious relationship. You and your lover or spouse are rethinking your relationship and many hidden resentments are coming to the surface for review and for resolution. Hang in there, it will work out. In addition to this there are many non-serious, fun-and-games types of romantic opportunities coming your way – especially after the 20th. But indulging in these might make your current relationship even shakier than it is. Your partner also has abundant romantic opportunities. Think before you act.

This is a month of great personal indulgence – in food and other sensual delights. Be careful not to put on the pounds. Female Librans are unusually fertile, especially from the 14th to the 16th.

This month you are getting a taste of the changes that are going on in your financial life. Pluto, your Money Planet, flirts with your Solar 3rd House of Communication – a prelude to its more permanent move at the end of the year. You are going to earn your money from sales, marketing and more cerebral activities than usual. You are going to earn money in your neighbourhood. Income from your investments is going to increase – forming a greater share of your earnings than ever before and giving you more leisure time. Rest and relax more until the 20th.

February

Best Days Overall: 8th, 9th, 10th, 18th, 19th, 26th, 27th, 28th

Most Stressful Days Overall: 3rd, 4th, 5th, 11th, 12th, 24th, 25th

Best Days for Love: 3rd, 4th, 5th, 6th, 7th, 13th, 14th, 15th, 16th, 17th, 22nd, 23rd, 24th, 25th

Best Days for Money: 3rd, 4th, 5th, 13th, 14th, 15th, 20th, 21st, 22nd, 23rd

Eighty to 90 per cent of the planets are clustered at the bottom half of your Horoscope this month, showing that career and worldly ambitions are less important to you than your emotional happiness and harmony. Feeling good is more important to you than your place in the world. Any employer who wants your talents will have to understand this and cater to this now. Venus, your Ruling Planet, moves into the 4th House of Home and Family early in the month and stays there. The pleasures of family life, of home and hearth, of giving and receiving emotional support, of nurturing and being nurtured, are all very attractive now. Family gatherings are likely to dominate the month ahead.

By now you have sated yourself with the 'pleasures of the flesh' and are ready to drop a few pounds and otherwise improve your health. Too much pleasure often leads to pain. It is likely that you will get into this diet or health regime early in the month, but definitely by the 19th. It seems like something strict – something requiring discipline and sacrifice.

Until the 19th you are very much involved in creative

projects and with children. This goes well but be careful of how you communicate with children, as misunderstandings are likely until the 16th. Make sure the children you are dealing with are really getting your message – and you are getting theirs. Take the time to ask questions if you don't understand.

Earnings are strong until the 19th. They come – as they did last month – through sales, marketing, advertising and promotion. Intellectual interests in general can be turned to profit. For example, if you enjoy a certain subject or hobby – such as bird watching, or cycling – you can find profit-making opportunities by either teaching about these things or writing about them.

After the 19th you work harder for your earnings than usual. Overspending on friends or on group activities during this period can tax your finances unduly.

With Mars, your Love Planet, still retrograde (travelling backwards) the entire month, caution is still necessary in love. It would not be wise to schedule either a marriage or a divorce now. The Cosmos wants you to review and 'backtrack' over a current relationship to reveal to you whether it is really what you want. If it is you will see what corrections can be made to make it better. If it is not you will be shown how to dissolve it and create a better 'mental blueprint' for future love. This retrograde involves serious committed relationships. Fun-and-games types of relationships are very abundant and easily available. Singles have ample opportunity to amuse themselves until they find Mr or Ms Right.

March

Best Days Overall: 8th, 9th, 17th, 18th, 26th, 27th

Most Stressful Days Overall: 3rd, 4th, 10th, 11th, 12th, 24th, 25th, 30th, 31st

Best Days for Love: 3rd, 4th, 8th, 9th, 13th, 14th, 17th, 18th, 21st, 22nd, 26th, 27th, 28th, 30th, 31st

Best Days for Money: 3rd, 4th, 13th, 14th, 19th, 20th, 21st, 22nd, 30th, 31st

Like last month, the planets are focused in the Western hemisphere of your Solar chart, denoting an interest in others above an interest in yourself. Though some Signs are uncomfortable with this, for you it is a piece of cake. You tend to do this anyway. You like getting your way through the grace of other people. This month you are merely being given opportunities to exercise your social genius.

Most of the planets are still clustered at the bottom half of your chart, showing a greater interest in personal happiness, family values and psychological harmony rather than in outward ambitions and career. But this is gradually changing as the months go by. You are getting ready to pursue your ambitions. In the mean time your paths of greatest fulfilment involve money-making, intellectual interests, children and creativity.

This month you are juggling between your fun-loving urges and the demands of the workplace. The pace at work has picked up. You know that your duty and responsibility lie there, yet you want some fun. Those with children feel the conflict of twin duties – duties to your children and to your employer. Happily both your employer and your children are understanding and you should be able to work out an acceptable compromise.

Though your health is basically good, you seem, as you were last month, involved in a strict dietary or exercise regime. This is probably not a health programme *per se* but more a vanity programme. You want to get in shape for spring. With Venus, your Ruler, in the 5th House of Fun and Self-indulgence it is quite a challenge to enter into this dietary discipline. You should persist, though, as this becomes easier towards the end of the month. Rest and relax more after the 21st.

In love, spring fever will hit you hard, Libra. Mars, the Lord of your Love Life, is finally moving forward on the 24th and the Sun moves into your (7th) House of Love and Marriage on the 21st. Romance is in the air. Singles find love opportunities among friends and through group activities – especially group sporting events or group entertainment events. You are now ready to accept someone you have kept at arm's length as something more than a friend. The major problem in the love department this month – and this applies to both singles and marrieds – is the need to balance your interests with those of your partner. You seem to be going in different directions, wanting to do different things and to go to different places. The problem is not one of lack of love, but of conflicting desires.

Earnings are unusually strong after the 21st. Be cautious in spending or making long-term financial commitments now, however, as Pluto, your Money Lord, is retrograde.

April

Best Days Overall: 4th, 5th, 6th, 14th, 15th, 22nd, 23rd

Most Stressful Days Overall: 1st, 7th, 8th, 20th, 21st, 26th, 27th, 28th

Best Days for Love: 1st, 7th, 8th, 9th, 10th, 16th, 17th, 18th, 19th, 26th, 27th, 28th

Best Days for Money: 1st, 9th, 10th, 16th, 17th, 18th, 19th, 24th, 25th, 26th, 27th, 28th

Your love/social life is clearly the main headline for the coming month. Not only are 60 to 70 per cent of the planets in the Western hemisphere of your chart, but your 7th House of Love and Marriage is unusually active. Yes, you are very much interested in other people this month, interested in 'people-pleasing' and catering to others. And, though some other Signs of the Zodiac find this difficult, for you it is great fun. By putting others first you know that your own needs will inevitably be fulfilled.

Singles are likely to find 'that special someone' this month. The workplace, doctors' surgeries, hospitals and professional organizations to which you belong are likely places where you will meet him or her. With Venus moving forward with great speed your personal confidence is strong and you are sure-footed socially. A platonic friend becomes a serious romantic prospect. You will get whomever you set your sights on right now as you seem willing to pay any price. Only remember, you might be stuck with your choice for a long time. You are also attending an unusual number of parties and weddings this month.

Personal earning power is much stronger before the 20th than afterwards. After the 20th there is a need for caution in your financial dealings. Review any financial proposals or investments very carefully. Though your personal earning power is weaker during the latter part of the month, the slack is taken up by the generosity of your partner – who is prospering – or by fortunate legal rulings in your favour.

Rest and relax more until the 20th. Take special care to maintain a harmonious rapport with your family until then as well. Lack of family harmony can really deplete you. Your vitality returns with a vengeance after the 20th. Domestic harmony is increased then as well.

The two eclipses this month activate the 1st House of the Body and Personal Image and the 8th House of Elimination, Transformation and Other People's Money. The Lunar Eclipse of the 15th signals a long-term career change and the resultant alterations in your personal image. A redefinition of your personality causes a career change and vice versa. The Solar Eclipse of the 29th in your 8th House signifies major changes in your partner's finances and in your relationship with an investor.

May

Best Days Overall: 1st, 2nd, 3rd, 11th, 12th, 19th, 20th, 29th, 30th

Most Stressful Days Overall: 4th, 5th, 17th, 18th, 24th, 25th, 31st

Best Days for Love: 6th, 7th, 8th, 15th, 16th, 17th, 24th, 25th, 26th, 27th, 28th

Best Days for Money: 4th, 5th, 6th, 7th, 8th, 13th, 14th, 15th, 16th, 21st, 22nd, 23rd, 24th, 25th, 31st

With so many of the planets clustered in the Western half of your Horoscope this month you get a real chance to exercise your social genius. What is genius for if not to be used? And because you attain your good through the grace of others this will be a happy and successful month for you. This is, after all, your speciality.

The way that the planets are evenly dispersed above and below the horizon of your chart shows a wonderful balance between and perspective regarding your career and home life. You are neither over- nor under-emphasizing either.

Your paths to greatest fulfilment this month continue to be money-making, intellectual interests and your love life. After the 17th, helping others to prosper and the elimination of undesirable things from your life are also happy and fulfilling pursuits.

Forty per cent of the planets are retrograde as the month begins; by the time it ends, 50 per cent of them will be retrograde. Though you will make much personal progress, the general climate is one of stalemate, delays and caution. Be patient with yourself and with others. Use delays to your advantage – to rethink and improve your plans, products and services.

As the month begins you are involved in elimination, transformation and re-inventing yourself. This is the time to eliminate undesirable habits, character traits and material possessions that you no longer need. This cleansing of the mind, body and surplus prepares you for the intellectual expansion that occurs after the 21st. You are more free to pursue religious studies and other forms of higher education because of this 'clear-out'. You are freer to travel mentally (through books and higher ideas) and physically and to profit from such travels. However, with both Jupiter and Mercury retrograde this month it would be best to postpone journeys abroad until next month. Plan them now, by all means, but execute these plans later on.

With Pluto (your Money Planet) retrograde all month, your personal earning power is not what it could be. Important financial deals or investments should be studied more carefully. This earning 'slack', however, is more than made up for by the generosity of your partner and by outside investors or lenders. These monies come to you much more easily than personal earnings. Your partner is prospering this month – and you are instrumental in this success.

Your love life is romantic until the 17th. Your lover is very happy with you. And why not? You are catering to his or her every whim and putting your partner's interest ahead of your own. The physical intimacy aspects of the relationship become more intense after the 17th. Though your health is good all month, your partner needs to rest and relax more.

June

Best Days Overall: 7th, 8th, 9th, 16th, 17th, 25th, 26th

Most Stressful Days Overall: 1st, 2nd, 14th, 15th, 20th, 21st

Best Days for Love: 3rd, 4th, 5th, 6th, 12th, 13th, 16th, 17th, 20th, 21st, 25th, 26th, 30th

Best Days for Money: 2nd, 3rd, 4th, 10th, 11th, 12th, 13th, 19th, 20th, 21st, 28th, 29th, 30th

This month's Solar Horoscope points to both unusual action and change and to equally unusual inaction and stalemate. What could these contradictory tendencies mean?

The call to action comes from the rare and stressful Grand Square aspect involving 60 per cent of the planets. After the 10th, Venus (your Ruling Planet) also becomes involved in this formation. The call to inaction comes from 50 per cent of the planets being retrograde most of the month.

It seems that the caution and delay come precisely because there is such a need for change and activity. The greater the need for change, the greater the need for caution and adequate planning and testing.

Though this month is not as stressful on you as it will be for other Signs, still you must deal with fundamental conflicts between religious studies and more mundane intellectual interests; between philosophical and moral beliefs and current sales projects; between personal work goals and the work goals of your partner; between personal health interests and the health interests of your partner. No one is better equipped to mitigate these conflicts than you are.

Opportunities for foreign travel are sure to come to you this month, but it would be better to delay them until after the 17th when Mercury goes forward again.

Pluto (your Money Planet) continues to be retrograde this month, suggesting a need for caution when it comes to investments and major purchases. Study things more carefully before committing resources to them. Earnings are strong after the 22nd. Your career and public prestige are also boosted around that time.

Singles are more idealistic – perhaps unrealistically so – in love this month. Love is stormy and tempestuous until the 22nd. Passions, both positive and negative, run high. Rows are more intense than usual but making up is all the sweeter afterwards. Criticism and undue perfectionism are the greatest dangers to romance right now. Small voluntary sacrifices made now will prevent larger involuntary ones in the future.

July

Best Days Overall: 5th, 6th, 13th, 14th, 22nd, 23rd

Most Stressful Days Overall: 11th, 12th, 17th, 18th, 25th, 26th

Best Days for Love: 2nd, 3rd, 4th, 7th, 8th, 11th, 12th, 15th, 16th, 17th, 18th, 21st, 22nd, 25th, 26th

Best Days for Money: 1st, 7th, 8th, 9th, 10th, 16th, 17th, 18th, 26th, 27th, 28th

As the month begins the planets are evenly dispersed in the different sectors of your chart, enhancing your already inborn sense of balance. But as the month progresses the fast-moving planets shift the power to the Eastern sector of your chart. The power between the upper and bottom halves of your chart continues to be evenly balanced.

This shows that you are becoming ever more self-assertive and in control. You are less dependent on others for your success. If you so choose, you have the power to go it on your own this month.

You've got the right perspective on your career this month and are much more ambitious than you have been earlier in the year. Earlier on you were actually ignoring your career, now at least you give it the attention it deserves. With two planets retrograde in your 4th House of Family, family issues can safely be put on hold now. Focus on your career.

Your paths of greatest fulfilment this month are money-making – both for yourself and for others – intellectual interests, communication, religious studies, career and – towards the end of the month – group activities.

Though parents and family members are unsure of where you are going in your career they support you nevertheless.

Finances are simply outstanding most of the month. Your Money Planet (Pluto) is going backwards, however, which helps you to maintain a healthy scepticism and caution when presented with new investments or financial deals. Study them thoroughly. Perhaps the most important thing you could be doing now is to set your financial goals for the coming year. Visualize your goals as already fulfilled.

Your love life is gradually heating up. As the month begins, love is idealistic and pure. Both you and your partner are sacrificing for each other. Singles meet romantic opportunities at charitable activities and spiritual meetings. After the 22nd love becomes more physical, tangible and actual. It is less idealistic and more concerned with fulfilling personal needs and giving pleasure. Part of the happiness of this period comes from your lover's willingness to put your interests ahead of his or her own. You are calling the shots in the relationship now.

Rest and relax more until the 23rd.

August

Best Days Overall: 1st, 2nd, 9th, 10th, 19th, 20th, 28th, 29th

Most Stressful Days Overall: 7th, 8th, 14th, 15th, 21st, 22nd

Best Days for Love: 1st, 2nd, 5th, 6th, 9th, 10th, 14th, 15th, 19th, 20th, 26th, 27th, 28th, 29th

Best Days for Money: 3rd, 4th, 5th, 6th, 12th, 13th, 14th, 15th, 21st, 22nd, 26th, 27th, 30th, 31st

Your unusual personal aggressiveness just gets stronger and stronger. Mars in your own Sign of Libra all month makes you fearless, courageous and willing to overcome any hardship to attain your ends. Combine this with the overwhelming power of the Eastern sector of your chart and you get a picture of someone who is dynamic, electric, strong and probably unaware of his or her own power. You've got the energy of 10 people this month and can accomplish whatsoever you will. You have a strong sense of self – very unusual for Libra – and a strong sense of your self-interest. You are very much in charge of your life right now, and if other people don't co-operate you can go it alone if you have to. You are the creator of your conditions and circumstances. Other people will just have to adapt to you.

In spite of all this energy you are curiously unambitious now. Most of the planets are below the horizon of your chart, making you more concerned with personal happiness, the past, family values and emotional security than with your place in the world. You get further in your career by supporting and fostering other people's careers than by pushing your own. You are a support person for now.

Your paths of greatest fulfilment are money-making, sensual pleasures, intellectual interests, friends, group activities and charity work.

Love is particularly happy now, though there are ups and downs and sudden shifts in your current relationship. The ups, downs and changes, however, only serve to make things more interesting. You are very much in charge of your current relationship and your lover is accommodating your every need. You are loved not only platonically but physically as well. Bonding with your beloved is almost total now. Your romantic partner fosters your platonic friends and seems to get on well with them. There is no special tension between your group activities and your love relationship – they merge well together. Singles find love close to home, in their immediate environment. Love comes as a result of your physical appeal now and not because of your intellect or any of your other virtues. Just look your best now and romance will find you.

The stalemate in your financial affairs is ending this month. Stalled projects, investments, payments and deals start to happen. Your financial confidence grows and grows – and this is 90 per cent of financial success. Your financial judgement is also improving. Earnings reach a new peak after the 23rd.

September

Best Days Overall: 6th, 7th, 15th, 16th, 24th, 25th

Most Stressful Days Overall: 4th, 5th, 10th, 11th, 17th, 18th, 19th

Best Days for Love: 4th, 5th, 8th, 9th, 10th, 11th, 12th, 13th, 14th, 18th, 19th, 24th, 25th, 27th, 28th

Best Days for Money: 2nd, 9th, 10th, 11th, 18th, 19th, 20th, 21st, 27th, 28th, 29th, 30th

With 60 to 70 per cent of the planets still in your Eastern sector you are very much your own boss this month, setting the pace, the trend and the conditions of your life. You are in the unusual position of not being dependent on others. You are independent and self-motivated, and though this goes against your nature it is healthy at times to be this way. You get to transcend yourself and become a deeper person. You are very much like an Aries now.

This 'me first' attitude extends even to love. Your lover is doing everything to adapt to your needs. You continue to call the shots in love this month.

The planets are still very much below the horizon of your chart, reinforcing your tendency to focus on emotional harmony and security rather than on your career. After the 23rd the top half of your chart empties completely at times, activated only by occasional transits of the Moon. This means that you are almost totally focused on your family and building your emotional base. Career issues are almost completely ignored. Your ambitions centre round your family – or your support group – as a whole, and not yourself. With many of your family planets going retrograde this month, take the long-term view in family matters, domestic projects and family relationships. There are no quick solutions here. Only time will build your emotional base.

Your paths of greatest fulfilment this month are charity and philanthropy, personal pleasure, the enhancement of your self-image, money-making and intellectual interests.

You are in one of the happiest months of your year and you should savour it to the full. This is a month in which you buy (or receive) new and fashionable clothing, jewellery and personal accessories. It is a month for enjoying good food, good restaurants and new sensual delights. Your personal glamour is at an all-time high now. Your aesthetic taste, both in clothes and art, is superb. You are a magnet for love and for the opposite sex in general. If you can make peace with your personal divinity before the 23rd – get into a state of grace through the expiation of guilt and sin – your personal appearance will shine even more.

Finances are not a big priority before the 7th. After this date they become more important. Your partner has shifted from fulfilling your every whim to fostering your financial goals, and seems hard at work on your financial behalf. Financial success is likely.

October

Best Days Overall: 3rd, 4th, 12th, 13th, 22nd, 23rd, 30th, 31st

Most Stressful Days Overall: 1st, 2nd, 7th, 8th, 9th, 15th, 16th, 28th, 29th

Best Days for Love: 3rd, 4th, 5th, 6th, 7th, 8th, 9th, 15th, 16th, 22nd, 23rd, 24th, 25th, 30th, 31st

Best Days for Money: 5th, 6th, 7th, 8th, 9th, 15th, 16th, 17th, 18th, 24th, 25th, 26th, 27th

The power of the planets continues to be focused in the Eastern sector of your chart this month, with Venus (your Ruler) among them. Seldom have you felt so centred and in tune with yourself. Your 'me first' attitude is a surprise to friends and associates and probably to yourself. You've got all the power you need to achieve your goals this month – or even the goals of 10 people.

Ninety per cent of the planets are moving forward after the 14th, so you can expect rapid progress towards your goals and objectives. Always adept at gaining co-operation from others, you nevertheless are not dependent on others right now and if you need to can go it alone. You are master of conditions and circumstances; what you create, others will accept.

Ninety to 100 per cent of the planets – an astounding percentage – are below the horizon of your chart, further reinforcing your 'me first' attitude. Right now, your personal happiness, emotional security and the fulfilment of personal and sensual desires come before your long-term goals and objective success. You don't really care what the world thinks of you now, you just want to be happy. You would rather stay in the background being supportive than out there on the world stage.

Your paths of greatest fulfilment are personal pleasures, the enhancement of your personal image, money-making, intellectual interests and domestic travel.

There are two eclipses this month. The first is a Lunar Eclipse on the 8th which occurs in your 7th House of Love and Marriage. The Second is a Solar Eclipse on the 24th which occurs in your (2nd) Money House. Thus long-term changes – brought on by long-repressed feelings – are occurring in your love life and financial life. When the dust settles a new and better blueprint for these matters will manifest itself.

Your health is excellent all month. You can enhance it further by maintaining harmony with children and through personal creativity.

Your financial life is excellent this month. There is a lot of support for your financial goals and many new earning opportunities. Both friends of the heart and platonic friends are bringing financial opportunities to you. Your understanding of technology translates into cash. Earning opportunities also come through astrology, astronomy, science and industries that deal with these things. Your partner is acting powerfully on your financial behalf as well. Look for a net increase in worth.

November

Best Days Overall: 8th, 9th, 10th, 18th, 19th, 27th, 28th

Most Stressful Days Overall: 4th, 5th, 11th, 12th, 25th

Best Days for Love: 2nd, 3rd, 4th, 5th, 14th, 15th, 23rd, 24th

Best Days for Money: 2nd, 3rd, 4th, 5th, 13th, 14th, 15th, 21st, 22nd, 23rd

With all the planets going forward this month and with so much power in your Eastern sector, you are in a month of action and achievement. You are making things happen and the Cosmos co-operates with you. In one month you make as much progress as you once did in three or four months. Your personal influence, charisma and ego are unusually powerful. You get your way and others have to adapt to you. It is good when a Libra becomes more self-assertive. Librans are unlikely to ride roughshod over other people's rights and they usually – by nature – think of the way in which their actions will affect others.

Ninety to 100 per cent of the planets are still beneath the horizon of your chart, making you less outwardly ambitious and more concerned with emotional security. Those seeking to lure a Libra executive into their corporation will need to focus on the amenities they have to offer the Libra, such as housing allowances, family leave, child carc and the like. Librans can best advance their own careers by being supportive of other people's careers.

Your paths of greatest fulfilment are money-making, intellectual interests, personal pleasure, and enhancing your personal image and home life.

Venus (your Ruling Planet) and Mars (your Love Planet) are both out of bounds at the same time – from the 16th onwards. This is highly unusual. They go out of bounds in your 3rd Solar House of Communication. This suggests that you and your partner are going way out of your normal 'orbits' in the pursuit of education and intellectual excellence. There are various scenarios as to how this plays out. Many of you will be travelling to distant cities for study. Many of you will be out of your social orbit, mixing with people you wouldn't mix with normally. You and your lover go to extreme lengths to please and woo each other. You and your lover are unusually compatible and communicative with each other. Seldom have you been able to combine the physical and intellectual sides of your union so happily.

Earnings are unusually strong this month. A lucky sale or

inspired idea translates into a financial windfall in the middle of the month. Your financial confidence is strong and your optimism great. New communication equipment and other 'big-ticket' (expensive, long-lasting) items come to you.

Your health is excellent all month.

December

Best Days Overall: 6th, 7th, 16th, 17th, 24th, 25th

Most Stressful Days Overall: 1st, 2nd, 8th, 9th, 22nd, 23rd, 28th, 29th

Best Days for Love: 1st, 2nd, 3rd, 4th, 13th, 14th, 22nd, 23rd, 24th, 28th, 29th

Best Days for Money: 1st, 2nd, 11th, 12th, 18th, 19th, 20th, 21st, 28th, 29th

With 100 per cent of the planets moving forward and with so much power in Cardinal Signs, this is going to be a month of action, achievement and great progress. Always a lover of action, this month your most active wishes are fulfilled. The pace of your life is dizzying. Try to rest and relax more after the 22nd.

The planets are shifting more and more to the Western sector of your chart. This is the sector that emphasizes social relationships. While other Signs are uncomfortable with this – as there is an accompanying feeling of dependence and lack of self-assertion – for you this is all very comfortable. You get to exercise your genius. You are never too comfortable with the notion of independence. To you this is a false notion. You see the world as interdependent and live your life that way. Well, the planets are headed for your comfort zone now and your life becomes more pleasurable. There's no need to advise a Libra on how to charm others or how to achieve consensus. You know how to do it and will do it well.

The planets are very much focused below the horizon and will peak at the lowest point of your chart after the 22nd. Your energy and attention are directed inwardly towards emotional goals. Your heart out-powers your head. The focus tends to be on the past rather than the future. Family interests and the need for domestic bliss outweigh career concerns. There is a mood of nostalgia and reminiscences of times long gone. Use this natural nostalgia to achieve psychological and therapeutic objectives. The more you come to terms with your past, the better equipped you are to face your future.

This is very much a month in which you spend time with your family and smooth out family relationships. A sudden move or sudden – surprising – renovation of your home takes place.

Your health and vitality are excellent until the 22nd, but after then rest and relax more.

Earnings are unusually strong this month and will be so for many years to come. Earnings come through your sales and marketing abilities, while intellectual hobbies can be converted into cold cash. Financial opportunities come from neighbours and siblings; all the earning opportunities you need are right there in your neighbourhood.

In your love life the mood is nurturing and supportive. Your ability to give and receive emotional support makes you irresistible to your lover this month – especially before the 22nd. Entertain your beloved at home with home-cooked meals. Introduce him or her to your family. After the 22nd romance is more playful and you will have more of a desire to go out and explore the hotspots around town.

Scorpio

♏

THE SCORPION

Birthdays from
23rd October
to 22nd November

Personality Profile

SCORPIO AT A GLANCE

Element – Water

Ruling planet – Pluto

Co-Ruling planet – Mars
Career planet – Sun
Health planet – Mercury
Love planet – Venus
Money planet – Jupiter
Planet of home and family life – Uranus

Colour – red-violet

Colour that promotes love, romance and social harmony – green

Colour that promotes earning power – blue

Gems – bloodstone, malachite, topaz

Metals – iron, radium, steel

Scents – cherry blossom, coconut, sandalwood, watermelon

Quality – fixed (= stability)

Quality most needed for balance – a wider view of things

Strongest virtues – loyalty, concentration, determination, courage, depth

Deepest needs – to penetrate and transform

Characteristics to avoid – jealousy, vindictiveness, fanaticism

Signs of greatest overall compatibility – Cancer, Pisces

Signs of greatest overall incompatibility – Taurus, Leo, Aquarius

Sign most helpful to career – Leo

Sign most helpful for emotional support – Aquarius

Sign most helpful financially – Sagittarius

Sign best for marriage and/or partnerships – Taurus

Sign most helpful for creative projects – Pisces

Best Sign to have fun with – Pisces

Signs most helpful in spiritual matters – Cancer, Libra

Best day of the week – Tuesday

Understanding the Scorpio Personality

One symbol of the Sign of Scorpio is the phoenix. If you meditate upon the legend of the phoenix you will begin to understand the Scorpio character, his or her powers and abilities, interests and deepest urges.

The phoenix of mythology was a bird that could recreate and reproduce itself. It did so in a most intriguing way: it would seek a fire – usually in a religious temple – fly into it, consume itself in the flames and then emerge as a new bird. If this is not the ultimate, most profound transformation, then what is?

Transformation is what Scorpios are all about – in their minds, bodies, affairs and relationships (Scorpios are also society's transformers). To change something in a natural and not an artificial way involves a transformation from within. This type of change is a radical change as opposed to a mere cosmetic make-over. Some people think that change means changing just their appearance, but this is not the kind of change that interests a Scorpio. Scorpios seek deep, fundamental change. Since real change always proceeds from within, a Scorpio is very interested in – and usually accustomed to – the inner, intimate and philosophical side of life.

Scorpios are people of depth and intellect. If you want to interest them you must present them with more than just a superficial image. You and your interests, projects or business deals must have real substance to them in order to stimulate a Scorpio. If they haven't, he or she will find you out – and that will be the end of the story.

If we observe life, the processes of growth and decay, we see the transformative powers of Scorpio at work all the time. The caterpillar changes itself into a butterfly, the infant grows into a child and then an adult. To Scorpios this definite and perpetual transformation is not something to be feared. They see this as a normal part of life. This acceptance of transformation gives Scorpios the key to understanding the true meaning of life.

Scorpios' understanding of life (including life's weaknesses) makes them powerful warriors – in all senses of the word. Add to this their depth and penetration, their patience and endurance and you have a powerful personality. Scorpios have good, long memories and can be at times quite vindictive – they can wait years to get their revenge. As a friend, though, there is no one more loyal and true than a Scorpio. Few are willing to make the sacrifices that a Scorpio will make for a true friend.

The results of a transformation are quite obvious, although the process of transformation is invisible and secret. This is why Scorpios are considered secretive in nature. A seed will not grow properly if you keep digging it up and exposing it to the light of day. It must stay buried – invisible – until it starts to grow. In the same manner, Scorpios fear revealing too much about themselves or their hopes to other people. However, they will be more than happy to let you see the finished product – but only when it is finished. On the other hand, Scorpios like knowing everyone else's secrets as much as they dislike anyone knowing theirs.

Finance

Love, birth, life as well as death are Nature's most potent transformations and Scorpios are interested in all of these. In our society money is a transforming power, too, and a Scorpio is interested in money for that reason. To a Scorpio money is power, money causes change and money rules. It is the power of money that fascinates them. But Scorpios can be too materialistic if they are not careful. They can be overly awed by the power of money, to a point where they think that money rules the world.

Even the term *plutocrat* comes from Pluto, the Ruler of the Sign of Scorpio. Scorpios will – in one way or another – achieve the financial status they strive for. When they do so they are careful in the way they handle their wealth. Part of this financial carefulness is really a kind of honesty, for

Scorpios are usually involved with other people's money – as accountants, lawyers, stockbrokers or corporate managers – and when you handle other people's money you have to be more cautious than when you handle your own.

In order to fulfil their financial goals, Scorpios have important lessons to learn. They need to develop qualities that are not naturally in their natures, such as breadth of vision, optimism, faith, trust and, above all, generosity. They need to see the wealth in Nature and in life as well as in the more obvious forms of money and power. When they develop this generosity their financial potential reaches great heights, for Jupiter, the Lord of opulence and good fortune, is Scorpio's Money Planet.

Career and Public Image

Scorpio's greatest aspiration in life is to be considered by society as a source of light and life. They want to be leaders, to be stars. But they follow a very different road than do Leos, the other stars of the Zodiac. A Scorpio arrives at the goal secretly, without ostentation; a Leo pursues it openly. Scorpios seek the glamour and fun of the rich and famous in a secretive, undisclosed manner.

Scorpios are by nature introverted and tend to avoid the limelight. But if they want to attain their highest career goals they need to open up a bit and to express themselves more. They need to stop hiding their light under a bushel and let it shine. Above all, they need to let go of any vindictiveness and small-mindedness. All their gifts and insights were given to them for one important reason – to serve life and to increase the joy of living for others.

Love and Relationships

Scorpio is another Zodiac Sign that likes committed, clearly defined, structured relationships. They are cautious about marriage, but when they do commit to a relationship they tend to be faithful – and Heaven help the mate caught or even suspected of infidelity! The jealousy of the Scorpio is legendary. They can be so intense in their jealousy that even the thought or intention of infidelity will be detected and is likely to cause as much of a storm as if the act had actually occurred.

Scorpios tend to settle down with those who are wealthier than they are. They usually have enough intensity for two, so in their partners they seek someone pleasant, hard-working, amiable, stable and easy-going. They want someone they can lean on, someone loyal behind them as they fight the battles of life. To a Scorpio a partner, be it a lover or a friend, is a real partner – not an adversary. Most of all a Scorpio is looking for an ally, not a competitor.

If you are in love with a Scorpio you will need a lot of patience. It takes a long time to get to know Scorpios, because they don't reveal themselves readily. But if you persist and your motives are honourable, you will gradually be allowed into a Scorpio's inner chambers of the mind and heart.

Home and Domestic Life

Uranus is Ruler of Scorpio's 4th Solar House of Home and Domestic Affairs. Uranus is the planet of science, technology, changes and democracy. This tells us a lot about a Scorpio's conduct in the home and what he or she needs in order to have a happy, harmonious home life.

Scorpios can sometimes bring their passion, intensity and wilfulness into the home and family, which is not always the place for these qualities. These virtues are good for the warrior and the transformer, but not so good for the nurturer and family person. Because of this (and also because of their need for change and transformation) the Scorpio may be prone to sudden changes of residence. If not carefully constrained, the sometimes inflexible Scorpio can produce turmoil and sudden upheavals within the family.

Scorpios need to develop some of the virtues of Aquarius

in order to cope better with domestic matters. There is a need to build a team spirit at home, to treat family activities as truly group activities – family members should all have a say in what does and does not get done. For at times a Scorpio can be most dictatorial. When a Scorpio gets dictatorial it's much worse than if a Leo or Capricorn (the two other power Signs in the Zodiac) does. For the dictatorship of a Scorpio is applied with more zeal, passion, intensity and concentration than is true of either a Leo or Capricorn. Obviously this can be unbearable to his or her family members – especially if they are sensitive types.

In order for a Scorpio to get the full benefit of the emotional support that a family can give, he or she needs to release conservatism and be a bit more experimental, to explore new techniques in child-rearing, be more democratic with family members and to try to manage more things by consensus than by autocratic edict.

Horoscope for 1995

Major Trends

1994 was a year of great personal expansion on almost every level for you, Scorpio. Your health, self-esteem and self-confidence were at an all-time high. You caught the lucky breaks. You prospered and enjoyed yourself physically. You travelled and otherwise conducted yourself as a wealthy person. This happy trend continues in 1995, only the emphasis shifts a bit this year. Where in 1994 you focused on sensual pleasures and creating your perfect image, in 1995 you focus on perfecting the substance behind the image. 1995 is very much a money year and when Pluto, your Ruling Planet, moves into your 2nd House of Money towards the end of the year this trend will become long term.

The importance of neighbours, intellectual interests and

communication continues in 1995, just as in 1994. This is a long-term trend. Your home and domestic life are much less depressing this year than they were last year. Saturn has moved out of your 4th House of Home and Domestic Life and into the 5th House of Creativity and Speculations. This is another signal that the fun and games are over and it's time to get serious about life. Saturn in your 5th Solar House shows that you have to be more selective and prudent about pleasures and creativity. Saturn is not going to deprive you of fun, but it is going to make you more discriminating about how you go about it. If fun can be integrated into your larger purpose and goals, by all means indulge. If it takes you away from these goals, shun it.

'High tech' is definitely in your life for a while, especially when it comes to cars and communication equipment. Only the latest and the best will do for you.

Health

Though your health was excellent in 1994, it gets even better this year. Saturn, the lone long-term planet which was making stressful aspects to you, has now moved away. Where for two years it was subtly blocking you, limiting you, testing and challenging you, now it is your best friend – co-operating and enhancing your physical energy. Your general well-being is at an all-time high.

Your 6th House of Health is not a House of Power this year, which is a positive health signal. Your health is so good that you are just not concerned about it. You operate on the principle of 'if it isn't broken, don't fix it.' The Cosmos pushes you neither one way nor the other. You have a lot of flexibility and freedom as far as diet and exercise regimes go.

Mars is the Lord of your 6th House of Health; if we keep our eyes on him we will understand your health needs. Mars makes an unusually long transit through your 10th House of Career this year – from 23rd January to 26th May. Not only does this show the driving urge and the aggressiveness with which you pursue career goals, it also shows that your public image and professional status are factors in your general physical well-being. You actually feel better physically when you are in charge and thought well of by others. The way in which you handle administrative power will have an impact on your health.

From 26th May to 2nd July Mars is in Virgo, your 11th Solar House of Friends, Group Activities and Fondest Wishes. This shows that harmony with friends is an important health factor. Before rushing off to see a doctor if an ailment arises, check to see that you are in harmony with your friends. If there is any disharmony, correct it. Chances are that the physical ailment will go away on its own.

22nd July to 8th September brings some temporary karmic cleansing and catharsis which leads to even greater vitality than before. This catharsis has to do with old baggage from past incarnations. 8th September to 24th October brings increased vigour and vitality and the need for exercise. You need to do something with all your excess energy. 21st October to 21st December is not only a financially prosperous time, but money and your health become intimately related. When you earn more you feel better physically and vice versa. You tend to define your health in terms of your 'bottom line'. After 21st December your health becomes more dependent on having a healthy nervous system. The pursuit of intellectual interests – the exercising of the intellect – will actually make you feel better physically. Read a good, educational book when you feel tired.

Home and Domestic Life

Though your 4th House of Home and Family is not as prominent as it was last year, Uranus, the Lord of the House, is still very much stimulated this year. Thus family interests are still prominent – and much happier than they were last year. The sense of burden and duty with regard to your family has gone away. Whatever burdens you carried have been resolved and there is a greater sense of freedom in your home and with your family. You have more living space, you feel less cramped. You are back to being experimental, creative and innovative with your décor and daily lifestyle. High-tech equipment makes domestic chores much easier to handle. Check the plumbing in your house this year, as there is a danger of water damage. Though relations with your family are still volatile – now up, now down, now on speaking terms and now not speaking – still there is no sense of depression and repression. People speak their minds forcefully without fear and let the chips fall where they may.

For the next two years you are dealing more with children – your own and other people's. This is quite challenging. Patience, persistence, fairness and a sense of limits are called for. There are no quickie solutions to your situation. Time and patience will resolve things. You are in conflict about how much freedom and how much discipline children need. You fluctuate between permissiveness and authoritarianism, perhaps in an unbalanced way. The cosmic message here is 'Freedom within Limits'. There are lines they cannot cross and they should know where those lines are.

A sibling becomes almost like your child – you have to care for him or her as you would a child. Though this sounds dire and stressful, actually it is not. For the sibling gives you a subtle energy that helps you.

Moves and changes in your residence are still likely this year. You are still searching for the 'ideal home' and though you get ever closer to it, you are not there yet. Enjoy the quest and you will handle this beautifully. It's fun to keep making improvements – to keep getting closer to your ideal.

Love and Social Life

Your 7th House of Love and Marriage is not prominent this year, Scorpio. Though unquestionably you are attracting the opposite sex – your physical appearance and personal magnetism are awesome – you are more concerned with your own personal needs and goals than with those of a partner. When you do get involved in relationships your partner has to conform to your will and needs. You are not bending over backwards for anyone. Those involved with Scorpios please take note.

Your social attitudes this year are related to the transformations you have been making to your personal image. As your self-concept changes and you re-invent yourself into the person that you want to be, you must develop the kind of social life you desire. These social attitudes are not yet fully formed, but they will be.

This lack of prominence in your Marriage House means that the Cosmos is giving you a free hand in this area. It is neither helping you socially nor obstructing you. It tends to favour the status quo. Married people will tend to stay married and singles will tend to stay single.

This lack of social interest should not be interpreted as an abnormality. On the contrary it is, perhaps, the highest wisdom. The sages have always counselled that before we can marry another we should marry ourselves. This is what you are doing this year – integrating your own self, unifying your own personality. When this is done correctly the right partner always appears – quite naturally and spontaneously.

Venus rules your House of Marriage – and it is a good Ruler to have, as this is its natural domain. Venus moves around the Zodiac quite rapidly and your social life will also change rapidly, as will your attitudes to love and mood for it. You can follow Venus' movements in the month-by-month forecasts below. Venus will be in certain parts of your Horoscope twice this year. Those places that it visits twice become important love indicators. For example, while Venus will transit most of your chart only once, it will be in your 1st, 2nd, 3rd and 4th Houses twice. Thus, people from your past and early childhood – perhaps old flames – are very likely to become romantic partners this year. You find love while pursuing your financial goals and through people involved in your finances. Love is very much close to home this year, there is no need to travel far and wide for it.

Those of you already married need to be careful of over-asserting yourself. You force your own position too strongly. You have some trouble appreciating your partner's viewpoint and you can come off as arrogant and domineering if you're not careful.

The marriage of a parent is in turmoil over financial issues. The marriage of a friend is not as happy as it looks.

Career and Finance

Your 2nd House of Money and Possessions is very much a House of Power this year. Your earning power is simply awesome. Jupiter, the Lord of your financial affairs, stays in his own Sign and House all year, which is very unusual. Jupiter normally moves through a Sign in 11 months. Jupiter will be in your Money House for approximately 13 months this year. This means that Jupiter is acting very powerfully on your behalf, and since wealth, riches and good luck are his natural domain, you can expect very strong earnings this year. This is a year to think big about financial goals. You will deny yourself a lot of good if you are too petty and small-minded. Demand a lot from the Cosmos and the Cosmos will certainly fill any measure you hold up to it.

Earnings are great and your spending habits are also more expansive. There is great financial optimism in you. You catch the lucky breaks. You are in the right place at the right time. You make fortunate financial connections. Money is earned easily and happily.

It is quite safe this year to spend generously and to acquire the expensive things you crave. You have plenty of income to cover their cost. Towards the end of the year you will need to do some pruning of wasteful expenditures, but not before then.

Rarely – except perhaps 11 years ago – have you

experienced such financial power. You have control over money and are very much in charge of your own financial destiny. You have no one to answer to in these matters except yourself.

You are not only spending on yourself but on others as well. You give generously to your friends and to those in need. And it seems that the more you spend the more you make.

Money comes to you in ways that are natural to you – in ways that you enjoy – through banking, investments, the stock market, foreign trade and the travel and publishing industries. A great financial key has been handed to you. It's as if you've learned some great, potent secret and you are using it to your advantage.

The income of your partner is basically stable – no major trend either way. The income of a parent is insecure. This parent disapproves slightly of your ultra-generosity while he or she is forced to budget and tighten the belt.

Self-improvement

Various areas of your life are getting improved this year, Scorpio. The improvements in your financial life and self-image have already been mentioned. These improvements will happen almost by themselves. Your part is just to receive and be grateful. Just flow with it.

Improvements in the home will take place in fits and starts. By all means be bold, creative and innovative there. Don't be afraid to forge new paths. Keep your attention focused on your ideal as you make these incremental changes.

Your moods will swing wildly high and wildly low again this year. Rather than repressing them you can direct them towards positive achievements. When your mood is up, schedule important things. When a successful attitude is just the one you want to project, take advantage of those times when you're feeling that failure is impossible. When your mood turns low, however, pull in your horns and finish up old business. Of course, mastering mood control, which comes from meditation exercises, is the best way to deal with these mood changes.

Your creativity can be greatly improved this year through work and discipline. A deeper study of the laws that govern the field you are interested in, coupled with persistent practice, will make your creative projects endure. If you are involved in dance, music or fine arts – practise, practise, practise. Practise when you feel like it and when you don't feel like it. In two years' time you won't believe what you will have achieved.

Month-by-month Forecasts

January

Best Days Overall: 5th, 6th, 15th, 16th, 24th, 25th

Most Stressful Days Overall: 3rd, 4th, 10th, 11th, 17th, 18th, 30th, 31st

Best Days for Love: 5th, 6th, 7th, 8th, 10th, 11th, 17th, 18th, 19th, 26th, 27th

Best Days for Money: 7th, 8th, 17th, 18th, 26th, 27th

Most of the planets are clustered in the Eastern and lower segment of your Horoscope this month. This shows great strength, initiative and creative power. You create your own conditions this month and others must accept these conditions. You are much more in control of your destiny and less at the mercy of other people. With most of the planets moving forward and with your Ruling Planet Pluto changing Signs, you can feel big changes going on in your life. You are making progress and you are in control of it.

Having most of the planets in the bottom segment of your chart shows that you are more interested in personal happiness than in outward success. True, finances are a major priority, but this seems unconnected with your career or status. You just want large earnings and are not concerned with glory or position or what the world thinks of you. In spite of this you will get lucky career breaks this month – and you seem to be able to mould them so you don't have to sacrifice your personal happiness. The pursuit of your financial goals is perhaps the area of greatest joy and fulfilment now.

This is a fabulous month for money. Money comes pleasurably and easily. You catch the lucky breaks. 'Big-ticket' (large, expensive) items are acquired this month. Investments prosper. You are supportive of your partner and your partner is supportive of you. Jupiter and Venus – your Lord of Money and Love respectively – are travelling together in your (2nd) Money House. This shows a very happy and mutually satisfying financial arrangement between you and your partner or lover. You are in a money-making cycle of your life both this month and over the long term.

Your health is basically excellent this month, but rest and relax more after the 20th. Until the 20th focus on intellectual and communication interests. After the 20th deal with home projects and spend more time with your family. Your emotional home base and support system are very important now. The higher you plan to go in your career, the deeper and stronger must your emotional support be.

Your love life is particularly rapturous from the 14th to the 16th.

February

Best Days Overall: 1st, 2nd, 11th, 12th, 20th, 21st

Most Stressful Days Overall: 6th, 7th, 13th, 14th, 15th, 26th, 27th, 28th

Best Days for Love: 4th, 5th, 6th, 7th, 16th, 17th, 24th, 25th

Best Days for Money: 3rd, 4th, 5th, 13th, 14th, 15th, 22nd, 23rd

Though 80 to 90 per cent of your planets are still at the bottom half of your chart, you are not exactly unambitious this month. Mars is still very much in your (10th) Career House and the Sun, your Career Planet, will be very much stimulated after the 19th. This points up an interesting contradiction which describes your feelings and attitudes exactly. You want career success but on your terms and without any sacrifice of your domestic or personal interests. You want the world – and employers – to accept you on your terms. You want to create career conditions that will enable you to spend time with your family. This requires some thought and planning – and this is what you seem to be doing this month.

There is some promotion at work – some added responsibilities that you will carry. You are called upon to exert authority over others, and you do it well.

Your earning power is still very strong, though not as strong as last month. After the 19th you have to work harder for your earnings. After the 19th you are thrust into a situation in which you are forced to decide whether money or public prestige is more important to you. This is not an easy decision, and you should not go too far in either direction. Both are equally important.

Financial opportunities still come through your family, real estate and family connections. Friends can be of help financially as well, but this more likely to happen after the 16th when Mercury goes direct. Your pursuit of wealth is still very much a path of fulfilment – now and over the long term.

Your love life is particularly exciting this month, as Venus (your Love Planet), gets stimulated by both Neptune and Uranus. Your partner is romantic but in unpredictable ways. He or she might bring flowers one day or throw a surprise party another. Your partner does unusual things to keep your interest. Singles are attracted to verbal, intellectual people this month. The more unconventional and untraditional they are, the better Scorpio likes them. Love talk is a particularly erotic turn-on this month. Those involved with Scorpios should take note of this. Singles in search of love should stick close to home – in the neighbourhood. There's someone close by just aching to meet you.

Rest and relax more until the 19th. Your vitality is not what is should be. After the 19th it comes back in full force.

March

Best Days Overall: 1st, 2nd, 10th, 11th, 12th, 19th, 20th, 28th, 29th

Most Stressful Days Overall: 5th, 6th, 7th, 13th, 14th, 26th, 27th

Best Days for Love: 5th, 6th, 7th, 8th, 9th, 17th, 18th, 26th, 27th, 28th

Best Days for Money: 3rd, 4th, 13th, 14th, 21st, 22nd, 30th, 31st

Most of the planets, like last month, are still in the bottom hemisphere of your Solar chart, denoting your interest in emotional harmony and family values above career and 'outer' success. There is, however, a shift of planetary power to the Western hemisphere of the chart. This shows that you are gradually becoming more social, interacting with others more and not being completely in control of circumstances and conditions. You need to depend on others for your good and for the success of your projects. You've got to start letting others have their way now. This relative lack of self-assertion is further reinforced by the retrograde (backward motion) of Pluto, your Planetary Ruler. You have initiated many projects in the past few months, have had things your way, and now you must take stock and see what you've created. Move cautiously and weigh the impact that your plans and projects have on others. This is a time to take stock and make corrections. You seem especially unsure now as to whether you should be focused on financial matters or on your personal image. You waver between the two. Perhaps you see that there are issues of image that you haven't fully dealt with yet. You need to retrace your steps.

Your paths of greatest fulfilment this month, however, continue to be money-making, image-creation and family interests. What confuses you is which should take priority – and as mentioned you are moving back to your interest in image-making and –enhancement.

Having said all this, you are nevertheless in a fun month. There are more parties, entertainment events and romantic opportunities. The urge to speculate this month is intense, only be very calculated and serious as to how you go about it. Recklessness will do you in now. If you must speculate, take a percentage of your income – after paying your bills – and devote that to speculating. Don't speculate with your whole 'nest egg'. Be proportional in all things.

Singles find love opportunities through family and through past relationships. Old flames with unresolved feelings are likely to come back into your life this month. These don't look too serious but they are useful in clearing the decks for the future. Scorpios want nurturing in love this month – those of you involved with Scorpios should take note.

Your health is excellent all month.

April

Best Days Overall: 7th, 8th, 16th, 17th, 24th, 25th

Most Stressful Days Overall: 2nd, 3rd, 9th, 10th, 22nd, 23rd, 29th, 30th

Best Days for Love: 2nd, 3rd, 7th, 8th, 16th, 17th, 26th, 27th, 28th, 29th, 30th

Best Days for Money: 1st, 9th, 10th, 18th, 19th, 26th, 27th, 28th

The planets are evenly dispersed between the Eastern and Western hemispheres of your Solar Horoscope. You cater to others but have not totally sacrificed your personal interests or creative power. You are quite well balanced between social urges and self-interest.

The planetary power is still very much in the bottom half of your Horoscope, once again showing that your primary drive is towards emotional harmony and subjective, introverted interests. You still would rather conquer yourself this month than conquer the world.

Pluto, your Ruling Planet, goes retrograde all month and actually shifts Signs. It moves from Sagittarius, which it visited briefly, back into your own Sign of Scorpio. This shows that you need to retrace your steps in certain personal desires. Get back and work on your self-image and personality before you focus too much on money. You may feel that you are going backwards in life, but this is not the case. You have been working on your image and personality for many years now, but you may have left 'fortresses unconquered' – now is the time to conquer them.

Jupiter, your Money Planet, is also retrograde all month – and in your (2nd) Money House no less. This reinforces the need for evaluating your financial drives, deals and projects and for making sure that you are on the right course. This is the time to perfect both yourself and your financial deals and investments. Think twice – perhaps three times – before entering into any long-term financial commitment or major purchase.

In spite of this need for caution your earnings are still

strong and your financial opportunities plentiful this month. Really, the problems stem from an embarrassment of riches – from too many opportunities and too many deals going forward at once. Clarifying your goal and purpose will guide you through this 'jungle'.

The pace at work has become hectic. It looks like you're doing the work of 10 people. Your work goals are achieved speedily and with enthusiasm.

Your social life becomes very active after the 20th. Not only do the Sun and Mercury activate your (7th) House of Love, but the Solar Eclipse of the 29th occurs in your Love House as well. Big, long-term changes happen in your love life. A current relationship either breaks up or changes drastically. The ground rules of the relationship change as hidden resentments come to the surface for resolution. Singles may well meet that special someone, as the Eclipse favours a change in marital status. Early in the month love is not serious but just fun and games. You really want a playmate more than a partner. Romantic opportunities come through parties, creative projects and in entertainment venues. Later on in the month love comes at the workplace or with health professionals.

The Solar Eclipse of the 29th also shows a major change in your career. Short-term upheavals lead to long-term promotion and progress.

May

Best Days Overall: 4th, 5th, 13th, 14th, 21st, 22nd, 23rd, 31st

Most Stressful Days Overall: 6th, 7th, 8th, 19th, 20th, 26th, 27th, 28th

Best Days for Love: 6th, 7th, 8th, 15th, 16th, 17th, 26th, 27th, 28th

Best Days for Money: 6th, 7th, 8th, 15th, 16th, 24th, 25th

The short-term, fast-moving planets are shifting the balance of planetary power above the horizon of your Horoscope. Most of the planets are still below the horizon, but not as many as in previous months. Thus, although you are still predominantly interested in personal harmony and emotional security, there is more ambition in you than there has been of late. You are less likely to ignore your career this month.

This month, as last month, the planets are focused in the Western sector of your chart, showing your greater concern for your social life and the interests of other people. With Pluto, your Ruler, retrograde this month you are much less assertive and more prone to put other people's desires ahead of your own. This is a wise thing to do, for you are now re-defining what your interests are. Until this process is complete it would be best not to assert your interests too strongly.

Your paths of greatest happiness and fulfilment this month are enhancing your personal image and appearance, money-making (though less so than in previous months), your health, work and your social life.

Your social life is active, dynamic and happy all month. Singles are attracting people who can help them in their career and who can boost their social status. They are mixing with those above them in status. New social contacts boost career prospects. Whom you know this month has more career clout than what you can do. Whom you know carries more weight than any personal merit. Until the 17th you want a partner who serves you and your interests. After that you want more of a true equal partnership. Singles are likely to find that special someone this month. You have great social confidence and charisma. You seem ready for romance and the Cosmos is giving it to you.

After the 21st the planetary power activates your 8th House of Elimination, Transformation and Other People's Money. Nobody loves a strong 8th House more than a Scorpio. This period will be comfortable and enjoyable for you. You will succeed with investors, with making money for others and through the use of other people's money. Your normal urges to eliminate and transform things will be reinforced and you can use this power to good effect by cleaning house, ridding yourself of 'excess baggage' and detoxifying both your character and body. With Mercury going retrograde in your 8th House after the 24th, be ultra-careful of the way you talk to investors or lenders. Spell everything out. Take nothing for granted as far as communication is concerned. Miscommunication is more likely at this time than usual.

Rest and relax more until the 21st.

June

Best Days Overall: 1st, 2nd, 10th, 11th, 18th, 19th, 27th, 28th, 29th

Most Stressful Days Overall: 3rd, 4th, 16th, 17th, 22nd, 23rd, 24th, 30th

Best Days for Love: 5th, 6th, 16th, 17th, 22nd, 23rd, 24th, 25th, 26th

Best Days for Money: 3rd, 4th, 12th, 13th, 20th, 21st, 30th

The planets are more or less evenly distributed throughout your Solar Horoscope this month, giving you a nice sense of balance, perspective and sound judgement. You are going to need it! There are many conflicts that need to be resolved this month.

Though your planetary Lord (Pluto) is not involved in the current Grand Square aspect, your Career Planet (the Sun) is. Major career changes are taking place. Part of this is voluntary – things that you are putting into motion; part of it comes from a shake-up in the corporate structure. At present no one sees where the chips will fall and there is much doubt and confusion involved. The people involved in the shake-up – those doing the shaking up – are not even sure where they are going, so how can you be expected to know? One thing you can be sure of: you have a place in all of this. After a few experimental changes in your position your right and true niche will be discovered.

Fifty per cent of the planets are retrograde this month – including Pluto, your Ruler. Be patient with yourself and with others. Try to see your feelings of doubt and indecision as cosmic signals to review and attain clarity concerning your goals. Research all moves thoroughly – in your career and otherwise.

Your health is good all month, but your self-esteem and self-confidence could be greater. They will improve after the 22nd.

Your Money Planet, Jupiter, is also involved in the Grand Square aspect mentioned earlier. Moreover, it is retrograde. Though financial fear will never help matters, a sense of caution will. Spend on necessities but avoid making major purchases and commitments until your situation becomes more clear. This will occur when Jupiter starts to go direct in August. In a current joint venture – and you need to study this carefully – you must make doubly sure that your personal financial interests are represented as well as the interests of the venture as a whole. While it is good to help other to prosper, don't neglect yourself.

Love is placid until the 10th, then Venus enters into the Grand Square aspect and passions start to run high. Physical intimacy becomes more important than courtship, and attempts to make your partner change in some way produce erupting tensions. Attempts at logical communication with your partner are troubled until the 17th. Conflicting financial interests also put stress on a current love relationship. If you can rise above the passions and see the highest interests of both parties – yours and your lover's – solutions will start to arise.

July

Best Days Overall: 7th, 8th, 15th, 16th, 25th, 26th

Most Stressful Days Overall: 1st, 13th, 14th, 20th, 21st, 27th, 28th

Best Days for Love: 7th, 8th, 15th, 16th, 20th, 21st, 25th, 26th

Best Days for Money: 1st, 9th, 10th, 17th, 18th, 27th, 28th

If you can maintain your patience and composure amid all the delays and stalemate going on you will find this to be one of your happiest months of the year. Many good things are happening for you behind the scenes, but if you lose your patience you could actually block them. Keep the 'art of the possible' as your guiding principle. Achieve in the areas where achievement is possible and let everything else go.

Your career is about to take off after the 23rd. Pay rises and promotions are coming, though they won't actually take effect when they are supposed to. Nevertheless, they will come. In the mean time, get all the education you need to fill the position that you covet. Prepare for promotion now.

Finances and earnings are outstanding this month, especially after the 23rd. The only fly in the ointment is the retrograde of your Money Planet, Jupiter. If Jupiter were going direct your earnings would in the stratosphere. As it is they are just outstanding. Be cautious, however, with investments and financial deals. Study them thoroughly before committing yourself. Early in the month there is a conflict with your partner over finances, but this gets resolved after the 5th. Your partner's 'firm and inflexible' position changes. He or she feels more secure as well as the month goes on and enjoys great prosperity.

Your health is excellent until the 23rd; after then rest and relax more. You are shining in the world after this date, but you need to give yourself some time to get in touch with who you are. Don't completely ignore your personal desires and inclinations either.

Your love life is active and constantly changing. Until the 5th physical intimacy is most important in romance. After the 5th you want a lover who can guide you and teach you things. You want to travel with your lover. You admire a partner who has culture and refinement. After the 30th you want a partner who has higher status than you and who can help you in your career. Those of you involved with Scorpios have your work cut out for you. You have to be many things to them.

August

Best Days Overall: 3rd, 4th, 12th, 21st, 22nd, 31st

Most Stressful Days Overall: 9th, 10th, 16th, 17th, 24th, 25th

Best Days for Love: 5th, 6th, 14th, 15th, 16th, 17th, 26th, 27th

Best Days for Money: 5th, 6th, 14th, 15th, 26th, 27th

Both Pluto (your Ruling Planet) and Jupiter (your Money Planet) start moving forward this month after many months of retrograde motion. The sense of personal and financial stalemate and delay is just about over. Rejoice.

Though most of the planets are below the horizon of your Solar chart, this is still an excellent career month. Your 10th House of Career gets unusual stimulation from the short-term, fast-moving planets. Friends, groups you belong to, lovers, partners and elders are all conspiring to promote you before the public and in your business life. Moreover, with your family planets retrograde at present there's not much you can do with family and domestic issues anyway. You might as well focus on the outside world for the short term.

With the planets concentrating ever more eastward you are becoming more assertive, self-interested and in control of the tone and tenor of your life. This is especially true in career issues. You are calling the career shots now. You are creating career circumstances and conditions. Others are quite willing to manifest your creations.

Your paths of greatest fulfilment this month are career, friendships, group activities, money-making and charitable endeavours.

Your health is delicate until the 23rd; try to rest and relax more. Your health can be enhanced through prayer, meditation, positive imagery and other metaphysical healing practices. After the 23rd your vitality returns to normal.

Your love life in general and a particular relationship is very high on your agenda this month. It is difficult to tell whether your career or your relationship is more important. They seem intertwined. You socialize more with the 'high and mighty' this month. Singles find love through career pursuits and through those involved with their careers. Singles will tend to marry upwards now. Marrieds will want career support from their partner and they will get it.

Finances are unusually good. The financial stalemate is over. As mentioned, Jupiter (your Money Planet) moves forward and receives beautiful aspects until the 23rd. Stalled payments finally come in. Arrested deals and projects start moving again. Your financial judgement is sound and your financial confidence strong. Elders, parents and those involved with your career are all assisting your financial goals and creating money-making opportunities. Save excess cash made before the 23rd for after that date. You have to work harder for earnings after the 23rd.

September

Best Days Overall: 8th, 9th, 17th, 18th, 19th, 27th, 28th

Most Stressful Days Overall: 6th, 7th, 12th, 13th, 14th, 20th, 21st

Best Days for Love: 4th, 5th, 12th, 13th, 14th, 24th, 25th

Best Days for Money: 2nd, 10th, 11th, 20th, 21st, 29th, 30th

The Eastern sector of your Horoscope simply overflows with planetary power as 80 to 90 per cent of the planets are there all month. Thus you are ready, willing and able to go it on your own if others don't accede to your demands. You are in charge of your life and have dominion over your personal circumstances. Others have to adapt to you. With many planets in the Sign of Libra for most of the month people in general are unwilling to fight with you and you tend to get your way.

The bottom half of your Horoscope outweighs the upper half this month, especially after the 7th. Thus you have attained enough career success last month to sate you for a while and your heart belongs to your family and emotional needs.

Your paths of greatest happiness this month are friendships, group activities, charity, spiritual practices, the clearing of guilt and wrongdoing and money-making.

Always a powerful personality, Scorpio, this month you are even more so. Mars, your co-Ruler, moves into Scorpio on the 7th. Thus you probably don't even realize your own strength. You make what you think is an offhand remark and the other person is devastated. You tap someone – you perceive it this way – and he or she experiences it as a knockout blow. Your tendency is to sweep others off their feet now. Go out of your way to be more gentle and sensitive this month.

Normally a courageous person, this month you are more so. Nothing scares you. You go after what you want with great vim and vigour. You excel in sport and exercise. You tend to be undiplomatic and brusque; if you're not careful you can be over-argumentative.

Love is cool and friendly until the 16th. It lacks passion but there is good intellectual communication. Love becomes more idealistic after the 16th. There is a also sense of mutual sacrifice with your beloved. Both of you are demanding sacrifices in the relationship. Singles are perfectionists this month. They are less capable of overlooking human flaws and frailties. Destructive criticism is the greatest threat to romance this month.

Your earning power is steadily improving now that your Money Planet Jupiter is moving forward. Until the 23rd you've got to work a little harder for your money than you are used to, but don't worry, you've got plenty of energy to spare. After the 23rd earnings come much more easily and you receive a lot of help from your intuitive powers, astrologers, psychics and those who minister to others. Look for a net increase in wealth.

October

Best Days Overall: 5th, 6th, 15th, 16th, 24th, 25th

Most Stressful Days Overall: 3rd, 4th, 10th, 11th, 17th, 18th, 30th, 31st

Best Days for Love: 3rd, 4th, 10th, 11th, 15th, 16th, 24th, 25th

Best Days for Money: 7th, 8th, 9th, 17th, 18th, 26th,, 27th

The planets continue to be strongly focused in the Eastern sector of your chart, with your Ruler, Pluto, among them. Most of the planets are also below the horizon of your chart this month. This gives a picture of someone who is unusually focused on the self, on personal goals and pleasures and personal emotional harmony. It shows a person who knows what his or her interests and desires are and who has all the energy necessary to achieve them. You have great independence, assertiveness and personal influence now. You create the conditions, you set the pace and you call the shots; other people must accept and adapt. You couldn't care less at this point what the world or other people think of you, you just want to be happy. If your projects and plans don't meet with their approval you will just go it alone.

This is a month for self-fulfilment rather than concern for others or for the world. And though you do good deeds for others – especially charitable endeavours and ministering activities – you are really doing so because this makes you feel better and not so much for altruistic reasons.

This is also a month of great personal achievement as 90 per cent of the planets – after the 14th – are moving forward. The universe favours action and change now. You will get more done this month.

Your health and vitality are strong all month and will get even stronger after the 14th, when Mercury, your Health Planet, goes forward again. Your health can be further enhanced by maintaining harmony with friends and with professional groups that you belong to.

Usually a 'me first' attitude is not conducive to love. It tends not to foster the romantic attitude. Yet you manage this right now and get away with it. Your lover or partner accommodates your every need and desire. You call the shots in love this month, especially after the 11th. With your personal magnetism and charisma so strong your appeal to the opposite sex is especially powerful. Your fondest romantic dreams come to pass this month.

Your earning power is getting stronger and stronger with each passing month. There is in you a combination of financial confidence and fearlessness now. You set your goals and you go after them aggressively. Money is earned easily and effortlessly. Money is probably spent lavishly as well. Your ability to work and achieve work goals is increased after the 21st, thus you are a more valuable employee at this time. Earnings opportunities come to you in fields involving health care, pharmaceuticals, health foods, international commerce and foreign travel. These opportunities could come in the form of employment or investment possibilities. Look for a net increase in wealth this month.

November

Best Days Overall: 6th, 7th, 16th, 17th, 25th

Most Stressful Days Overall: 6th, 7th, 14th, 15th, 27th, 28th

Best Days for Love: 2nd, 3rd, 4th, 6th, 7th, 14th, 15th, 23rd, 24th

Best Days for Money: 4th, 5th, 14th, 15th, 23rd

With the Sun, Venus and Mercury – your Career, Love and Health Planets respectively – moving through your own Sign of Scorpio at various times during the month you are in one of the happiest months of your year. Your health is excellent, your self-esteem and confidence are strong and your appeal to the opposite sex is unusually powerful. With most of the planets in the Eastern sector you are especially assertive and influential this month as well. People are bending over backwards to please you.

With 100 per cent of the planets moving forward you are in a month of action and achievement. You get your way. What you will is created and with speed. Prayers are answered quickly.

After the 4th, 90 to 100 per cent of the planets are below the horizon of your chart. Thus 'outer' ambitions take a back seat to your need for emotional harmony and security. Yet, in spite of this lack of interest, you make real career gains this month – perhaps because of your disinterest. Your urge for greater earnings, not your need for glory or status, leads you to accept a career promotion.

Your paths of greatest fulfilment are meditation, prayer, spiritual studies, charitable activities, the enhancement of your personal image, personal pleasure and money-making.

Earnings hit the stratosphere this month. Everything you touch turns to gold. Elders, superiors, your lover, partners, friends – almost everyone – are lending their support to your financial goals. More important, Pluto, your Ruling Planet, makes a major long-term move into your (2nd) Money House on the 11th. You will be preoccupied with attaining wealth for many years to come. You will apply your unique and ferocious concentration to this and of course you will succeed. Nothing will make you swerve from your financial goals. The planetary power shows that you are not just satisfied with 'earning a living', you are interested in the attainment of great wealth – opulence is what you're after.

Your health is excellent all month. It can be enhanced through keeping harmony with those involved in your finances. Your financial well-being affects your physical well-being.

Love, too, is happy and rapturous this month. Your lover can't do enough for you. Singles will find love in the pursuit of their financial goals, perhaps with someone involved in their finances.

December

Best Days Overall: 8th, 9th, 18th, 19th, 26th, 27th

Most Stressful Days Overall: 3rd, 4th, 11th, 12th, 24th, 25th, 31st

Best Days for Love: 3rd, 4th, 13th, 14th, 24th, 31st

Best Days for Money: 1st, 2nd, 11th, 12th, 20th, 21st, 28th, 29th

The planets are still very much clustered in the Eastern sector of your chart, making you unusually independent, self-reliant and personally influential. You are concerned with your personal interests – earning power, your own neighbourhood, personal intellectual interests – and feel, 'if I don't take care of myself, who will?' This is very much a month in which you make things happen and in which your personal will is like a law of the universe.

The planets continue to be focused below the horizon of your chart and are headed lower and lower. Thus the urge is to come to terms with your past, to indulge in nostalgia and looking back over your life, to create emotional harmony and security for yourself.

Your paths of greatest fulfilment are money-making, shopping, charities, intellectual interests and your domestic life.

Earnings are still unusually good this month and your financial judgement is sound. Though you are not necessarily seeking this, your earning ability does boost your public prestige. Elders and people of power are very helpful in fulfilling your financial goals. Shared resources – monies that are pooled with other people – prosper as well.

Though money-making is a priority all month, after the 22nd your attention shifts to your intellectual life and to your neighbourhood. You seem very active around the neighbourhood, making short trips, running errands and visiting people. Opportunities for education come to you and are favourable. Though your career is not a priority right now you can nevertheless boost it by furthering your education or taking courses.

Your love life is dramatic and exciting, with many wild swings of affection – ultra-highs and ultra-lows. Ride the roller-coaster and try to enjoy it. Don't take your partner for granted now. Romance blooms through good intellectual communication until the 22nd. Let your partner or lover know that you appreciate his or her mind as well as all his or her other attributes. After the 22nd love becomes less intellectual and more nurturing. It is OK to be a 'couch potato' with your beloved then. Entertain him or her at home and with your family. Make your beloved feel like part of the family.

Sagittarius

♐

THE ARCHER

Birthdays from
23rd November
to 20th December

Personality Profile

SAGITTARIUS AT A GLANCE

Element – Fire

Ruling planet – Jupiter
Career planet – Mercury
Love planet – Mercury
Planet of wealth and good fortune – Jupiter

Colours – blue, dark blue

Colours that promote love, romance and social harmony – yellow, yellow-orange

Colours that promote earning power – black, indigo

Gems – carbuncle, turquoise

Metal – tin

Scents – carnation, jasmine, myrrh

Quality – mutable (= flexibility)

Qualities most needed for balance – attention to detail, administration and organization

Strongest virtues – generosity, honesty, broad-mindedness, tremendous vision

Deepest need – to expand mentally

Characteristics to avoid – over-optimism, exaggeration, being too generous with other people's money

Signs of greatest overall compatibility – Aries, Leo

Signs of greatest overall incompatibility – Gemini, Virgo, Pisces

Sign most helpful to career – Virgo

Sign most helpful for emotional support – Pisces

Sign most helpful financially – Capricorn

Sign best for marriage and/or partnerships – Gemini

Sign most helpful for creative projects – Aries

Best Sign to have fun with – Aries

Signs most helpful in spiritual matters – Leo, Scorpio

Best day of the week – Thursday

Understanding the Sagittarius Personality

If you look at the symbol of the archer you will gain a good, intuitive understanding of the people born under this astrological Sign. The development of archery was humanity's first refinement of the power to hunt and wage war. The ability to shoot an arrow far beyond the ordinary range of a spear extended humanity's horizons, wealth, personal will and power.

Today, instead of using bows and arrows we project our power with fuels and mighty engines, but the essential reason for using these new powers remains the same. These powers represent our ability to extend our personal sphere of influence – and this is what Sagittarius is all about. Sagittarians are always seeking to expand their horizons, to cover more territory and increase their range and scope. This applies to all aspects of their lives: economic, social and intellectual.

Sagittarians are noted for the development of the mind – the higher intellect – which understands philosophical, metaphysical and spiritual concepts. This mind represents the higher part of the psychic nature and is motivated not by self-centred considerations but by the light and grace of a higher power. Thus, Sagittarians love higher education of all kinds. They might be bored with formal schooling but they love to study on their own and in their own way. A love of foreign travel and interest in places far away from home are also noteworthy characteristics of the Sagittarian type.

If you give some thought to all these Sagittarian attributes you will see that they spring from the inner Sagittarian desire to develop. To travel more is to know more, to know more is to be more, to cultivate the higher mind is to grow and to reach more. All these traits tend to broaden the intellectual – and indirectly, the economic and material – horizons of the Sagittarian.

The generosity of the Sagittarian is legendary. There are many reasons for this. One is that Sagittarians seem to have an inborn consciousness of wealth. They feel that they are rich, that they are lucky, that they can attain any financial goal – and so they feel that they can afford to be generous. Sagittarians don't carry the burdens of want and limitation – which stop most other people from giving generously. Another reason for their generosity is their religious and philosophical idealism, derived from the higher mind. This higher mind is by nature generous because it is unaffected by material circumstances. Still another reason is that the act of giving tends to enhance their emotional nature. Every act of giving seems to be enriching, and this is reward enough for the Sagittarian.

Finance

Sagittarians generally entice wealth. They either attract it or create it. They have the ideas, energy and talent to make their vision of paradise on Earth a reality. However, mere wealth is not enough. Sagittarians want luxury – earning a comfortable living seems small and insignificant to them.

In order for Sagittarians to attain their true earning potential they must develop better managerial and organizational skills. They must learn to set limits, to arrive at their goals through a series of attainable sub-goals or objectives. It is very rare that a person goes from rags to riches overnight. But a long, drawn-out process is difficult for Sagittarians. Like Leos, they want to achieve wealth and success quickly and impressively. They must be aware, however, that this over-optimism can lead to unrealistic financial ventures and disappointing losses. Of course, no Zodiac Sign can bounce back as quickly as Sagittarius, but only needless heartache will be caused by this attitude. Sagittarians need to maintain their vision – never letting go of it – but must also work towards it in practical and efficient ways.

Career and Public Image

Sagittarians are big thinkers. They want it all: money, name, fame, glamour, prestige, public acclaim and a place in history. They often go after all these goals. Some attain them, some don't – much depends on each individual's personal Horoscope. But if Sagittarians want to attain public and professional status they must understand that these things are not conferred to enhance one's ego but as rewards for the amount of service that one does for the whole of humanity. If and when they figure out ways to serve more, Sagittarians can rise to the top.

The ego of the Sagittarian is gigantic – and perhaps rightly so. They have much to be proud of. If they want public acclaim, however, they will have to learn to tone the ego down a bit, to become more humble and self-effacing, without falling into the trap of self-denial and self-abasement. They must also learn to master the details of life, which can sometimes elude them.

At their jobs Sagittarians are hard workers who like to please their bosses and co-workers. They are dependable, trustworthy and enjoy challenging work assignments and situations. Sagittarians are friendly to work with and helpful to their colleagues. They usually contribute intelligent new ideas or new methods that improve the work environment for everyone. Sagittarians always look for challenging positions and careers that develop their intellect, even if they have to work very hard in order to succeed. They also work well under the supervision of others, although by nature they would rather be the supervisors and increase their sphere of influence. Sagittarians excel at professions that allow them to be in contact with many different people and to travel to new and exciting locations.

Love and Relationships

Sagittarians love freedom for themselves and will readily grant it to their partners. They like their relationships to be fluid, loose and ever-changing. Sagittarians tend to be fickle in love and to change their minds about their partners quite frequently.

Sagittarians feel threatened by a clearly defined, well-structured relationship, as it tends to limit their freedom. The Sagittarian tends to marry more than once in life.

Sagittarians in love are passionate, generous, open, benevolent and very active. They demonstrate their affections very openly. However, just like an Aries they tend to be egocentric in the way they relate to their partners. Sagittarians should develop the ability to see another's point of view, not just their own. They need to develop some objectivity and cool intellectual clarity in their relationships so that they can develop better two-way communications with their partners. Sagittarians tend to be overly idealistic about their partners and about love in general. A cool and rational attitude will help them to perceive reality more clearly and help them to avoid disappointment.

Home and Domestic Life

Sagittarians tend to grant a lot of freedom to their family. They like big homes and many children and are one of the most fertile Signs of the Zodiac. However, when it comes to their children Sagittarians generally err on the side of allowing them too much freedom. Sometimes their children get the idea that there are no limits. However, allowing freedom in the home is basically a positive thing – so long as some measure of balance is maintained – for it enables all family members to develop as they should.

Horoscope for 1995

Major Trends

1994 was a year of great inward expansion, cleansing and catharsis. It was a year of clearing the decks and preparing for the new. It was a year of dissolving old ties and connections, of being secluded and of being a power behind the scenes. You were so secluded as to be almost monastic. This is so uncharacteristic of you that there was probably a lot of confusion in your mind while you were going through all of this. In 1995 you are going to see the reasons for it all. In 1995 you become more like your natural self. You emerge with a new, shined-up, glamorized image. You are 'out there', asserting yourself in the spotlight. There is a new confidence in you, which really is your old, natural confidence and optimism resurfacing.

This is going to be one of the happiest and most fulfilling years of your life. It's not going to be 'perfect' – the Cosmos has thrown in a few challenges to keep you on your toes and to keep things interesting – but it's going to be good. The challenges are nothing that you can't handle – in fact they will make your successes all the sweeter.

Jupiter, your Ruling Planet, will be in your own Sign for an unusually long period of about 13 months. Usually it moves through a Sign in 11 months. Jupiter is the planet of luck, benevolence and wealth and is very comfortable in the Sign of Sagittarius – acting very powerfully on your behalf. Another unusual factor in your happiness and success is shown by the fact that Venus, which normally visits your Sign once during the year, visits your Sign twice this year. A double measure of love, happiness and wealth.

In 1994 you were called upon to sacrifice. You learned deeper things about sacrifice and the secret glory of it. Your sacrifices of 1994 are the measure for your indulgence and personal pleasures of 1995. In other words, the more you sacrificed in 1994 the more you are going to enjoy yourself in 1995. The Cosmos is going to provide you with both the means and the inclination. A very happy year overall.

Health

Overall your health and vitality are excellent. You have unusual physical energy. You excel in sports and exercise this year. Jupiter in your own Sign is jazzing you up. Saturn, however, does make stressful aspects to you all year, putting your energy to periodic tests. You probably think that you can swim a hundred laps and run a hundred miles. You feel your body can do anything. But Saturn is going to put you to the test and will curb any physical over-indulgence on your part. Saturn will remind you of your limitations. Saturn by itself is not enough to cause a health problem. It needs assistance from other planets and it's not getting it this year, except for a few short periods which will be analysed later. Basically Saturn is just going to signal when you're overdoing things.

There are only two threats to your health this year. One threat comes from over-indulgence in physical pleasure. Over-eating, over-exercise, etc. The other threat comes from family relationships, which could depress you if you allow them to. Relationships with family members are challenging this year and this could dampen your buoyant enthusiasm. Don't allow it. It doesn't seem that you will allow it – you've got too much going for you – but the temptation is there. Don't sink in the quicksand of negative feeling, of identifying with the trials and traumas of those close to you. Be sympathetic, kind and of practical service where possible, but don't identify emotionally.

Try to rest and relax more from 26th May to 22nd July and from 23rd August to 23rd September.

Home and Domestic Life

When Saturn entered the Sign of Pisces towards the end of 1994 your 4th House of Home and Family became very prominent for the long term. This is your one area of challenge in a year that is basically happy and fulfilled.

For a few years now there has been instability at home. There have been many moves, changes of residence and renovations. You haven't been able to settle in one place or domestic situation. Relations with your family have been turbulent – sometimes deliriously happy and sometimes deeply sad. There has seemed to be no rhyme or reason for all of this, except that in the school of life you have needed to learn how to deal with volatile and unpredictable relations and emotions. Saturn's movement into your family situation shows that at long last some stability is happening at home. The loyalty of family members – parents, siblings and those who are part of your 'support system' – is undergoing a trial by fire. Many will collapse under this, others will survive. Though you will be disappointed at the disloyalty of certain people, at least you will have discovered who is for real and who is not.

Exactly how is Saturn going to do all this? There are various scenarios, but basically Saturn will provoke a crisis requiring help or support. In this time of need you will discover who is for you and who is not. You are then free to act accordingly and make more realistic domestic plans. In this way you will establish a more realistic support system. Every crisis has its silver lining.

Your new image and self-confidence are also going to be tested by family members who might feel that you are getting too big for your boots.

For many years now many of you have expressed your feelings – positive or negative – in a free and uninhibited manner. There is nothing wrong with that, as long as it works. If you're already in an emotional state you might as well express it and get it over with. But this year you discover a better way of handling your emotions. A new way of controlling them is being given to you. Techniques for avoiding negative states are being offered you. In short, you will be able to manage your emotions better. Make no mistake, this year you are not as free to express every mood and feeling as you once were. The wrong expression of feeling could have serious consequences for your finances – for some delicate deal that you are working on. Better to keep your feelings positive from the start.

After the family tests you are going through, loyal family

members are going to provide financial opportunities for you. You will reciprocate as well. You are spending more money on the home, perhaps even overspending. Your basic urge is to create a secure, safe domestic and emotional situation that will endure over time. It won't be easy but you can do it.

Love and Social Life

Your 7th House of Love and Marriage is not especially prominent this year, Sagittarius. You seem blasé about love and commitment, totally unconcerned about them. Home, finances and personal pleasures are more important to you than marriage. With the Cosmos pushing you neither one way nor another, you have a lot of freedom in love this year – which is the way you like things. By nature you tend to be fickle in love. That is, you want your lover to be many different things to you at different times. You like to express love in a variety of ways – depending on where Mercury happens to be at a given time. This trend continues this year. You are calling the shots in relationships. Others have to bend to your will and desires.

You have unusual power to assert yourself and your personal needs this year, and there always seem to be plenty of prospective partners who are willing to do this. An embarrassment of riches is the phrase that springs to mind. You seem to think 'there are many fish in the sea and only those who meet my whim of the moment need be considered'. No, you are not mistreating your friends and lovers. On the contrary, you are more generous than ever. It's just that you don't value them as much as you could. Your real love this year is yourself. Nothing wrong with that – on the contrary, until you love yourself fully you will not be able to love another. So continue loving yourself and when you are ready, see the other as an extension of your own self whom you love so deeply.

With your 7th House relatively inactive, Mercury's quick

and ever-changing movements and aspects are going to determine how your love life goes this year. When Mercury moves at its highest velocity your love life accelerates and your social confidence is high. When Mercury slows down you become more cautious in love. When it goes backwards – which happens three times a year – you actually feel that your relationships are going backwards. When Mercury is in one Sign you want one thing from your lover; when it moves into another Sign you want something else. Those involved with a Sagittarius should take note of this. You can read about these short-term trends in the month-by-month forecasts below.

Career and Finance

Your 2nd House of Money and Possessions has been prominent in your Horoscope for many years now and will continue to be prominent this year. Your financial experimentation is beginning to pay off. Not because you've hit some powerful 'money button', but because your self-esteem and feeling of self-worth are greater. Financial deals which were always on the cards but were blocked off due to your lack of confidence will come to fruition this year. You are in a long-term trend of upward financial expansion. 1995 brings increased travel, education, money and promotions. You are perceived as being more valuable to your employer or to your clients. Next year you will make even more money than this year.

Your family is a burden to you this year but you carry it because they are either supporting you financially or are providing you with lucrative financial opportunities. Not all of these opportunities are particularly pleasant – they force you to stay close to home and limit your desires to 'wonder and wander'.

Real estate seems a particularly lucrative field this year. Because of your domestic wanderings in the past few years you have gained much experience in the dynamics of this pursuit. You need to pay attention to detail, be on time for appointments and take a businesslike attitude towards any plans you make. In a sense, you go a bit against your nature to achieve financial goals.

Other lucrative fields this year are nursery care for children, restaurants, home decorating and furnishings, hotels, inns, spas, footwear and shipping. You might find employment in these industries or come across investment opportunities here.

If you are married or involved in a business partnership, you seem to be the one who is earning the money and carrying the weight. Your partner seems unconcerned about these things. The income of your partner is neither helped nor obstructed by the Cosmos, so the status quo is likely to continue. If he or she earned a lot in 1994 these strong earnings will continue in 1995. If the reverse was true, this trend will continue. Check your partner's Sun Sign and read the Horoscope for it in this book to get more details on his or her earning capabilities this year.

The income of a sibling is diminished this year. Budgets and spending controls are called for. If the sibling just avoids wastefulness, the earnings, though somewhat diminished, will suffice to carry him or her through. Later in the year this sibling will be in a 'leaner, fitter' condition for expansion.

The income of your religious affiliation – your church, mosque, synagogue or ministry – is booming and you have a lot to with it.

Self-improvement

Your personal image and self-confidence are improving this year almost by itself. You just have to be open to it and go along with it. You are in a year of self-indulgence and personal pleasure. But too much of a good thing can be harmful, so try to keep a balance. Your family situation and domestic life are going to improve as well this year – but through hard, disciplined work on your part and through many tests, challenges and crises. Your ability to control your moods and emotions will play a key role in this. Your emotions will have a dramatic impact not only on your home, but on your 'bottom line' as well. Crucial financial deals could fall through if you are 'emotionally promiscuous' – going along with every feeling that passes through your mind. You must become selective of the feelings that you entertain in your 'aura' – adhering and magnifying those that are constructive and healthy, and shunning those that are destructive and unhealthy. Emotional self-indulgence is much worse for you than physical self-indulgence; it is more expensive as well.

Month-by-month Forecasts

January

Best Days Overall: 7th, 8th, 17th, 18th, 26th, 27th

Most Stressful Days Overall: 5th, 6th, 12th, 13th, 19th, 20th, 21st

Best Days for Love: 1st, 2nd, 6th, 7th, 8th, 12th, 13th, 17th, 18th, 19th, 22nd, 23rd, 26th, 27th, 30th, 31st

Best Days for Money: 1st, 2nd, 5th, 6th, 7th, 8th, 15th, 16th, 17th, 18th, 24th, 25th, 26th, 27th

This is one of your great months in a great year. You have so much going for you in so many areas that it's difficult to know where to begin.

First off, the overwhelming percentage of planets are clustered in the Eastern half of your Horoscope, showing that you have great control over circumstances and conditions. You do not need to adapt to situations but create them according to your wishes. With Jupiter, your Ruling Planet, travelling with Venus in your own Sign, you are most definitely creating a happy reality for yourself.

This is a month of great personal pleasure and happiness. There are numerous opportunities for self-indulgence – parties, lovers, good food, extra money – and you probably take them. Remember not to overdo it.

The emphasis on personal happiness is further reinforced by the fact that 80 to 90 per cent of the planets are in the bottom half of your Solar chart. You consider personal happiness and emotional harmony to be greater achievements than worldly success or status. Your ambitions centre round your personal goals – such as developing your mind, mastering your studies, creating a stable home base – rather than goals that involve others. You set the tone and pace of events now; others either adapt or are left behind.

Many years of financial struggle and experimentation – of mixed success and failure – are coming to an end. With Jupiter and Venus in your 1st House of the Body and Personal Image, and with Pluto flirting with this 1st House as well, you begin to see that wealth begins with you. You earn more because you have become more. As you create your image of glamour and wealth, tangible wealth simply follows – logically and inexorably. At last you are dealing with basics and it's paying off.

You are dressing for success these days, perhaps even overdoing it. You are redecorating your home or personal environment lavishly and opulently. You attract both money and love like a magnet. You are also calling the shots in your current relationship. This seems disconcerting to your partner, who now needs to rethink the relationship. Give him or her the space to think.

Your health and finances are excellent all month. Don't commit to any major career moves after the 26th when Mercury (your Career Planet) is retrograde (travelling backwards). Tell the people involved that you need time to think things through.

February

Best Days Overall: 3rd, 4th, 5th, 13th, 14th, 15th, 22nd, 23rd

Most Stressful Days Overall: 1st, 2nd, 8th, 9th, 10th, 16th, 17th

Best Days for Love: 4th, 5th, 6th, 7th, 8th, 9th, 10th, 16th, 17th, 18th, 19th, 24th, 25th, 26th, 27th, 28th

Best Days for Money: 1st, 2nd, 3rd, 4th, 5th, 11th, 12th, 13th, 14th, 15th, 20th, 21st, 22nd, 23rd, 24th, 25th

Most of the planets are in the bottom and Eastern halves of your Solar Horoscope this month, Sagittarius. Moreover, 80 to 90 per cent of them will be moving forward as well. Combine this with your normal fiery, independent nature and you have a pretty good picture of the kind of month this will be. You tend to be intensely self-centred this month. You feel your power and you have the strength to create, shape and dictate events. It is a month for creating Karma – a month of action, achievement and progress. Onwards and upwards all the way. If your plans, goals and desires are positive and constructive, then your Karma (conditions, circumstances and the effect of your actions) will be happy and successful. Even if your plans are not well thought out, they will still succeed – but you will have to deal with the negative repercussions of this very success.

Yes, you shape events now, while others have to conform to you. You assert yourself with great confidence and have greater influence over others than usual. You are less concerned with your career than with personal happiness and emotional harmony. Very uncharacteristically for a Sagittarius, you are concerned with your 'selfish' desires – your personal pleasures, your earning power, your neighbours and neighbourhood and your family. This, of course, will not be a permanent condition – this is not your nature – but for now this is the state of play.

Your health is excellent until the 19th; after then you should rest and relax more. Whether you will actually heed this advice is another story. The pace of events and of your enthusiasm will make it difficult for you to slow down.

Your earnings – just like last month – continue to be excellent. The 'Financial Gods' are with you all the way. You earn money easily and pleasurably. Women – friends and co-workers – are especially helpful in reaching your financial goals. A sale or contract with a professional or social organization to which you belong looks lucrative.

Your love life is rather arrested for the first half of the month. Mercury, your Love Planet, retrogrades until the 16th, making you tentative and overly cautious when it comes to romance. Though you are personally confident now, in social matters you are less so. It takes two to tango, after all, and your exuberant over-assertiveness can make your lover or partner feel intimidated. This will pass after the 16th, however, when Mercury starts going direct again. If you are already involved in a relationship it will probably go forward again. If you are single you will feel more confidence and social magnetism. Singles looking for love should stick close to home. Love can be found in your own neighbourhood.

March

Best Days Overall: 3rd, 4th, 5th, 13th, 14th, 21st, 22nd, 30th, 31st

Most Stressful Days Overall: 1st, 2nd, 8th, 9th, 15th, 16th, 28th, 29th

Best Days for Love: 8th, 9th, 17th, 18th, 19th, 20th, 26th, 27th, 28th, 29th

Best Days for Money: 1st, 2nd, 3rd, 4th, 10th, 12th, 13th, 14th, 20th, 21st, 22nd, 24th, 25th, 30th, 31st

Most of the planets are still at the bottom half of your Solar Horoscope, showing that, as was true last month, you continue to favour emotional and psychological harmony to outward, career success. This month there is a slight shift, however – a shift that will get stronger with each passing month – towards the Western hemisphere of your chart. This shows an ever-increasing social urge and need to adapt to the desires of others. Although you basically get your own way, you need to begin to balance your interests with those of others.

With 80 per cent of the planets moving forward now, this is a month of action, progress and achievement. Your plans and projects are moving forward nicely.

The action at the bottom half of your Horoscope is even further accentuated by the power in your 4th House of Home and Family. You are interested in your personal history this month, particularly in events from your early childhood. This is not just idle curiosity but a recognition on your part that the further you want to go in life the deeper must be your connection to the past. All progress takes place in the context of tradition. You must understand your personal and family traditions now. Those of you involved in some form of psychological therapy or study will make much progress now.

You are also spending a great deal of money on the home or in the home. Family members come to you for financial assistance and you give it them. They are also supportive of your financial goals as well. Financial opportunities come through family connections, family businesses and real estate deals.

If you take the time to clear away your emotional baggage before the 21st of the month you will experience an unbelievable influx of life-force come the spring. Jupiter, your Ruling Planet, becomes involved in a happy and fortunate Grand Formation aspect after the 21st. Rarely have you experienced spring fever as strongly as you will this month. From the 21st onwards you are on 'cosmic holiday'. You are in a period of personal pleasure and self-indulgence. Speculations are favourable. Your normally boundless optimism is even more pronounced. Your personal magnetism and charisma become unusually strong, your creativity is intense and romantic opportunities abound. This is a very happy month. But take care to rest and relax more until the 21st.

Your love life is becoming more active. Mercury, your Love Planet, moves forward with great speed. Your social confidence is great. Singles are probably dating a lot. Though you will probably travel after the 21st – for pleasure – there is no need to do so in pursuit of love. Love is close to home. Those who want to win over Sagittarians this month need to nurture them and appeal to their intellect.

April

Best Days Overall: 1st, 9th, 10th, 18th, 19th, 26th, 27th, 28th

Most Stressful Days Overall: 4th, 5th, 6th, 11th, 12th, 13th, 24th, 25th

Best Days for Love: 4th, 5th, 6th, 7th, 8th, 9th, 10th, 16th, 17th, 20th, 21st, 26th, 27th, 28th, 29th, 30th

Best Days for Money: 1st, 7th, 8th, 9th, 10th, 16th, 17th, 18th, 19th, 20th, 21st, 24th, 25th, 26th, 27th, 28th

Perhaps it is good that Jupiter, your Planetary Ruler, goes retrograde this month. There is so much happening in your life, you are so filled with energy, vim, vigour and high spirits that you are in danger of over-extending yourself, of going too far too fast. Your life right now could be likened to someone driving a car at 150 mph: if you don't slow down and look at the signposts you could find yourself in strange territory – very far from home – very quickly.

You are in a happy period now. This is a month surging creativity, fun and games, non-serious love affairs and evenings out to entertainment venues. If you are involved in the fine arts, the Muses are all around you now. If you are a writer you are particularly inventive and original.

Most Sagittarians are optimistic people, but this month optimism surges to new heights – and many people consider you unrealistic. To you, however, this optimism is very realistic, based on your vision and perception. There is a fearlessness, a boldness, an unwavering courage and a feeling of invulnerability about you these days.

With most of the planets still in the bottom half of your chart your ambitions in the world are not that important. You just want to have a good time. And, since you attract money in lucky ways this month, you feel you don't need to concentrate on the career. Leave the work for later. Sufficient unto the day are the tasks of that day. The future will take care of itself.

You have an uncanny knack with children this period. They are drawn to you and you derive much joy from them.

Enjoy your 'cosmic holiday' until the 20th, for after then the demands of the workplace call you. The pace at work quickens and you must handle it. Your new creativity is very useful in achieving work goals and you seem to be able to have a good time even when you work. Nothing daunts your optimism.

Needless to say, your health is excellent. A repression of your creative urges could cause some problems – some feelings of discomfort – however.

Your Love Planet, Mercury, moves forward at exceptional speed this month, showing your social confidence and charisma. Social goals are achieved easily. There is much dating and fun and games. There is a lot of jumping into and out of relationships. There are a lot of 'love at first sight' kind of experiences. This is not a problem. The real problem in love is your lack of seriousness. A word of advice for those of you romantically involved with Sagittarians: until the 17th, be their playmate, after then try to make yourself useful to them. Serve their interests.

May

Best Days Overall: 6th, 7th, 8th, 15th, 16th, 24th, 25th

Most Stressful Days Overall: 1st, 2nd, 3rd, 9th, 10th, 21st, 22nd, 23rd, 29th, 30th

Best Days for Love: 1st, 2nd, 3rd, 6th, 7th, 8th, 12th, 15th, 16th, 17th, 19th, 20th, 26th, 27th, 28th, 29th, 30th

Best Days for Money: 4th, 5th, 6th, 7th, 8th, 13th, 14th, 15th, 16th, 17th, 18th, 21st, 22nd, 23rd, 24th, 25th

The planetary power is still very much below the horizon of your chart, making your ambitions and career less important now. Family and emotional values still take precedence over your career. The behaviour of Mercury, your Career and Love Planet, this month reinforces this and is worthy of mention. First off, it moves slowly and cautiously and on the 24th it starts going backwards. Secondly, it goes 'out-of-bounds' from the 6th to the 24th. This shows that you are going out of your normal career 'orbit' and feel less confident about it. Perhaps you are going in over your head in a career venture and will be forced to retrace your steps later on. Your caution is well placed, for when you drive off the main road you should drive more slowly and keep your headlights on. Think deeply before making any major career changes now.

Though the planets are evenly dispersed between the Eastern and Western sectors of your Horoscope, your social life is going to get more active from the 21st onwards. The main challenge in love this month is to keep a balance between your personal interests and desires and those of your partner. These interests are unusually divergent and threaten to pull the whole relationship apart. Good will and compromise can salvage things, but this divergence of interest is causing both you and your partner to rethink the relationship and your feelings for each other. This rethinking is not coming from just one party but from both sides. You are less self-assertive than you have been in the past, but then again so is your partner. Neither side dominates.

Singles are meeting romantic opportunities this month but seem confused as to where they want to go with these opportunities. The New Moon in your 7th House of Love on the 29th will help clarify things, but the real clarification will come when Mercury starts going direct next month. Sagittarians are looking for partners who can make them feel important, give them prestige and who can also teach them things. They want someone they can look up to and learn from. Avoid scheduling either a marriage or divorce this month.

Your health is fine until the 21st, but after then rest and relax more.

Finances are healthy before the 21st, but after then seem stressful. You need to work harder for your earnings than usual. Forty to 50 per cent of the planets are going retrograde – including one in your (2nd) Money House – and this suggests a sense of temporary stalemate in your financial dealings. Use the delays to your advantage by improving your plans, concepts, products and services. Try to spend less cash after the 21st.

June

Best Days Overall: 3rd, 4th, 12th, 13th, 20th, 21st, 30th

Most Stressful Days Overall: 5th, 6th, 18th, 19th, 25th, 26th

Best Days for Love: 5th, 6th, 7th, 8th, 9th, 16th, 17th, 25th, 26th

Best Days for Money: 1st, 2nd, 3rd, 4th, 10th, 11th, 12th, 14th, 15th, 18th, 19th, 20th, 21st, 28th, 29th, 30th

Happily for you, Sagittarius, it is not often that 50 per cent of the planetary power goes retrograde as it does this month. The frustration would drive you wild. As it is you are forced to go against your grain right now and learn patience. There is no use trying to force things or make things happen, no use being in a rush or getting anxious. Things will happen in their own time – and most probably not in the time you would set. Victory over frustration and discouragement this month should be your goal. If you achieve it you can legitimately call yourself a success.

There are lessons we learn from having power and lessons we learn when we have no power. When we have no personal power we need to rely on a Higher Power than ourselves to take care of things – and to trust it implicitly. This is one of the lessons of the coming month. Stand firm in your trust in the Great Order of things even while your world seems to be shaking at its foundations. The shaking will eventually stop and all that will have been destroyed is some old unpleasantness.

Your social life is active and fundamentally happy. It is not without its tensions, however. Mercury, your Love Planet, is retrograde in your 7th House of Love. This means that, though you are very much the social butterfly and attract abundant romantic opportunities, you are unsure as to what you really want and need in a relationship. It is quite possible that part of this confusion comes from having too many romantic opportunities. You feel cautious and unwilling to commit to anything. You feel unsure of your affections. Happily, this is a short-term trend and by the 17th your normal social confidence is back. Those romantically involved with Sagittarians now need to have patience with them. They can't tell you how they feel because they don't really know how they feel.

Another important challenge to love this month is the feeling that your partner and you enjoy different things and have different – even diametrically opposed – desires. When you want to go to the cinema your partner wants to go to the zoo. When you want to go to restaurant *x* your partner wants restaurant *y*. A power struggle is going on in terms of your personal desires. This is short term but nevertheless it creates some tension.

There is also an important power struggle going on concerning your career and ambitions. This could involve rivals at the office or in your business. Defend yourself by all means, but don't launch any counter-assaults until after the 17th when you are more sure of your career direction. Mercury, which is retrograde until the 17th, is not just your Love Planet but your Career Planet as well.

Rest and relax more this month. Conserve your energy for real priorities.

July

Best Days Overall: 1st, 9th, 10th, 17th, 18th, 27th, 28th

Most Stressful Days Overall: 2nd, 3rd, 4th, 15th, 16th, 22nd, 23rd, 30th, 31st

Best Days for Love: 5th, 6th, 7th, 8th, 15th, 16th, 22nd, 23rd, 25th, 26th, 27th

Best Days for Money: 1st, 7th, 8th, 9th, 10th, 11th, 12th, 15th, 16th, 17th, 18th, 25th, 26th, 27th, 28th

As was true last month, you are learning difficult lessons in patience and non-attachment. Fifty per cent of the planets continue to be retrograde – including Jupiter, your Personal Ruler. Maintain the attitude of 'letting things occur' rather than trying to force them to occur. You will get further with less stress. The time for 'making things happen' will come in future months; you're not quite there yet.

With most of the planets still in the Western hemisphere of your chart (this period is rapidly coming to an end) your key to success lies in your ability to adapt to situations and to charm others. You can't go it alone just yet.

Most of the planets are currently above the horizon of your chart – a trend which continues for the next few months – making you ever more ambitious, worldly and status conscious. The timing for this is just right, too. With Saturn and Neptune going retrograde there is little you can do with your home or family situation anyway. You might as well focus on your career.

Your paths to greatest fulfilment this month are the rediscovery of yourself, the enhancement of your physical image, making money for others, spiritual studies and charitable activities.

Your health is excellent all month but especially after the 23rd. Good health can be enhanced through a fulfilling social life, harmony with friends and your lover, meeting the normal needs of physical intimacy, detoxifying the body and having 'good health concepts'. A sound philosophy of health and disease is always vital to good health, but later on this month it becomes even more so.

Earnings are temporarily slow in coming right now as most of your wealth indicators are retrograde. Payments due you and pending financial deals will eventually materialize, but not straight away. Study all investment and earning opportunities really thoroughly and don't make a move until everything is crystal clear. Your lack of personal earning power is more than made up for by the prosperity of your partner – who is also very generous with you.

Now that Mercury moves speedily forward, your social charisma is stronger. Disputes with your lover or partner get resolved by the 11th. You are making good social progress. A current relationship moves forward again. Singles are dating more than usual and seem more interested in physical intimacy than mere romance. A romantic jaunt to a foreign land is on the cards late in the month.

August

Best Days Overall: 5th, 6th, 14th, 15th, 24th, 25th

Most Stressful Days Overall: 12th, 19th, 20th, 26th, 27th

Best Days for Love: 5th, 6th, 14th, 15th, 16th, 17th, 19th, 20th, 26th, 27th

Best Days for Money: 3rd, 4th, 5th, 6th, 7th, 8th, 12th, 13th, 14th, 15th, 21st, 22nd, 26th, 27th, 31st

Much of the stalemate of recent months is over now, and the unusual number of planets in Fire Signs makes you feel the way you like to feel: hot, active, optimistic, ebullient and playful.

By the 10th the planetary power will be mostly in your Eastern sector, putting you in charge of events and circumstances and making you – in a sense – master of your own house. As the month progresses, this sense of self-mastery and dominion gets stronger and stronger as more and more of the fast-moving, short-term planets move eastward. Combined with Jupiter's forward motion, this presents a picture of your tremendous self-confidence and happiness. You know who you are and where you want to go.

Until the 23rd you are in one of the happiest periods of your year. There is fun, personal pleasure, sensual delights, foreign travel and religious illumination happening for you. Your health is unusually good and your personal charisma is strong. This is a month in which you get your way and others have to start adapting to you.

Your paths of greatest fulfilment this month are foreign travel, religious studies, sports, career (after the 23rd), friendships, group activities and the enhancement of your personal image.

Since you feel more optimistic and have a greater sense of your self-worth it is no surprise that your career will blossom after the 23rd. It is merely the public and superiors recognizing things that you've been feeling for some time. Pay rises and promotions – as well as a lot of work – come to you after the 23rd. With family issues at an impasse for a while you might as well push your 'outer' goals and have some fun.

Your love life is fast-paced this month. Those of you involved in something serious are making good progress in the relationship. The relationship moves forward speedily. Those of you not currently involved with anyone have numerous and various opportunities for meeting someone. Until the 10th look at universities, church or religious functions and, if you can afford it, in foreign lands. After the 10th romance comes to you through the intervention of elders, bosses and other superiors at work. Many of you will find love at a government office. Others will find love with those who are involved with your career. There is much dating and much going out. Your social judgement is sound and you are not likely to make any mistaken choices now. Trust yourself.

Your financial life is still rather stalemated but you are less depressed about it. You are handling it much better than last month. Financial caution is still called for with any proposed investments or major purchases. Do your homework.

September

Best Days Overall: 2nd, 10th, 11th, 20th, 21st, 29th, 30th

Most Stressful Days Overall: 8th, 9th, 15th, 16th, 22nd, 23rd

Best Days for Love: 4th, 5th, 6th, 7th, 12th, 13th, 14th, 15th, 16th, 24th, 25th

Best Days for Money: 2nd, 4th, 5th, 8th, 9th, 10th, 11th, 17th, 18th, 19th, 20th, 21st, 27th, 28th, 29th, 30th

With Jupiter (your Ruler) moving forward and with 80 to 90 per cent of the planets in the Eastern sector of your Horoscope, things are just the way you want them to be. If you don't like the circumstances you're in, you have the freedom, the power and the assertiveness to make the needed changes. You are in command and control now. You have the cosmic luxury of truly being yourself. True, there are some obstacles and conflicts to deal with – most notably with your family and in your career – but you have all the firepower, drive and energy to overcome them.

Most of the planets are above the horizon of your chart and two powerful planets are in your (10th) Career House this month. Thus your worldly ambitions are being activated. You want to rise to the top. You want to take your place in the world. You want to exercise your rightful authority in your company and in society. You seek outer, temporal power these days – not for yourself but in order to serve and do good. Though you are vitally interested in family issues and your personal domestic sphere there is little you can do now to break the deadlock. Instead you channel your drives into helping other people's families. You want your work to foster the emotional security and sustenance of other people.

Career issues are going well this month. Pay rises and promotions are likely. The only catch to all this is the need to juggle your domestic duties, career responsibilities and your personal inclinations. All of these are at odds with each other this month.

Your paths of greatest happiness are your career, helping other people's families, friendships, group activities, personal pleasures and the enhancement of your personal image.

Rest and relax more until the 23rd. Your health can be enhanced through harmony with elders, cultivating your true life's work, finding your true duty in life and keeping things harmonious with friends.

Though over the long term your earnings outlook is super, at present finances are still delayed. Part of the problem is that your goals are very high and thus more is involved in their manifestation. Your ship is coming in, but be patient. Spend cautiously this month.

Mercury, your Love Planet, moves slowly and cautiously for most of the month. This shows that you are dating less this month and are more careful about whom you go out with. After the 22nd Mercury starts to go backwards, making you feel that your social life is also going backwards. Your social confidence is not as strong as it normally is. Be careful of how you communicate with lovers or partners. Spell out all the details, as mis-communication is the biggest potential hurdle to romance this month. Don't schedule either a marriage or divorce after the 22nd.

October

Best Days Overall: 7th, 8th, 9th, 17th, 18th, 26th, 27th

Most Stressful Days Overall: 5th, 6th, 12th, 13th, 20th, 21st

Best Days for Love: 3rd, 4th, 12th, 13th, 15th, 16th, 22nd, 23rd, 24th, 25th, 30th, 31st

Best Days for Money: 1st, 2nd, 5th, 6th, 7th, 8th, 9th, 15th, 16th, 17th, 18th, 24th, 25th, 26th, 27th, 28th, 29th

Think about what you want and go after it boldly – you will get it now. You are an action-orientated person in an action-orientated month. The stalemate, delay and obstructions of recent months have just melted away. Ninety per cent of the planets, after the 14th, are moving forward. You are in a period of achievement and accomplishment.

With the planets so concentrated in the East you are a 'me first' type of person now, which is unusual for a Sagittarius. If others don't co-operate with your plans and projects you have ample energy to go it alone. You have greater personal influence with others, greater confidence and self-esteem, greater dominion over the conditions of your life. If you don't like existing conditions just change them into something you do like. Others will have to adapt to you.

The planets are also very much focused above the horizon until the 21st. Thus you continue to be career-orientated and you have the power to make your career goals a reality now. You are making friends with people who are above you in status and who are in a position to make your fondest career desires come to pass – only be patient about your career progress until the 14th.

After the 21st Mars moves into your own Sign of Sagittarius, making you even more active, self-assertive, courageous and independent than usual. You sweep the opposition off their feet. Your life becomes unusually fast-paced. You excel in sport, exercise regimes and entertainment. You are the perfect show-off this month. Up till now you have been like a high-powered automobile driving through dense, heavy traffic. You were driving well below your true capacity. But when Mars goes into your own Sign and with most of the planets going forward, you are on the open road and can safely step on that accelerator. You do the work of 10 people this month.

Your paths of greatest fulfilment are friendship, group activities, charitable works, ministering to others, personal pleasures and the enhancement of your image.

You are attractive to the opposite sex because of your sheer energy. You charge them up, fire them up, inspire them and lift them to new physical and mental vistas. It is impossible for anyone to be dull or depressed around you now. You are an exciting person to be around. There's never a dull moment.

Needless to say, your health is excellent all month. In addition the financial stalemate is finally over and many stalled deals and payments are now coming to you.

November

Best Days Overall: 4th, 5th, 14th, 15th, 23rd

Most Stressful Days Overall: 1st, 2nd, 3rd, 8th, 9th, 10th, 16th, 17th, 29th, 30th

Best Days for Love: 2nd, 3rd, 4th, 8th, 9th, 10th, 11th, 12th, 14th, 15th, 21st, 22nd, 23rd, 24th

Best Days for Money: 2nd, 3rd, 4th, 5th, 11th, 12th, 14th, 15th, 21st, 22nd, 23rd, 24th, 25th, 26th, 29th, 30th

Your dream life is overactive until the 23rd of this month – and understandably so. You are flooded with premonitions, intuitions, hunches and visualizations. Even stark materialists are confronted with psychic phenomena which they cannot deny. The Cosmos is signalling you that major changes and momentous events are about to take place. Happily they are positive. Your dreams are likely to take the form of meetings with gods, illuminated masters and faraway places. These foreshadow things to come.

You are now in the peak period of a very peak year in your life. Enjoy. It's as if you can't make mistakes or do anything wrong. This is the luckiest period in a very lucky year. Kiss stalemate goodbye. All the planets are moving forward and you are achieving the goals of 10 people. You are doing in one month what previously took four or five months to accomplish.

The planets are 80 to 90 per cent in the Eastern part of your chart. Thus you are having things your way and your personal influence is strong. If you are involved in some power struggle you are the sure winner now – unless you are fighting another Sagittarius! You create beautifully and well, and people are adapting to what you create.

After the 23rd all the planets – with the exception of the Moon at times – will be below the horizon of your chart. This combined with the planetary power in the East shows that you are taking a holiday from the outside world and the stresses of outward success to focus on doing things that are meaningful to you. You are more interested in fulfilling your personal desires, in giving your body pleasure, in emotional harmony and well-being and in coming to terms with your past. You are more 'feeling'-orientated than success-orientated. The impasse in the domestic scene is over and domestic projects and family relationships go forward. The domestic scene is still far from your ideal and family members still pull you from your personal desires, but progress is being made.

Speculations are favourable and your financial intuition is sharp. You have so much energy and vitality that work goals are achieved very easily, leaving you plenty of free time to excel in sport, games and exercise regimes. Personal creativity translates into cash this month and gives you a great sense of satisfaction. Some of you feel that you would like to make a career out of enhancing your image. You vacillate between total self-indulgence – it is so easy to come by now – and over-exercise.

December

Best Days Overall: 1st, 2nd, 11th, 12th, 20th, 21st, 28th, 29th

Most Stressful Days Overall: 6th, 7th, 13th, 14th, 26th, 27th

Best Days for Love: 1st, 2nd, 3rd, 4th, 6th, 7th, 12th, 13th, 14th, 22nd, 23rd, 24th, 31st

Best Days for Money: 1st, 2nd, 8th, 9th, 11th, 12th, 18th, 19th, 20th, 21st, 22nd, 23rd, 26th, 27th, 28th, 29th

Your current optimism and good cheer are well founded. You are in one of the happiest periods of your year and perhaps your life. With most of the planets in the East – many of them in your own Sign of Sagittarius – your personal influence, energy and magnetism are unusually powerful. Your personal efforts are supported. Your personal will is a 'law of the universe'. You have dominion over your life and over your conditions and circumstance and are exercising it to the full.

After the 22nd you will see how your self-esteem – which is sky-high right now – translates into increased earnings. You command higher prices for your work and services. People believe in you because you believe in yourself. This translates into more business, more financial support and greater earnings. You earn more because you have become more.

Ninety to 100 per cent of the planets are below the horizon of your chart, making you less ambitious and less concerned with the future. You are more interested in the past and the here and now than in the future. You feel that if the present is OK the future will take care of itself. You are correct.

You are still very much in a month of personal pleasure and self-indulgence. Fantasies are being fulfilled now, only don't overdo things.

After the 22nd you become more preoccupied with money-making and are quite successful at it. Sales and marketing ventures go well. Real estate dealings are lucrative. Speculations are favourable, though you should calculate the risks and not make any rash decisions. You are an astute shopper and earn as much through your eye for good bargains as through your income. A legal judgement goes in your favour and positively affects your 'bottom line'. This legal ruling might not affect you personally *per se* but could affect a company you own stock in. Money is managed wisely and you know how to make the most of what you've got.

Your love life, too, is very happy. You are in command of a current relationship and your lover is pleased to fulfil your every whim. After the 12th your partner or lover shifts to helping you to achieve financial goals. Be careful about treating your lover as some sort of inanimate possession this month. His or her desire to please comes from love and not from lack of self-esteem.

Your health is excellent all month.

Capricorn

♑

THE GOAT

Birthdays from
21st December
to 19th January

Personality Profile

CAPRICORN AT A GLANCE

Element – Earth

Ruling planet – Saturn
Career planet – Venus
Love planet – Moon
Money planet – Uranus
Planet of health and work – Mercury
Planet of home and family life – Mars

Colours – black, indigo

Colours that promote love, romance and social harmony – puce, silver

Colour that promotes earning power – ultramarine blue

Gem – black onyx

Metal – lead

Scents – magnolia, pine, sweet pea, wintergreen

Quality – cardinal (= activity)

Qualities most needed for balance – warmth, spontaneity, a sense of fun

Strongest virtues – sense of duty, organization, perseverance, patience, ability to take the long-term view

Deepest needs – to manage, take charge and administrate

Characteristics to avoid – pessimism, depression, undue materialism and undue conservatism

Signs of greatest overall compatibility – Taurus, Virgo

Signs of greatest overall incompatibility – Aries, Cancer, Libra

Sign most helpful to career – Libra

Sign most helpful for emotional support – Aries

Sign most helpful financially – Aquarius

Sign best for marriage and/or partnerships – Cancer

Sign most helpful for creative projects – Taurus

Best Sign to have fun with – Taurus

Signs most helpful in spiritual matters – Virgo, Sagittarius

Best day of the week – Saturday

Understanding the Capricorn Personality

The virtues of Capricorns are such that there will always be people for and against them. Many admire them, many dislike them. Why? It seems to be because of Capricorn's power urges. A well-developed Capricorn has his or her eyes set on the heights of power, prestige and authority. In the Sign of Capricorn ambition is not a fatal flaw but rather the highest virtue.

Capricorns are not frightened by the resentment their authority may sometimes cause. In Capricorn's cool, calculated, organized mind all the dangers are already factored into the equation – the unpopularity, the animosity, the misunderstandings, even the outright slander – and a plan is always in place for dealing with these things in the most efficient way. To the Capricorn, situations that would terrify an ordinary mind are merely problems to be managed, bumps on the road to ever-growing power, effectiveness and prestige.

Some people attribute pessimism to the Capricorn Sign, but this is a bit deceptive. It is true that Capricorns like to take into account the negative side of things. It is also true that they love to imagine the worst possible scenario in every undertaking. Other people might find such analyses depressing, but Capricorns only do these things so that they can formulate a way out – an escape route or 'golden parachute'.

Capricorns will argue with success. They will show you that you are not doing as well as you think you are. Capricorns do this to themselves as well as to others. They do not mean to discourage you but rather to root out any impediments to your greater success. A Capricorn boss or supervisor feels that no matter how good the performance there is always room for improvement. This explains why Capricorn supervisors are difficult to handle and even infuriating at times. Their actions are, however, quite often effective – they can get their subordinates to improve and become better at their jobs.

Capricorn is a born manager and administrator. Leo is better at being king or queen, but Capricorn is better at being prime minister – the person who administrates the monarchy, government or corporation, the person actually wielding power.

Capricorn is interested in the virtues that last, in the things that will stand the test of time and trials of circumstance. Temporary fads and fashions mean little to a Capricorn – except as things to be used for profit or power. Capricorns apply this attitude to business, love, to their thinking and even to their philosophy and religion.

Finance

Capricorns generally attain wealth and they usually earn it. They are willing to work long and hard for what they want. They are quite amenable to forgoing a short-term gain in favour of a long-term benefit. Financially, they come into their own later on in life.

However, if Capricorns are to attain their financial goals they must shed some of their strong conservatism. Perhaps this is the least desirable trait of the Capricorn. They can resist anything new merely because it *is* new and untried. They are afraid of experimentation. Capricorns need to be willing to take a few risks. They should be more eager to market new products or explore different management techniques. Otherwise, progress will leave them behind. If necessary, Capricorns must be ready to change with the times, to discard old methods that don't work in modern conditions.

Very often this experimentation will mean that Capricorns have to break with existing authority. They might even consider changing their present position or starting their own ventures. If so, they should be willing to accept all the risks and just get on with it. Only then will a Capricorn be on the road to highest financial gain.

Career and Public Image

A Capricorn's ambition and quest for power are evident. It is perhaps the most ambitious Sign of the Zodiac – and usually the most successful in a worldly sense. However, there are lessons Capricorns need to learn in order to fulfil their highest aspirations.

Intelligence, hard work, cool efficiency and organization will take them a certain distance but won't carry them to the very top. Capricorns need to cultivate the social graces, to develop a social style along with charm and an ability to get along with people. They need to bring beauty into their lives as well as efficiency and to cultivate the right social contacts. They must learn to wield power and have people love them for it – a very delicate art. They also need to learn how to bring people together in order to fulfil certain objectives. In short, Capricorns require some of the gifts – the social graces – of the Libra to get to the top.

Once they've learned this, Capricorns will be successful in their careers. They are ambitious, hard workers who are not afraid of putting in the required time and effort. Capricorns take their time in getting the job done – in order to do it well – and they like, slowly but surely, moving up the corporate ladder. Being so driven by success, Capricorns are generally liked by their bosses, who respect and trust them.

Love and Relationships

Like Scorpio and Pisces, Capricorn is a difficult Sign to get to know. They are deep, introverted and like to keep their own counsel. Capricorns don't like to reveal their innermost thoughts. If you are in love with a Capricorn be patient and take your time. Little by little you will get to understand him or her.

Capricorns have a deep romantic nature, but they don't show it straight away. They are cool, matter of fact and not especially emotional. They will often show their love in practical ways.

It takes time for a Capricorn – male or female – to fall in love. They are not the love-at-first-sight kind. If a Capricorn is involved with a Leo or Aries, these Fire types will be totally mystified – to them the Capricorn will seem cold, unfeeling, unaffectionate and unspontaneous. Of course none of this is true, it's just that Capricorn likes to take things slow. They like to be sure of their ground before making any demonstrations of love or commitment.

Even in love affairs Capricorns are deliberate. They need more time to make decisions than is true of the other Signs of the Zodiac, but given this time they get just as passionate. Capricorns like a relationship to be structured, committed, well regulated, well defined, predictable and even routine. They prefer partners who are nurturers and they in turn like to nurture their partners. This is their basic psychology. Whether such a relationship is good for them is another issue altogether. Capricorns have enough routine in their lives as it is. They might be better off in relationships that are a bit more stimulating, changeable and fluctuating.

Home and Domestic Life

The home of a Capricorn – as with a Virgo – is going to be neat, orderly and well organized. Capricorns tend to manage their families in the same way they manage their businesses. Capricorns are often so career-driven that they find little time for the home and family. Capricorns should try to get more actively involved in their family and domestic life. Capricorns do, however, take their children very seriously and are very proud parents, particularly should their children grow up to become respected members of society.

Horoscope for 1995

Major Trends

1994 was primarily a social and financial year. Many of you realized your fondest hopes and wishes last year. New and important friends came into your life, friends who were powerful and in a position to help you. It was a year in which you needed to juggle your financial interests with your social interests. By now you have succeeded in doing this and you're on to other things. 1995 will be a year of spiritualism and intellect. Money, of course, continues to be important, but your focus has definitely shifted. Jupiter, your Lord of Wisdom, stays for an unusually long time in your 12th House of Wisdom, and Pluto is poised to make a long-term shift into that House at the end of the year. 1995, therefore, becomes a year of relative seclusion, a year in which you prefer being the 'power behind the throne' than actually on the throne, in which you undertake charitable and philanthropic activities and do good deeds for their own sake. This is a year of preparation for a new cycle that will begin in 1996, a new cycle of success and expansion.

Your spirit is calling you to get closer to it. It has many gifts to bestow on you and is already showering you with them. However, you need to be able to understand these gifts and especially to appreciate the value of what is being given. Consultations with astrologers, priests, ministers or spiritually-orientated psychics will help you to understand the specifics of your dreams and intuitions. Deeper powers are being awakened in you this year – and for the long term – and these need to be incorporated and digested properly.

Health

Your health is very much improved over 1994. Seldom have you felt this good, so full of life and vitality. The changes that you are making to your physical image are no longer causing physical upheavals but are pleasant and harmonious. You are still somewhat experimental with your body and physical energy. You continue to test your limits, but with the planetary aspects so favourable you get pleasant surprises. You can do more than you thought you could – you can swim further, run faster and do more press-ups than you previously believed possible. Your physical limitations are being shattered.

Your 6th House of Health is not prominent this year. This means that you are not overly concerned about health issues. You are much more concerned about your body from a cosmetic perspective – from the viewpoint of looking your best – rather than from a health perspective. The lack of prominence of the 6th House is a positive health signal. With the major long-term planets so kind to you this year, no news is good news.

Your urge to change your physical image continues this year. This has been going on for many years now. You still haven't settled on the 'perfect you' – your Divine Image. You dress in one style for a bit, then shift to another and then another. Though by nature you are conservative and traditional you are probably not dressing that way because you don't want to give that impression. You want to look ultra-modern, ultra-chic. You like to express a little rebellion in the way you dress, making personal – perhaps even political – statements through fashion. Your Horoscope presents an image of you equipping yourself with all kinds of modern gadgets: cameras (computer-driven, no doubt) hang from your shoulders, a palm-sized computer/organizer is in your pocket, and lurking in your briefcase is a portable fax machine. You are definitely 'high-tech' chic.

Home and Domestic Life

Though your 4th House of Home and Family is not prominent this year, Capricorn, there is still a lot of moving around and changing of residence. For the past few years you have been almost like a nomad, a wanderer from one home to another. You can't seem to get settled. Every time you think of a 'more perfect you', you see yourself in another environment. This can be quite disconcerting. Your friends have a hard time keeping track of you and you are making quite a mess of their address books! All this chopping and changing is coming from Uranus and Neptune moving through your 1st Solar House of the Body and Personal Image. Those of you born later on in the Sign (birthdays after 5th January) are feeling this more intensely than those born earlier. Those of you with earlier birthdays have already gone through the worst part of the 'itinerant' phase.

All of this moving around has some positive aspects to it. First off, you are forced to get rid of useless possessions in the home. You cannot take everything with you every time you move. You take only the essentials, leaving the rest behind or giving it to charity. You are learning to travel lighter, to let go of things, to be more flexible in your living habits. You are in fact learning some of the deeper secrets of happiness. The result is very liberating. You are not weighed down with excess baggage – physical or psychological. You can enter new experience clean, pure and prepared. You are poised to receive the new and the better.

Your family seems to give you freedom this year. They are not obstructing or hindering you in your goals and plans. You are becoming much closer with your eldest sibling – entering into a happier and more co-operative relationship. Only be careful not to be overbearing or a burden to him or her.

Love and Social Life

Your 7th House of Love and Marriage is not a House of Power this year, so marriage is not high on your list of priorities. Yet you are definitely attracting the opposite sex. The lack of romantic or matrimonial interest is coming from you and not from others.

Curiously – again because of unpredictable Uranus/Neptune in your 1st Solar House – many of you will change your romantic status quo this year. That is, marrieds are likely to become 'unmarried' and singles are likely to become married. These changes don't come as a result of love or lack of love, but more from a blind desire for change – change for its own sake. Those of you involved romantically with a Capricorn should understand this and flow with it. If you can satisfy your Capricorn partner's craving within your existing relationship you can save the relationship. If you resist it, your relationship is likely to explode. Be experimental with your Capricorn lover – offer excitement and change. Explore different ways of expressing romance. Probe the realm of fantasy to enhance your relationship. Use fantasy to create more glamour in your affair.

Many of you Capricorns, especially those born later in the Sign (birthdays after 5th January), are likely to change your names this year. This can happen in a variety of ways – through marriage or divorce, through numerology, through taking on a stage or professional name, or through the intervention of a Guru who gives you your True Spiritual Name.

Lovers will find Capricorn assertive – yet unstable – in financial and intellectual matters. Capricorns are definitely in control of the purse strings this year, make no mistake about it. However, their generosity or lack thereof can change quickly and unexpectedly.

Those of you who are older have seen one of your children divorce and remarry. This has either already happened or is about to happen. An employee or co-worker enters into a happy marriage this year, and you have something to do with it. Someone involved in your health also gets married this year.

The Moon is the Lord of your love life. Your love life, therefore, tends to wax and wane with the Moon. Sometimes it is passionate and exciting, then ebbing and lifeless. These are your normal rhythms. Respect them, for they are cosmic. You can read about these short-term rhythms in the month-by-month forecasts below.

Career and Finance

Money and career are always important to you, Capricorn, but this year they are less important than usual – and definitely less important than last year. Of the two, money-making is more important to you now than career status and prestige. 'Keep the glory and give me the money' is your attitude this year.

Your experimentation with financial matters continues this year, as it has for many years now. You are exploring all avenues, all gimmicks, every known technique to enhance your 'bottom line'. New technology and the latest communication equipment still play a role in your financial success. You are either in one of these industries or use such equipment a great deal in your work.

Those of you who have found their true 'life's work' are being innovative and creative in the way they earn money. Those who have not yet found it are shifting from job to job, investment to investment, in search of the ideal of 'economic freedom and liberation'. Through trial and error it will be found.

In financial matters you are wildly generous or wildly tight – it is difficult for you to keep the middle ground. Earnings come in very strongly or not at all. It's a financial roller-coaster ride all year long. You should save excess monies from the good times to carry you through the leaner periods.

Your physical appearance and image are still vital to your power to earn. You must make that 'right impression', so dress for success.

This year sales, marketing, advertising and communication skills in general are important to your 'bottom line'. Cultivate your ability to communicate. Equip yourself with the best gear. Get the best advertising agency or public relations firm working for you. Advertise, advertise,

advertise. Publicize through all the media – electronic, print, tele-marketing and the post. Sales rather than production is the essential success ingredient this year.

Many of you who are not in the business world will earn money through teaching, lecturing or writing. Those of you who do not yet have a degree can do well in the transportation business – especially locally. Driving people around by car or rail is lucrative.

The media or transportation business might present profitable investment opportunities to those of you looking to invest. And which Capricorn isn't looking for a good investment?

Your partner seems less interested in money than you are. You are more the bread-winner this year than your partner. Financial opportunities come to your partner from your side of the family, especially from 23rd January to 26th May. This is a period in which you can make progress in clearing off debts and obligations. This will also attract investors to your projects. Your family is more likely to invest in your ideas at this time as well.

Though your personal spending proceeds in fits and starts, your charitable spending is steadily generous. You are very much interested in 'making peace with God/the universe' this year, and you see charitable contributions as part of the way to achieve this. You are also giving of yourself – your time, energy and expertise – in volunteer work. Have no fear, what you give will come back to you many times over – as will your motives for giving. This year, unlike 1993, your motives are purer. You will see the practical, financial results this brings in 1996.

Self-improvement

Your spiritual life, ESP and prophetic abilities are going to improve this year with little effort on your part. You are not initiating this expansion. A Higher Power is calling you and you are merely responding. Let it happen.

Your intellectual and communication abilities need improvement this year, through some work and discipline on your part. First of all, learn all you can about the technical details of communication equipment. Hardware and software. Second, check the equipment you have now – let an expert check it for you. You don't want crucial equipment failing when you need it most. Have your car checked as well. Nip any problems in the bud. Take seminars and courses in sales and marketing. There are always new discoveries and techniques being developed in this field. Brush up on your writing skills in your spare time. All of this is going to affect your 'bottom line' in a positive way. Learn good study habits; study how to study. Your ability to absorb information accurately and quickly is going to be a financial life-saver. There are all kinds of books, tapes and courses on these things once you start looking.

Month-by-month Forecasts

January

Best Days Overall: 1st, 2nd, 10th, 11th, 19th, 20th, 21st, 28th, 29th

Most Stressful Days Overall: 7th, 8th, 15th, 16th, 22nd, 23rd

Best Days for Love: 6th, 7th, 8th, 10th, 11th, 15th, 17th, 18th, 19th, 22nd, 23rd, 26th, 27th, 30th, 31st

Best Days for Money: 1st, 2nd, 3rd, 4th, 7th, 8th, 10th, 11th, 17th, 18th, 19th, 26th, 28th, 29th, 30th, 31st

This is a good month to start off what is shaping up to be a good year. With Saturn (your Ruling Planet) moving forward speedily and with 80 to 90 per cent of the planets in the Eastern half of your chart, you are confident and energetic. You make rapid progress towards your goals. You are the creator of circumstances rather than having to adapt to circumstances not of your making. You assert yourself strongly and have great personal influence with others.

The planets are more or less equally balanced between the top and bottom halves of your Solar chart, showing that you are trying to achieve both 'outer' success and personal happiness. You are trying to have it all – a happy home life and a happy career. The movements of the Moon as it goes through the entire Zodiac during the month will tend to tip the balance in favour of either your career or personal happiness. When it moves through the top half of your Horoscope – from the 15th to the 29th – you will be more ambitious in the world. When it moves through the bottom half of your Horoscope – from the 1st to the 15th and from the 29th onwards – you will be more home and family-orientated.

Your health and physical vitality are strong all month, though stronger before the 20th than afterwards. Your physical appearance also shines and, have no fear, others will let you know about it. You radiate vitality, glamour, mystery and a kind of avant-garde modernism.

This is a banner financial month. Money comes from your partner, shareholders and outside investors. Debts are easily paid this month – but are also easily incurred. You are able to make money on your own account and also for others. You have the ability to work equally well with your own money and with other people's money. Your financial judgement is sound, sharp and realistic. You gamble, perhaps, but in a very measured and calculated way.

Your love life is happy and fulfilling. The Moon, your Love Planet, becomes full – reaching its peak of power and influence – in your 7th House of Marriage this month. This is a happy love omen.

Perhaps the happiest events this month come in your

spiritual and charitable activities. Your status in a charitable organization is raised. Charitable functions bring both financial and romantic opportunities.

You hear good news about the health of your partner.

February

Best Days Overall: 6th, 7th, 16th, 17th, 24th, 25th

Most Stressful Days Overall: 3rd, 4th, 5th, 11th, 12th, 18th, 19th

Best Days for Love: 4th, 5th, 6th, 7th, 8th, 9th, 10th, 11th, 12th, 16th, 17th, 18th, 19th, 20th, 24th, 25th

Best Days for Money: 3rd, 5th, 6th, 7th, 13th, 14th, 15th, 16th, 17th, 22nd, 23rd, 24th, 25th, 26th, 27th, 28th

Like last month, the planets are overwhelmingly congregated in the Eastern and bottom halves of your Solar chart. Unlike last month, however, 80 to 90 per cent of the planets will be moving forward. You are full of vim and vigour, in charge of events and your own life and intensely interested in your private concerns. An unambitious Capricorn is a contradiction in terms, yet this month you seem to lack ambition. You want to be personally happy and to build a more profound psychological support system for your future career growth. Many of you probably feel satisfied with your career just the way it is and now want to focus on having some fun and doing what makes you happy. Venus, your Career Planet, will be in your 1st House of the Body and Personal Image almost all month, suggesting that personal pleasure, physical fitness and creating the right image become your 'career' this month.

Right now you are spending the 'invisible capital' of your

current career status rather than building up new capital. Your current status brings you earning opportunities this month. Money comes to you through elders, people in positions of authority, and women. Money comes to you through some government programme as well.

Ever since the end of 1994 you have been interested in communication and the pursuit of intellectual interests. Learning has become a priority for you. This trend is further reinforced this month, especially after the 19th. By all means take advantage of the learning opportunities that will come your way this month.

Until the 19th money comes from investors or from selling investments. The urge now is to become leaner and tougher financially; to reduce costs and get rid of unnecessary possessions and expenses. Few Signs are as good at this as you are, so go ahead.

Your health is basically excellent, but it would be best to reserve judgement on a proposed dietary and/or exercise regime that you're contemplating. Check out all the details. Not every regime is good for everybody. Proceed cautiously and see how you feel.

Your 7th House of Love is not very active this month, so marriage and a social life are not high on your agenda right now. However, you are unusually attractive and glamorous this month – dressing with style and elegance and presenting yourself attractively. There are plenty of romantic opportunities for you. Also, the Cosmos is giving you a lot of social and romantic freedom now. Any lack of interest comes from you and not from others.

March

Best Days Overall: 5th, 6th, 15th, 16th, 24th, 25th

Most Stressful Days Overall: 3rd, 4th, 10th, 11th, 12th, 17th, 18th, 30th, 31st

Best Days for Love: 1st, 2nd, 8th, 9th, 10th, 12th, 17th, 18th, 19th, 20th, 21st, 26th, 28th, 30th, 31st

Best Days for Money: 3rd, 5th, 6th, 13th, 14th, 15th, 16th, 21st, 22nd, 24th, 25th, 26th, 27th, 30th, 31st

The planets are still overwhelmingly clustered in the Eastern and bottom halves of your Solar chart this month. Thus you are still calling the shots, creating your own circumstances and conditions and not taking other people's viewpoints, objections or scepticism too much to heart. You believe in what you're doing and others will just have to adapt themselves to it. Basically you are involved with the things that bring you personal fulfilment now. You are doing what you really want to do – and who can ask for more than that? 'Let the world give or withhold recognition as it pleases, but I'm going to do what makes me happy' – this is your general attitude now. With 80 per cent of the planets moving forward there is no question that this policy is paying off now. Your progress is rapid, probably faster than your cautious nature would have believed possible.

Your paths of greatest fulfilment this month are platonic friendships, group activities, scientific interests and money-making.

Your unusual self-assertiveness – your willingness to be true to yourself – makes you more magnetic and appealing to others right now. There are many positive love signals in the Cosmos this month. Venus is in your own Sign of Capricorn until the 4th, making you glamorous and charming. The Moon, your Love Planet, will wax as it moves through your House of Love on the 10th, 11th and 12th – giving you more social confidence, charm and charisma. There are two New Moons this month – highly unusual – which shows that a current relationship is making more rapid progress than usual. You feel that you have been with this person much longer than you actually have. Psychologically you go through more experiences with your lover or partner than usual. Love begins close to home this month but could end up in some foreign, exotic land. This is probably a romantic holiday with your partner.

Finances are favourable this month as well. Early in the month money comes to you suddenly and unexpectedly as a result of some speculation or creative project. Money is earned pleasurably and harmoniously. Women are gracing and aiding your financial efforts. Money comes through work and through your ability to sell and communicate. Someone involved in the health field becomes either a client or an instrument of increased earnings in some other way. A co-worker presents you with a lucrative proposition.

Your health is excellent all month.

April

Best Days Overall: 2nd, 3rd, 11th, 12th, 13th, 20th, 21st, 29th, 30th

Most Stressful Days Overall: 1st, 7th, 8th, 14th, 15th, 26th, 27th, 28th

Best Days for Love: 7th, 8th, 9th, 10th, 16th, 17th, 18th, 19th, 20th, 26th, 27th, 28th, 29th, 30th

Best Days for Money: 1st, 3rd, 4th, 5th, 9th, 10th, 13th, 14th, 18th, 19th, 22nd, 23rd, 26th, 27th, 28th

The combination of having most of the planets at the bottom half of your Horoscope and the Lunar Eclipse in your 10th House of Career shows that your urges for a happy family life and emotional well-being are forcing long-term changes in your career. The trend towards putting your career in proper perspective has been going on for many months now; this month something gives. The change is provoked by a crisis. Resentments built up over time surface so that they can be dealt with. Your career will have to adapt itself to your emotional needs – and so it changes now.

The Lunar Eclipse of the 15th is important to you for other reasons as well. The eclipsed planet, the Moon, happens to be your Love Planet. Thus much-needed long-term changes in a current relationship or in your social attitudes are coming to pass. Ride through the initial upheaval and see where the pieces fall. Something much better is coming through for you.

Rest and relax more until the 20th. After that your vitality improves considerably. Until the 20th you feel somewhat uncomfortable as people in general – but especially your family – seem to be rushing hither and thither. The pace of life, especially your family life, is too quick for your cautious nature. You resent being forced into actions without thinking them through. Things slow down after the 20th, however, and you feel much more comfortable.

The change in your career corresponds to the change in your financial life. There is much greater financial freedom – both in the way you earn and in the way you spend. You are more in control of things this month. New high-tech possessions come to you this month. After the 20th your urge to have fun conflicts with your money-making urges; you need to balance the two. Don't go too far either way. Try to combine work with fun.

A charitable project you're working on needs more review and study. Don't jump into unwarranted philanthropy just yet – perhaps what is needed to help someone unfortunate is different than what you think.

May

Best Days Overall: 9th, 10th, 17th, 18th, 26th, 27th, 28th

Most Stressful Days Overall: 4th, 5th, 11th, 12th, 24th, 25th, 31st

Best Days for Love: 4th, 5th, 6th, 7th, 8th, 9th, 10th, 15th, 16th, 17th, 18th, 26th, 27th, 28th, 29th, 30th, 31st

Best Days for Money: 1st, 2nd, 6th, 7th, 8th, 11th, 12th, 15th, 16th, 19th, 20th, 24th, 25th, 29th

The planets are evenly dispersed in the Eastern and Western parts of your Horoscope, showing – like last month – your healthy perspective on your own personal desires and those of others. You are not riding roughshod over others in pursuit of your personal whims, but neither are you kowtowing to them or sublimating your own interests. You attain your ends by a combination of personal creativity and social skill.

With most of the planets still very much below the horizon you are uncharacteristically unambitious. Your focus on family values and domestic harmony boosts your career indirectly, however – especially early in the month. Your family supports your career right now and a pay rise or promotion comes through them.

Your paths of greatest happiness and fulfilment are platonic friendships, group activities, spiritual and philanthropic activities (though less so this month than in previous months), family and domestic interests, children and creativity.

With the Sun in your 5th Solar House of Fun, Entertainment, Creativity, Speculations and Love Affairs until the 21st you are very much into a fun period now. Fun, games, children, personal creativity and entertainments of all sorts are highlighted. Capricorns tend to get too serious; a brief period of lighthearted fun is very much in the cosmic plan. There is plenty of time for work after the 21st.

Your 7th House of Love and Marriage is not very active this month, showing that you have less interest in romance than usual. However, you have got plenty of social freedom now. Singles are more interested in love affairs than in serious committed relationships – but this is only short term. Your Love Planet, the Moon, will visit your House of Marriage twice this month – this is a bit unusual – and will be waxing both times. This shows some happy – but short-term – romantic experiences.

Earnings are stronger before the 21st than afterwards. Recent radical changes in the way you make money are delayed and need further thought. Get-rich-quick schemes – though very alluring – are neither quick nor profit-making. A co-worker or religious leader provides a financial opportunity early in the month. Your partner is unexpectedly generous around the 21st. Rethink financial goals after the 5th and avoid making major purchases, investments or long-term financial commitments then. Do your homework and make your moves when Uranus goes forward in a few months' time.

June

Best Days Overall: 5th, 6th, 14th, 15th, 22nd, 23rd, 24th

Most Stressful Days Overall: 1st, 2nd, 7th, 8th, 9th, 20th, 21st

Best Days for Love: 1st, 2nd, 5th, 6th, 7th, 8th, 9th, 16th, 17th, 25th, 26th, 27th, 28th, 29th

Best Days for Money: 3rd, 4th, 6th, 7th, 12th, 13th, 15th, 16th, 17th, 20th, 21st, 24th, 30th

You have an unusual month coming up. There is a combination of conflict, change, imperatives to action and a sense of stymied action and stalemate. Most zodiacal temperaments would have a problem with this, but you are well-equipped to handle it. Stalemate brings out your managerial and administrative genius. Thus you will be at your best this month and people will be relying on you and your judgement.

There is no need to instruct a Capricorn about the virtues of patience and taking the long-term view. Capricorns know all about the 'art of the possible' and the attainment of goals by degrees. You will apply your wisdom in these matters instinctively.

The Grand Square aspect forces you to build a practical consensus between your personal work goals – those you get paid for – and your charitable works – any volunteer work you do. Consensus is also needed to bridge the gap between your personal health interests and those of your partner; between your personal work goals and those of your partner; between your urges for long-term intellectual growth and your short-term intellectual interests; between the thinking of the everyday world and your religious philosophy; and between your own inclinations and the needs of your family. All of these issues conflict with each other and pull you in diverse directions. Most other people will also be experiencing similar conflicts and will be looking to you to see how you deal with yours. You are a teacher, an example to others right now – not by words but by deeds.

Fifty per cent of the planets are also retrograde (travelling backwards) for most of the month. Thus superficial, knee-jerk reactions get delayed or otherwise stymied. This is one of those impossible situations which the Celestial Powers love to throw at us every now and then to foster our growth. As we work through these 'impossible' situations we find that they are not as hopeless as we'd thought.

Your Money Planet (Uranus) is still retrograde all month but receives reasonably favourable aspects. Your earnings are average and you should maintain a healthy scepticism regarding major new purchases and investments. Investigate them even more thoroughly than you would usually do.

Until the 22nd you seem most focused on your work and achieving work-related goals. The pace at work has speeded up, but not in a clear, steady way. It speeds up chaotically, frenziedly, causing a lot of confusion among your co-workers. After the 22nd the focus turns to love and romance. The New Moon of the 27th occurs in your 7th House of Love and is going to clarify your next romantic steps.

Rest and relax more all month.

July

Best Days Overall: 2nd, 3rd, 4th, 11th, 12th, 20th, 21st, 30th, 31st

Most Stressful Days Overall: 5th, 6th, 17th, 18th, 25th, 26th

Best Days for Love: 7th, 8th, 15th, 16th, 25th, 26th, 27th, 28th

Best Days for Money: 1st, 3rd, 4th, 9th, 10th, 11th, 12th, 13th, 14th, 17th, 18th, 21st, 27th, 28th

Fifty per cent of the planets continue to be retrograde this month, including Saturn, your Personal Ruler. Patience, caution and taking the long-term view are vital for your success now. This is not the time for self-assertion and power struggles, but for allowing things to happen as they will.

The fact that the planets are clustered in the Western half of your chart further reinforces this. You need the good graces of others to get ahead, you can't do it on your own – temporarily, anyway.

The planets are shifting with ever-increasing intensity above the horizon of your chart, making you more ambitious than even you are used to. Yet this is deceptive, for family interests are still close to your heart. Mars (Lord of your Home and Domestic Life) continues to be the most elevated planet in the Horoscope. Thus your ambitions centre round your family as a whole and you are more ambitious for family members than you are for yourself. Many of you are reaching for greater corporate power because you want to help other people's families. You like the idea that you are 'the source of supply' for many other families as well as your own. Your family as a whole does attain greater social status and recognition come the 22nd and after.

Rest and relax more until the 23rd. A current health problem is rapidly disappearing. You have the confidence you need to eliminate it. Your health is enhanced by keeping to work goals, harmony at the workplace and maintaining good feelings with your current lover and with friends.

Your paths of greatest fulfilment this month are charitable activities, spiritual studies, friends, group activities, dietary regimes and your love life.

There seems little you can do about a current financial entanglement except wait and let the Cosmos work it out. All your financial indicators are retrograde now. This implies that it would not be wise to make major purchases or large investments at this time – but if you do, make sure you read the fine print before signing anything. With your personal earning power at a bit of an impasse you may as well socialize and enjoy yourself. Invest in your current relationship – not necessarily in a financial way – but with your time and attention. Invest in your friends in the same way. Network more. Build up your social connections. Money comes to you through these activities.

Your partner prospers and becomes more generous with you after the 23rd. Your love life in general is happy and active. Romantic opportunities are abundant; lovers are nurturing and sentimental.

August

Best Days Overall: 7th, 8th, 16th, 17th, 26th, 27th

Most Stressful Days Overall: 1st, 2nd, 14th, 15th, 21st, 22nd, 28th, 29th

Best Days for Love: 5th, 6th, 14th, 15th, 21st, 22nd, 26th, 27th

Best Days for Money: 5th, 6th, 7th, 8th, 9th, 10th, 14th, 15th, 16th, 17th, 26th

The planets are moving inexorably Eastward in your Solar chart, giving you ever greater independence, mastery and dominion over your life. You are calling the shots now; others will have to adapt to you. Take note, however, that your Ruler, Saturn, is still retrograde, showing that you are still not sure of the kind of conditions and circumstances that you want to create. You have the power, but more reflection is needed to decide how it should be used.

The planets are also clustered above the horizon of your chart, making you ambitious and worldly. Yet, like last month, you are most definitely not ignoring your family or your emotional happiness. Your Family Planet, Mars, is still the most elevated planet of the Horoscope. Your ambitions centre round your family and home. Many of you are thinking that 'I owe it to my family to become prominent and well respected.' (Those looking to motivate Capricorns now might do well to use some of this logic with them.) Many are thinking 'If I'm lifted up in the world my family will also be lifted up.' Others of you are ambitious for your family as a whole and not so much for yourself. Still others want to help not only your own family but other people's families as well. You get a particular joy out of the fact that your efforts in the world are helping others to feed and provide for their families, and this is true whether you are a boss with employees or a worker.

Your paths of greatest fulfilment now are charities, spiritual studies, making peace with your divinity, cost-cutting, friendships, your career, and eliminating the useless and undesirable from your life.

Though your health is excellent all month you can enhance it further with a pure diet, detoxification regimes, prayer and meditation and maintaining harmony with your elders.

Your love/social life is not a big priority this month. You are not being pushed in any particular direction and the Cosmos is neither helping nor obstructing your social progress. You have the freedom to make of your social life what you want – although you can't really be bothered about it right now.

Your financial life still seems rather stalemated and earnings are lacklustre. Your financial goals need to be clarified. Deals, investments and perhaps payments due to you are delayed and you must be patient. Spend cautiously now.

September

Best Days Overall: 4th, 5th, 12th, 13th, 14th, 22nd, 23rd

Most Stressful Days Overall: 10th, 11th, 17th, 18th, 19th, 24th, 25th

Best Days for Love: 4th, 5th, 12th, 13th, 14th, 17th, 18th, 19th, 23rd, 24th, 25th

Best Days for Money: 2nd, 4th, 5th, 6th, 7th, 10th, 11th, 13th, 14th, 20th, 21st, 22nd, 23rd, 29th, 30th

The delays and cautiousness in your personal life of late turn out to have been blessings in disguise this month. As the planets move increasingly Eastward you have ever greater power to create things as you'd like them to be. You can go it alone now if need be. This power brings responsibility – and you've had plenty of opportunity to be sure of what you really want and to clarify your true interests. As the months progress you become increasingly assertive and in control of things. A part of you knows that you will have to live with your creations, hence your caution.

The planets are also mostly above the horizon of your chart this month. This fosters ambition in the world. You crave outer success rather than inner success. Outer security takes priority over emotional security. Other people's families take priority over your own. Too much preoccupation with your personal home and domestic situation leads to stagnation.

Your paths of greatest happiness this month are foreign travel, religious studies, your career and search for status, and charitable works.

Personal finances are still rather stalemated this month but your partner's income is on the rise. Maintain your caution regarding all investments and financial deals. You are in one of the best periods of your year in terms of your career, however. Thus your public/professional status is increased, regardless of what your personal earnings might be. Money and status often bear no relationship to each other.

Love is not a big priority this month and you have lots of freedom to shape it as you will. The Moon, your Love Planet, wanes as it moves through your 7th House of Love – a further indication of your lack of social enthusiasm. Ambitions and career take priority over your love life.

Your health is excellent until the 23rd, but after then rest and relax more. Your health is enhanced through harmony with elders and superiors and by career fulfilment.

October

Best Days Overall: 1st, 2nd, 10th, 11th, 20th, 21st, 28th, 29th

Most Stressful Days Overall: 7th, 8th, 9th, 15th, 16th, 22nd, 23rd

Best Days for Love: 3rd, 4th, 12th, 13th, 15th, 16th, 23rd, 24th, 25th

Best Days for Money: 2nd, 3rd, 4th, 7th, 8th, 9th, 10th, 11th, 17th, 18th, 21st, 26th, 27th, 29th, 30th, 31st

Ninety to 100 per cent of the planets are now in the Eastern sector of your chart; after the 14th 90 per cent of the planets are moving forward. These are unusually high percentages. Normally these planetary signals would foster unusual self-assertiveness, confidence, self-esteem and personal power directed towards personal ends. You can have things your way right now. Yet, though the universe rockets forward, you remain cautious. Is it merely innate Capricorn conservatism? Partly. The real cause, however, is that Saturn, your Ruling Planet, is the only planet that still goes retrograde after the 14th. This creates a contradiction – an ambivalence – in the nature of things. You are moving forward, but cautiously, measuring every step. You are still clarifying to yourself what your real and true desires are.

Sixty to 70 per cent of the planets are above the horizon of your chart, fostering your ambitions and the need for outer success. Though you are not so concerned about what your lover or other people you know think of you, you are quite concerned about your public image, about what superiors and the general public think of you. This, after all, affects your place in society. This is a month of work on your public image.

Your paths of greatest fulfilment are your career, friendships, group activities, the study of science and technology, astrology and charitable activities.

Career activities, self-promotion and dealings with elders and superiors continue to go well this month. When Mercury moves forward after the 14th these activities become even more favourable. Pay rises and promotions are likely now. New responsibilities come to you. Because you have fostered other people's careers your own is now boosted and supported. You enjoy great public popularity until the 11th.

Happily the stalemate in your financial life is over. Stalled deals, payments due to you and the acquisition of luxury possessions all proceed ahead. Your focus on career does not stop you from making sacrifices for your family and their needs. You know that you will have to give up small things to achieve long-term emotional harmony and security.

Rest and relax more until the 24th. After then your vitality returns to normal levels. Your health can be enhanced through harmony with elders, parents and those involved in your career.

November

Best Days Overall: 6th, 7th, 16th, 17th, 25th

Most Stressful Days Overall: 4th, 5th, 11th, 12th, 18th, 19th

Best Days for Love: 1st, 2nd, 3rd, 4th, 11th, 12th, 14th, 15th, 21st, 22nd, 23rd, 24th

Best Days for Money: 4th, 5th, 7th, 14th, 15th, 17th, 23rd, 25th, 27th, 28th

Ninety to 100 per cent of the planets are in the Eastern sector of your chart, making you increasingly self-reliant, independent and influential. You are self-orientated rather than 'other'-orientated. Nor has this trend reached its peak. You can have things your way if you choose. You can create the conditions and circumstances that you desire, custom-designed to your personal specifications. Others will adapt to you.

The planets are still very much above the horizon of your chart, spurring your personal ambitions and your view of the future. Always a person who is conscious of his or her duty to life, this month you are even more so. Your duty to the world comes before your duty to your family.

Paths of greatest fulfilment this month are your career, friendships, group activities, creativity within a group, charitable endeavours, ministering to others and cleansing the mind of guilt and error.

With 100 per cent of the planets moving forward you are in a period of action and achievement. Your level of activity is high.

Your health is good all month and can be enhanced even further by maintaining harmony with elders and friends, by fulfilling your duty to the world and by meditation and prayer.

Social relationships and group activities are very pleasant until the 23rd, but then you feel more altruistic and want to engage in charitable and more 'meaningful' activities. If you belong to a spiritual or charitable organization your status becomes elevated now. You give of yourself both financially and personally. Your dream life becomes super-activated after the 23rd. Psychic experiences are commonplace. You are forced by these things to look deeper into life and to discern the meaning of these messages. Some are cleansings and some are personal messages. They hold the key to certain family relationships, creative projects, the destiny of children and life's-work issues. Study them well.

The 7th and 2nd Houses of Love and Money respectively are not active this month, showing that these are not priorities for you. Earnings are stable and you have a free hand in how you spend and invest. You have the freedom to shape both of these areas of your life into what you will.

December

Best Days Overall: 3rd, 4th, 13th, 14th, 22nd, 23rd, 31st

Most Stressful Days Overall: 1st, 2nd, 8th, 9th, 16th, 17th, 28th, 29th

Best Days for Love: 1st, 2nd, 3rd, 4th, 8th, 9th, 11th, 12th, 13th, 14th, 20th, 21st, 24th, 30th, 31st

Best Days for Money: 1st, 2nd, 4th, 11th, 12th, 14th, 20th, 21st, 23rd, 24th, 25th, 28th, 29th, 31st

With 90 to 100 per cent of the planets in the Eastern sector of your chart and with 50 per cent of them in your own Sign of Capricorn you are totally involved with your own self now. You have unusual independence, self-reliance, assertiveness and personal influence this month. You have little tolerance of fools and bumblers and want things done in a hurry. With all the planets moving forward this month you will make unusual progress towards your goals.

With all this power in your own Sign you 'don't know your own strength' right now. Your short fuse (as far as patience is concerned) has been mentioned, but there is also an aggressiveness – a martial quality – that makes you combative even when you don't want to be. You simply plough through all obstacles as if they were nothing. While this attitude is wonderful for achievement in the wide world, it can wreak havoc on relationships. True, you don't care what other people think right now and are not in need of their good opinion, but you don't need to alienate or offend them either.

You will not walk away from a fight this month. In truth, you will prevail in any power struggle – as long as it's not with another Capricorn! You excel in sports, exercise programmes and militaristic activities. Those of you serving in the military should experience a rise in status and greater recognition.

With most of the planets now at the bottom half of your chart your ambitions in the world are abating and you become more concerned with your family relationships. Your highest aspiration now is personal pleasure and self-indulgence. Work around the home goes well. Start construction projects after the 22nd.

With all this toughness, however, there is still a soft side to your nature. Your concern for the poor, underprivileged and needy is genuine and you continue to be active in charity work. Your dream life continues to be active until the 22nd. The New Moon of the 21st will clarify the correct interpretations of these dreams – often in strange and unexpected ways. Be on the look-out for the cosmic signals.

Your health is excellent all month. The greatest danger to your health is hyperactivity – doing more than you can physically handle.'

Those involved with a Capricorn romantically will have to be very patient this month. Avoid conflicts and confrontations, and give in on the little things. Your Capricorn is not purposely or maliciously riding roughshod over you – he or she just isn't aware of doing so at all.

Aquarius

♒

THE WATER-BEARER

Birthdays from
20th January
to 18th February

Personality Profile

AQUARIUS AT A GLANCE

Element – Air

Ruling planet – Uranus
Career planet – Pluto
Health planet – Moon
Love planet – Venus
Money planet – Neptune
Planet of home and family – Venus

Colours – electric blue, grey, ultramarine blue

Colours that promote love, romance and social harmony – gold, orange

Colour that promotes earning power – aqua

Gems – black pearl, obsidian, opal, sapphire

Metal – lead

Scents – azalea, gardenia

Quality – fixed (= stability)

Qualities most needed for balance – warmth, feeling and emotion

Strongest virtues – great intellectual power, the ability to communicate and to form and understand abstract concepts, love for the new and the avant-garde

Deepest needs – to know and to bring in the new

Characteristics to avoid – coldness, rebelliousness for its own sake, fixed ideas

Signs of greatest overall compatibility – Gemini, Libra

Signs of greatest overall incompatibility – Taurus, Leo, Scorpio

Sign most helpful to career – Scorpio

Sign most helpful for emotional support – Taurus

Sign most helpful financially – Pisces

Sign best for marriage and/or partnerships – Leo

Sign most helpful for creative projects – Gemini

Best Sign to have fun with – Gemini

Signs most helpful in spiritual matters – Libra, Capricorn

Best day of the week – Saturday

Understanding the Aquarius Personality

In the Aquarius-born, the intellectual faculties are perhaps the most highly developed of any Sign in the Zodiac. Aquarians are clear, scientific thinkers. They have the ability to think abstractly and to formulate laws, theories and clear concepts from masses of observed facts. Geminis might be very good at gathering information, but Aquarians take this a step further, excelling at interpreting the information gathered.

Practical people – men and women of the world – mistakenly consider abstract thinking as impractical. It is true that the realm of abstract thought takes us out of the physical world, but the discoveries made in this realm generally end up having tremendous practical consequences. All real scientific inventions and breakthroughs come from this abstract realm.

Aquarians, more so than most, are ideally suited to explore these abstract dimensions. Those who have explored these regions know that there is little feeling or emotion there. In fact, emotions are a hindrance to functioning in these dimensions; thus Aquarians seem – at times – cold and emotionless to others. It's not that Aquarians haven't got feelings and deep emotions, it's just that too much feeling clouds their ability to think and invent. The concept of 'too much feeling' cannot be tolerated or even understood by some of the other Signs. Nevertheless, this Aquarian objectivity is ideal for science, communication and friendship.

Aquarians are very friendly people, but they don't make a big show about it. They do the right thing by their friends, even if sometimes they do it without passion or excitement.

Aquarians have a deep passion for clear thinking. Second in importance, but related, is their passion for breaking with the establishment and traditional authority. Aquarians delight in this, because for them rebellion is like a great game or challenge. Very often they will rebel strictly for the fun of rebelling, regardless of whether the authority they defy is right or wrong. Right or wrong has little to do with the rebellious actions of an Aquarian because to a true Aquarian authority and power must be challenged as a matter of principle.

Where Capricorn or Taurus will err on the side of tradition and the status quo, an Aquarian will err on the side of the new. Without this virtue it is doubtful whether any progress would be made in the world. The conservative-minded would obstruct progress. Originality and invention imply an ability to break barriers; every new discovery represents the toppling of an impediment to thought. Aquarians are very interested in breaking barriers and making walls tumble – scientifically, socially and politically. Other Zodiac Signs, such as Capricorn, also have scientific talents. But Aquarians are particularly excellent in the social sciences and humanities.

Finance

In financial matters Aquarians tend to be idealistic and humanitarian – to the point of self-sacrifice. They are usually generous contributors to social and political causes. When they contribute it differs from when a Capricorn or Taurus contributes. A Capricorn or Taurus may expect some favour or return for their gift; an Aquarian contributes selflessly.

Aquarians tend to be as cool and rational about money as they are about most things in life. Money is something they need and they set about scientifically to acquire it. No need for fuss; they get on with it in the most rational and scientific ways available.

Money to the Aquarian is especially nice for what it can do, not for the status it may bring (as is the case for other Signs). Aquarians are neither big spenders nor penny-pinchers and use their finances in practical ways, for example to facilitate progress for themselves, their families or even strangers.

However, if Aquarians want to reach their fullest financial potential they will have to explore their intuitive nature. If they follow only their financial theories – or what they believe to be theoretically correct – they may suffer some losses and disappointments. Instead, Aquarians should call on their intuition – which knows without thinking. For Aquarians, intuition is the short-cut to financial success.

Career and Public Image

Aquarians like to be perceived not only as the breakers of barriers but also as the transformers of society and the world. They long to be seen in this light and to play this role. They also look up to and respect other people in this position and even expect their superiors to act this way.

Aquarians prefer jobs that have a bit of idealism attached to them – careers with a philosophical basis. Aquarians need to be creative at work, to have access to new techniques and methods. They like to keep busy and enjoy getting down to business straight away, without wasting any time. They are often the quickest workers and usually have suggestions for improvements that will benefit their employers. Aquarians are also very helpful with their co-workers and welcome responsibility, preferring this to having to take orders from others.

If Aquarians want to reach their highest career goals they have to develop more emotional sensitivity, depth of feeling and passion. They need to learn to narrow their focus on the essentials and concentrate more on their job. Aquarians need 'a fire in the belly' – a consuming passion and desire – in order to rise to the very top. Once this passion exists they will succeed easily in whatever they attempt.

Love and Relationships

Aquarians are good at friendships, but a bit weak when it comes to love. Of course they fall in love, but their lovers always get the impression that they are more best friends than paramours.

Like the Capricorn they are cool customers. They are not prone to displays of passion nor to outward demonstrations of their affections. In fact, they feel uncomfortable when their mate hugs and touches them too much. This doesn't mean that they don't love their partners. They do, only they show it in other ways. Curiously enough, in relationships they tend to attract the very things that they feel uncomfortable with. They seem to attract hot, passionate, romantic, demonstrative people. Perhaps they know instinctively that these people have qualities they lack and so seek them out. In any event, these relationships do seem to work, Aquarius' coolness calming the more passionate partner while the fires of passion warm the cold-blooded Aquarius.

The qualities Aquarians need to develop in their love life are warmth, generosity, passion and fun. Aquarians love relationships of the mind. Here they excel. If the intellectual factor is missing in a relationship an Aquarian will soon become bored or feel unfulfilled.

Home and Domestic Life

In family and domestic matters Aquarians can have a tendency to be too nonconformist, changeable and unstable. They are as willing to break the barriers of family constraints as they are those of other areas of life.

Even so, Aquarians are very sociable people. They like to have a nice home where they can entertain family and friends. Their house is usually decorated modernly and full of state-of-the-art appliances and gadgets – an environment Aquarians find absolutely necessary.

If their home life is to be healthy and fulfilling Aquarians need to inject it with a quality of stability – yes, even some conservatism. They need at least one area of life to be enduring and steady; this area is usually their home and family life.

Venus, the planet of love, rules the Aquarian's 4th Solar House of Home and Family as well, which means that when it comes to the family and child-rearing, theories, cool thinking and intellect are not always enough. Aquarians need to bring love into the equation in order to have a great domestic life.

Horoscope for 1995

Major Trends

For many years now you've been making radical and important changes to your image and self-concept. This has been a long, drawn-out process, filled with many experiments, mistakes and successes. In 1993 and 1994 your self-concept was put through a severe trial by Saturn, that powerful but eminently just Tester. Your ego and your body were put under intense pressure, just as Nature puts pressure on a lump of coal in order to make it a diamond. Only those elements that could withstand the pressure survived. The rest were cast aside.

This year Saturn has moved away from your Sign, leaving you more realistic about and more secure with who you are. You know your limits, it's true, but you also know your infinite potential. Saturn has also taught you that although limitation is real – at any given time – it is not permanent, and every day brings new opportunities to expand and extend our limits. This applies especially to the realms of sport, exercise and career goals.

In 1994 you suppressed much of your personal interests in order to focus on your career. And you succeeded. This year the ambitiousness eases off and you become a little kinder to yourself. In 1995 you reap some of the rewards of career success and increased status. You fulfil some of your fondest wishes and make friends who are interested in helping you make your dreams come true. You could not have met these people had you not focused on your professional success in 1994. Your increased status has catapulted you into 'new company' – a new social sphere.

Three areas dominate your interest in 1995 – friendships, spirituality and earning power. Each will be fulfilling in its own way.

Health

One of the first improvements you are experiencing, now that Saturn has at long last moved away from you, is in your health. Your vitality is much stronger than it has been because you are carrying less burdens. It is not that you are stronger this year than last year, but you feel stronger because you are carrying less weight, both physically and psychologically.

Moreover, Pluto, the lone long-term planet that has been plaguing you, is getting ready to move into harmonious aspect to you by the end of the year. Therefore, the long-term health forecast is super. In 1993 and 1994 you probably have lost a lot of weight – this is typical of a Saturn transit. The challenge in 1995 is to keep those pounds off.

Keep in mind, though, that just like when in a difficult year there are periods in which your health is 'less difficult', so too in a positive health year there are periods in which your vitality is not as great as other times. You should take note of these periods and try to rest and relax more – from 20th April to 21st May, 23rd July to 23rd August and 23rd October to 22nd November.

The fact that your 6th House of Health is not prominent this year should be considered further good news. You are so healthy and vital that you are just not concerned about it. You are more concerned with healing others than you are with your own personal health.

The health of your partner is more delicate. His or her physical vitality goes radically up and down. Your partner is experimenting with all kinds of diets and health regimes, pursuing every health fad going. This is not to be ridiculed as it is a stage in the process of attaining truly good health. Good health will come to your partner through the new, the unconventional and the untried.

The Moon is the Lord of your 6th House of Health. Pay special attention to its phases, movements and positions when dieting or pursuing a health regime – or when healing others. Your personal healing power will always be stronger on the waxing Moon than on the waning Moon. Dieting and all purification regimes will also be more successful on the waning Moon, while exercise regimes will proceed better on the waxing Moon. To follow these lunar phases more closely, consult the month-by-month forecasts below.

Home and Domestic Life

Your 4th House of Home and Family is not a House of Power this year, Aquarius. You have freedom this year to make of your home and family relationships what you will. Your family grants you freedom and latitude in the pursuit of your true goals and interests. Yes, you have all the freedom you want, but what you lack is interest.

A long-standing problem with a parent is being resolved this year. This parent will either change or be out of your life. The same is true of your partner's parent. If you have children, it is your partner who seems to carry the burden of looking after them this year – and, by the way, he or she enjoys doing so.

This year you are much more interested in going out with your friends, attending organizational meetings and political rallies and the like, than being at home with your family.

You will tend to be most preoccupied with your family and domestic projects from 3rd to 28th March, 20th April to 11th June, and 22nd December to the end of the year.

Your financial advisor, accountant or attorney will move to larger quarters this year, as does someone involved in your partner's finances.

Love and Social Life

Your 7th House of Love and Marriage is not prominent this year, Aquarius, but your 11th House of Friends is. This shows that you are more interested in friendship than in romance. You shine as a friend this year. The ideals of friendship, which are always fascinating to you, are even more fascinating this year. You attain your childhood dream of becoming the perfect friend, and the friends you make are your vision of perfection.

The lack of interest in romance can come from two reasons. One, you are already in a stable relationship and are basically pleased with it. You feel free to develop your friendships. Two, you are single and marriage is just not on your mind this year. The lack of prominence of the 7th House will tend to foster the status quo. Marrieds will tend to stay married and singles will tend to stay single.

Naturally, the short-term movements of the planets will make you more or less romantic at different times during the year. There are always passionate periods even in the most lacklustre year. This year these are 21st May to 21st June and 23rd July to 23rd August. Your partner will tend to be most amorous from 20th January to 18th February and 23rd October to 22nd November. However, every month brings periods of increased romantic ardour. You can find out about these short-term trends in the month-by-month forecasts below.

One word of warning: Be careful that you don't overdo your lack of romantic interest – especially if you are in a relationship. Your partner has ample romantic opportunities this year. Don't lead him or her into temptation. Those romantically involved with Aquarians should be patient. Their lack of interest is not a rejection of you and should not be interpreted in this way. You are still loved. You just need to make special efforts to rekindle the mood and spirit of romance.

A parent or authority figure seems to have recently remarried or to have become involved in a new relationship.

This new relationship seems happy and passionate indeed. The eldest child and the second sibling in your family also find romance this year and are very happy with it.

Career and Finance

Both your 2nd House of Money and your 10th House of Career are prominent this year, Aquarius. Your interest in career status is, however, waning. By the end of the year you are more interested in the fruits of career success – the money and the social opportunities it brings – than in the success itself.

The 2nd House of Money, though prominent for many years, takes on a different kind of prominence now that Saturn has moved in for the long term. Whereas for years you have been experimenting and innovating in money matters, you must now look to 'tradition' to carry you through. Innovation and invention are wonderful qualities. They are important and we all need them. But don't ignore the financial techniques that have withstood the tests of time. These have weathered all kinds of conditions whereas your financial experiments are basically unproven.

If you feel that you have discovered a new financial technique, a new idea for a business or a new invention, this is the year that it will undergo trials to see whether it is really worth it. If it passes the test and the pressures put on it, you really have something wonderful. Welcome the trials and the opposition, as they are the only way of finding out if your new ideas are worth pursuing.

For many years now you have been taking a creative approach to business and perhaps were weak on the management side. You've kept looking to ever-greater earnings, and in the process allowed a lot of waste to go unchecked. This is the year in which you will have to 'stop the rot'.

You need to manage existing resources better. Become a more discerning shopper. Cut waste. Learn how to create budgets and live by them. Get some control over your spending. Save money from prosperous periods to tide you over the lean ones. Beware of 'white collar' irregularities that will incur the wrath of the government or your corporate superiors. These improprieties can cost you money.

Saturn is the Lord of your 12th House of Wisdom and Philanthropy. You are possibly giving too much to charities – more than you can afford. There is nothing wrong with giving to charity, it's a wonderful act. But don't put a burden on yourself in the process.

Your partner's income is stable and he or she is a very lucky speculator this year. Tensions could develop between the two of you over finances. Your partner feels that you are bit too mean. This is not a major tension, as your partner does appreciate all the other things you are doing, particularly to further his or her career and health goals.

The income of a parent is skyrocketing this year, as are the incomes of your superiors at work.

Financial opportunities come through large spiritual, charitable and religious organizations. Industries involved in health care on a large scale are good sources of investments for you. You might find yourself working for one of these organizations, either as a paid employee or as a volunteer. Either way, the financial opportunities will come. You make useful connections and one thing leads to another.

Oil and shipping are also lucrative industries for you, either as an employee or an investor.

As far as your career goes, you are still prospering and things are going much more easily for you this year than last year. Last year superiors were tougher on you. They helped you, it is true, but they also had high expectations. This year they go easier on you. You've proved yourself and they are not breathing down your neck any longer. Parents and elders in general are also less demanding of you. There is still a lot of forward motion in your career this year, but as mentioned earlier your interest in this area of life is waning.

Your career prestige has not only brought you into new

company socially, but has opened financial doors as well. Financial opportunities come strictly because of the position that you now hold.

Self-improvement

There is major expansion going on in your social life. You are making many new – and powerful – friends. You are getting more involved in political causes on a national and international level. You will have many happy opportunities to increase your knowledge of science, technology and astrology. By all means grab these opportunities. Your political consciousness is being raised and you carry more political clout than you ever did. You will be travelling in a group, probably internationally and probably more than once. All of this is going to happen more or less of its own accord. Your job is only to accept and be grateful.

Your real challenge this year will be in the realms of money matters and investments. Budgeting, financial planning and traditional methods of investing are all called for now. Financial discipline, never comfortable for an Aquarius, is required. Understand that you manage money not to limit yourself but to be assured that your money goes where you really want it to go and is not wasted on passing fancies. Financial guidance will come to you in dreams, through intuition and from psychics and astrologers. Pay attention but test out what is being conveyed by all of these.

Towards the end of the year – 10th November – Pluto will make a major move into your 11th House of Friends. When that happens you are going to become more selective about your friendships and more aware of others' hidden motives. This uncovering of hidden motives will also be illuminating in the political causes that you are involved in. If the cause is pure, stay with it; if not, sever all connection to it.

Month-by-month Forecasts

January

Best Days Overall: 3rd, 4th, 12th, 13th, 22nd, 23rd, 30th, 31st

Most Stressful Days Overall: 10th, 11th, 17th, 18th, 24th, 25th

Best Days for Love: 1st, 2nd, 5th, 6th, 7th, 8th, 10th, 11th, 17th, 18th, 19th, 22nd, 23rd, 27th, 30th, 31st

Best Days for Money: 5th, 6th, 7th, 8th, 10th, 11th, 17th, 18th, 19th, 20th, 21st, 26th, 27th, 28th, 29th

One could not ask for a more fortunate circumstance than for an Aquarian being thrust into happy group situations, seminars and media activities. This is precisely what happens this month and it is happy indeed. Your circle of friends not only expands in quantity but in quality as well. These are also friends who enjoy making your fondest hopes and wishes come to pass.

With 80 to 90 per cent of the planets in the Eastern half of your Horoscope you seem in charge of your life – the Lord and Creator of your circumstances and condition. You go forth with confidence and have no inhibitions about asserting yourself and knowing where your interests lie. Others need to adapt to you this month.

Though you have been active in charitable groups for some years now, this month you are more active than usual. Your dream life and ESP abilities are heightened this month as well.

Uninvolved singles need to spend the early part of the month setting out a pattern for future love. This is more of an introspective process than an extroverted one. Rather than running around looking for love in all the wrong places, your energies would be better spent clarifying what you want in a lover and what you want in a relationship. Once this is clear your mental pattern will attract what you want after the 20th. Love will come to you; you don't need to run after it.

Finances are strong all month with both the Sun and Mercury stimulating your Money Planet (Neptune). This month you learn that social contacts and friendships are another form of wealth – an intangible asset and resource that is nevertheless real. These things don't show up on financial statements but nevertheless operate in your favour this month. Your partner and social contacts lead you to earning opportunities. Your generosity to charities enriches you in subtle ways. As you give so do you receive. Wealth ideas come through your dreams and intuitive hunches. Psychics, mystics and astrologers lead you to hidden wealth and resources.

Your health is excellent all month – but gets exceptionally good after the 20th when the Sun moves into your own Sign.

February

Best Days Overall: 8th, 9th, 10th, 18th, 19th, 26th, 27th, 28th

Most Stressful Days Overall: 6th, 7th, 13th, 14th, 15th, 20th, 21st

Best Days for Love: 4th, 5th, 6th, 7th, 8th, 9th, 10th, 13th, 14th, 15th, 16th, 17th, 18th, 19th, 20th, 24th, 25th

Best Days for Money: 1st, 2nd, 3rd, 4th, 5th, 6th, 7th, 13th, 14th, 15th, 22nd, 23rd, 24th, 25th

The overwhelming predominance of the planetary power is in the Eastern sector of your Solar chart – just like last month. Thus you are in charge of your life. You call the shots. You create conditions and circumstances and you set the ground rules. You can pretty well have life on your own terms right now – so enjoy.

Eighty to 90 per cent of the planets are moving forward this month, so take advantage of this to set your plans into motion. This is a month for action, achievement, boldness and initiative.

With both the Sun and Mercury in your own Sign of Aquarius – for most of the month – you are physically radiant and magnetic. As the Sun is your Lord of Love, your social charisma is strong. You are attracting the opposite sex without even trying – in fact, most of you are involved in some romantic relationship right now. And you seem to be in charge. Your partner or lover is willing to go to any lengths to please you. There is some short-term disagreement with your partner early in the month but this passes quickly. The problem was due to a lack of communication and understanding, not malice or anything like that. Relations with a sibling and neighbour are more delicate. Try to understand that the problem is not with you but with them. They need to review their behaviour and correct it. Your partner feels threatened by the attentions paid to you by a neighbour who has romance on his or her mind. Relations with a child are delicate until the 16th. Patience, patience and more patience is the answer. Take the time to get at the *real* source of the dispute or problem – it is probably not what you think it is.

Personal earnings are positive all month. Your family is supportive financially, especially towards the end of the month, and a legal decision has a positive impact on your bank account. After the 19th, your partner or lover takes an interest in your financial affairs, supporting and perhaps providing financial opportunities. The help of your partner can come in various ways – via outright financial gifts, for example, or by steering you towards his or her connections which enrich you financially. Your partner is sincere, idealistic and unusually self-sacrificing in his or her financial support.

Your health is excellent all month.

March

Best Days Overall: 8th, 9th, 17th, 18th, 26th, 27th

Most Stressful Days Overall: 5th, 6th, 7th, 13th, 14th, 19th, 20th

Best Days for Love: 1st, 2nd, 8th, 9th, 10th, 11th, 14th, 17th, 18th, 19th, 20th, 21st, 27th, 28th, 31st

Best Days for Money: 2nd, 3rd, 4th, 5th, 6th, 14th, 15th, 16th, 22nd, 24th, 25th, 28th, 29th, 30th, 31st

Like last month, most of the planets are still heavily concentrated in the Eastern hemisphere of your Solar chart, making you more self-assertive, independent and basically in charge of conditions and circumstances. You are doing what you want to do and letting other people adapt to your actions.

Unlike last month, there is a shift of power from the top to the bottom half of your chart. Thus, though your ambitions are still strong – and by no means should you neglect them – there is an ever-growing need for you to get your emotional and family life in order. Remember, the higher your aspirations in the world the deeper and more stable must your emotional life be. Healthy careers are built on stable emotional foundations.

Your paths of greatest happiness and fulfilment this month are your career, platonic friendships, scientific interests and creating and enhancing your personal image. With 80 per cent of the planets going forward you can expect rapid progress towards your goals now.

Your love life is starting to stabilize this month, though you could do with more ardour and less 'duty'. You and your lover are dutiful to each other, but cool. Still there is much to be said for a sense of duty when things get rough. It holds things together. Early in the month a dispute with your partner can be solved by mutual sacrifice. Each of you must sacrifice certain small things for the sake of the relationship. Keep the big picture in mind at all times and you will both feel less like martyrs. By the 21st romance starts blooming again. The heat and passion return. Past disappointments are forgotten, swallowed up by the inrush of spring fever. Singles will do better romantically after the 21st than before. Romantic opportunities are abundant and close to home. You attract relationships because you are more in the mood for them. Love is active and extroverted this month, especially after the 21st. There are a lot of evenings out, hustling, bustling, sharing sport activities, etc. A lot of running around. Singles are apt to fall in love at first sight. Relationships are entered into impulsively – and perhaps rashly. Yet they seem to work out because your love intuition is strong now.

Your health is excellent all month but especially after the 21st. Finances are important this month and you take a more serious approach to them. Budgets and astute, realistic financial management will bring you increased prosperity. Avoid putting financial burdens on your partner this month. There's enough on his or her plate.

April

Best Days Overall: 4th, 5th, 6th, 14th, 15th, 22nd, 23rd

Most Stressful Days Overall: 2nd, 3rd, 9th, 10th, 16th, 17th, 29th, 30th

Best Days for Love: 7th, 8th, 9th, 10th, 16th, 17th, 18th, 19th, 20th, 26th, 27th, 28th, 29th, 30th

Best Days for Money: 1st, 3rd, 9th, 10th, 12th, 13th, 18th, 19th, 20th, 21st, 24th, 26th, 27th, 28th, 30th

This is a happy but tumultuous month, Aquarius. Uranus, your Planetary Ruler, makes a major move out of Capricorn and into your own Sign of Aquarius. Though there are many other important things happening this month, this is the major headline.

Uranus in your own Sign is going to release pent-up rebellious urges in you. The urge for change is simply overwhelming – perhaps stronger than any mere mortal can withstand. You must direct this urge towards positive ends. Change just for the sake of change will leave you worse off than before. This is the great challenge and the great opportunity now.

Always an experimental, avant-garde person, always original and freedom-loving, now you become even more so. You become a 'super Aquarian' these days. Get used to this feeling, for though Uranus will retrograde (move backwards) out of your Sign in June, in the future it will go back in and stay there for many years. You are getting a taste of the future this month.

You are likely to move house this month. This is only the first of a series of moves over the next few years. The Solar Eclipse of the 29th – which occurs in your 4th House of Home and Family – is a further indication of a move. You are also making major changes to your personality and personal appearance, dressing and 'packaging' yourself in radically different ways.

The Solar Eclipse of the 29th is important to you in other ways. The eclipsed planet, the Sun, also happens to be your Love Planet. A major change in a current relationship is brewing. Your partner had better give you more personal freedom or else you are gone. If you can find this freedom within your existing relationship it's got a good chance of surviving. But your partner will have to make major adjustments.

The Lunar Eclipse of the 15th occurs in your 9th House of Religion and Philosophy, signalling long-term changes in these areas of your life, particularly in your personal philosophy. This eclipse will affect the workplace and your job situation as well – perhaps you move or are transferred to a different branch of your company.

The most active area this month has to do with your intellectual interests. You are involved with studying and taking courses, and with sales activities. These go very successfully.

May

Best Days Overall: 1st, 2nd, 3rd, 11th, 12th, 19th, 20th, 29th, 30th

Most Stressful Days Overall: 6th, 7th, 8th, 13th, 14th, 26th, 27th, 28th

Best Days for Love: 6th, 7th, 8th, 9th, 10th, 15th, 16th, 17th, 18th, 26th, 27th, 28th, 29th, 30th

Best Days for Money: 6th, 7th, 8th, 9th, 15th, 16th, 17th, 18th, 21st, 22nd, 23rd, 24th, 25th, 26th, 27th, 28th

The planets are quite evenly dispersed through the various sectors of your Horoscope this month, showing a nice balance between personal interests and the needs of others and between career urges and family values.

When the planets are spread throughout an entire chart like this, the tendency is to have many interests and perhaps to spread yourself too thin. It is good to have a few projects going at one time, but not more than you can handle comfortably.

Your paths of greatest fulfilment this month are your career and the search for status, friendships, group activities, intellectual interests and – after the 17th – your home and family.

Forty to 50 per cent of the planets will be going retrograde this month, including your Ruler, Uranus. This creates a sense of impasse, delay, caution and inaction in the environment. You must be patient with yourself and with others. You can't make things happen now, nor can you rush things. The proper attitude is just to let things to happen. Use this period to review your plans, goals and projects and to apply any correctives or improvements necessary. There is no rush; you have plenty of time to do things properly.

Earnings are mixed this month – better before the 21st than afterwards. You are hard pressed to stick to a budget after the 21st as the pressure to spend is enormous. You need to work harder for your earnings after the 21st than before. Aside from this there are no financial disasters and your earning power will rebound late next month. All this seems true for your partner as well. He or she really needs to work hard after the 21st. Your partner is unusually aggressive in money matters and perhaps rushes into ventures and spending sprees too rashly.

You are trying a new and unexplored strategy with children this month and seem very hesitant about it. You won't really know whether you are on the right track until next month when you've had a chance to see the results. Your caution is well placed.

You also go way out of your normal 'orbit' in pursuit of fun and entertainment from the 5th to the 26th. After you go through the experience you may never want to repeat it again! There's a lot of backtracking and review involved in this. This 'reviewing' could apply to a love affair as well.

Your health is better after the 21st. Rest and relax more before then.

June

Best Days Overall: 7th, 8th, 9th, 16th, 17th, 25th, 26th

Most Stressful Days Overall: 3rd, 4th, 10th, 11th, 22nd, 23rd, 24th, 30th

Best Days for Love: 3rd, 4th, 5th, 6th, 7th, 8th, 9th, 16th, 17th, 25th, 26th, 27th, 28th, 29th

Best Days for Money: 3rd, 4th, 5th, 6th, 12th, 13th, 14th, 15th, 18th, 19th, 20th, 21st, 23rd, 24th, 30th

As a natural lover of change you should feel comfortable this month. Changes are occurring not only in your own life but in the world around you. A part of you thrills to all of this, because the changes going on are working in your favour.

Nevertheless you are not exempt from the demands of the Heavenly Grand Square aspect going on all month. Like your partner, you must deal with the conflict between meeting your children's demands and meeting those of a socio-political or professional organization close to your heart; between manifesting your own fondest wishes and fulfilling the needs of your children; between your personal creativity and the interests of a wider group of people; between your personal financial interests and those of your partner; between making money for yourself and the need to make money for others; between the concerns of investors and your own personal concerns.

Change will happen in these areas, but in fits and starts. With 50 per cent of the planets retrograde for most of the month there is a general climate of stalemate and caution. Be patient. Take whatever action you can take and let the rest go. Time will resolve many conflicts.

Singles seem confused on the love front. The confusion comes not from a lack but rather an abundance of romantic opportunity. The urge to have fun and enjoy life is strong this month, but you wonder whether you can build something worthwhile with someone who is only a 'playmate'. You wonder whether a current love affair is just an affair or something deeper than that. The answers should come after the 17th when Mercury starts to go direct. The lover who is right for you will begin to be of practical service to you after the 22nd. He or she will want to support your interests and not just entertain you.

Earnings come in rather slowly this month as the retrograde of your Money Planet (Neptune) fosters a sense of caution and lack of financial confidence. Your financial judgement may not be as sound as it usually is right now, thus you should avoid major investments, purchases or long-term financial commitments. If you do enter into any of these, let it be only after really thorough study.

Your health is excellent all month.

July

Best Days Overall: 5th, 6th, 13th, 14th, 22nd, 23rd

Most Stressful Days Overall: 1st, 7th, 8th, 20th, 21st, 27th, 28th

Best Days for Love: 1st, 7th, 8th, 15th, 16th, 25th, 26th, 27th, 28th

Best Days for Money: 1st, 3rd, 4th, 9th, 10th, 11th, 12th, 15th, 16th, 17th, 18th, 21st, 27th, 28th

The planetary patterns in your chart are especially interesting this month and worthy of some comment. The long-term, slow-moving planets are all in the Eastern half of your chart (and all going retrograde as well), while the fast-moving, short-term planets are all in the Western sector of your chart and are all going forward.

Thus, the long-term picture is one of self-assertion and personal creativity which are temporarily halted in favour of your social life, people-pleasing and adapting to unfamiliar conditions. You definitely can – and should – make it on your own over the long term, but right now you need or want others. You are flirting with the idea of a business partnership now. You are testing your ability to adapt, as if you want to learn more about yourself in this area.

As the month progresses the short-term planets shift – with ever greater intensity – above the horizon of your chart, spurring your worldly ambitions and making you less interested in family and emotional concerns. Nevertheless you need to spend more time formulating and perfecting your career goals. Career success is coming, but you need to prepare.

Your paths of greatest fulfilment this month are friendships, group activities, science, astrology, your career, personal creativity, children, dietary regimes and work goals.

As the month begins you are working to translate your personal creativity into action. You are bringing creativity to the workplace, achieving goals in creative ways. The workplace is hectic but enjoyable these days.

There is help available for a long-standing health problem. It will be resolved. Your health is better before the 23rd. Rest and relax more after then.

Singles have an active romantic life this month. This is one of the few areas of life in which nothing is being delayed. Romantic opportunities are abundant and your social charisma is strong. Those already in a relationship are seeing it progress. Those who are not yet involved with anyone are highly likely to meet that special someone after the 23rd. Aquarians want lovers who serve their interests and who want to do things for them. This is the way they give (and receive) love early in the month. After the 23rd they want more courtship and romantic indulgences. Candle-lit dinners, roses, champagne, sweet words and romantic settings work all the right magic.

Be patient in finance – the deadlock is temporary. Don't count your chickens before they hatch, but on the other hand have faith in yourself and your earning abilities. Prudence and caution should govern expenditures now.

August

Best Days Overall: 1st, 2nd, 9th, 10th, 19th, 20th, 28th, 29th

Most Stressful Days Overall: 3rd, 4th, 16th, 17th, 24th, 25th, 31st

Best Days for Love: 5th, 6th, 14th, 15th, 24th, 25th, 26th, 27th

Best Days for Money: 5th, 6th, 8th, 12th, 14th, 15th, 16th, 17th, 26th, 27th

The planets are overwhelmingly concentrated above the horizon of your chart this month, fostering your ambitions and need for outwardly success. This trend is further reinforced by your Career Planet (Pluto) going forward this month after many months of retrograde motion. Career stalemate is ending and much progress begins.

Though most of the planets are in the Eastern sector of your chart, the fast-moving, short-term planets are temporarily activating your 7th House of Love and Marriage, making you more socially conscious than you would ordinarily be. This is an excellent month socially but you are not a doormat for others nor do you cede your personal power to them.

Your paths of greatest fulfilment this month are your love life, friendships, fine art, religious study, physical intimacy and eliminating what is useless from your life.

Singles are very likely to meet that special someone this

month. You are in the mood for romance and you attract it. You attract your ideal very easily. Only remember that your ideal tends to change as you mature. Right now you meet the ideal person for this stage of your life. Go to parties, entertainment venues or sporting events, for there are you most likely to meet potential partners. Early in the month the emphasis is on romance and courtship; later on the emphasis shifts to physical intimacy.

Your health is more delicate until the 23rd. Try to rest and relax more. Your health can be enhanced by proper mood control;-try to direct your moods in positive directions.

Your financial life still seems rather deadlocked. Be patient with the delays going on. Spend cautiously and do your homework before making investments or big financial commitments. What you lack in personal earning power is more than made up for by your partner, who not only prospers after the 23rd but shares that prosperity with you. Focus on enriching others and your own financial needs will be taken care of.

September

Best Days Overall: 6th, 7th, 15th, 16th, 24th, 25th

Most Stressful Days Overall: 12th, 13th, 14th, 20th, 21st, 27th, 28th

Best Days for Love: 4th, 5th, 12th, 13th, 14th, 20th, 21st, 23rd, 24th, 25th

Best Days for Money: 2nd, 4th, 5th, 8th, 9th, 10th, 11th, 13th, 14th, 20th, 21st, 22nd, 23rd, 29th, 30th

As of the 7th the Eastern sector of your chart begins to outweigh the Western sector. Thus you are becoming more assertive, more in tune with your own needs and interests, more independent and more able to go it alone should other people not co-operate. Yet Uranus (your Ruler) is retrograde, showing that you should think and plan more before setting too many things into motion. Do your homework.

The upper half of your Horoscope continues to dominate the lower half. Eighty to 90 per cent of the planets are above the horizon this month, indicating that you are very 'career-driven' right now. Your focus on personal domestic bliss must give way to concern about the domestic bliss of others. Giving support to your own family, though admirable, nevertheless must widen to giving emotional support to other people's families.

Your paths of greatest fulfilment this month are physical intimacy, elimination and transformation, religious and metaphysical studies, higher education, foreign travel, friendships and group activities.

Your health is going to be excellent all month due in part to favourable planetary aspects and in part to the New Moon (your Health Planet) in the 9th House of Philosophy. New and better health concepts are being born.

Your partner continues to prosper for most of the month, but the retrograde of Mercury (your partner's Money Planet) indicates a need to consolidate and regroup in business. Your partner must be cautious about signing contracts and making long-term financial commitments. Your personal financial life could be better as well. The problem is stale-mate and delay. Though you will have enough for your needs you must spend cautiously. Money is easily obtained through credit or investors until the 23rd. Your credit limit is raised.

Your love life is not a priority this month and you have the freedom to make of it what you will. The Cosmos isn't pushing you in one direction or another. Singles find love at funerals and wakes – don't laugh, many romantic meetings have taken place at these gatherings – at doctors' surgeries and in the offices of accountants and stockbrokers. After the 23rd romantic opportunities are likely to come at church socials, at universities or colleges or in bible classes. Singles who are students are likely to fall in love with their teachers.

October

Best Days Overall: 3rd, 4th, 12th, 13th, 22nd, 23rd, 30th, 31st

Most Stressful Days Overall: 10th, 11th, 17th, 18th, 24th, 25th

Best Days for Love: 3rd, 4th, 12th, 13th, 15th, 16th, 17th, 18th, 23rd, 24th, 25th

Best Days for Money: 2nd, 5th, 6th, 7th, 8th, 9th, 11th, 17th, 18th, 21st, 26th, 27th, 29th.

Most of the planets are in the Eastern sector of your chart; as the month continues the percentage gets higher and higher. Moreover, Uranus (your Ruling Planet) starts moving forward again on the 6th after many months of retrograde motion. Add to this brew the fact that 90 per cent of the planets are moving forward after the 14th and you get a picture of an aggressive, self-assertive, no-nonsense achiever – perhaps even an over-achiever. You can and will have things your way this month. You can and do achieve what you want to achieve. Of course you would prefer it if others went along with you, but if they don't you will go it alone, on your own. Most of the obstructions in your path are removed, but if any remain you have more than enough energy to overcome them. You are ready, willing and able to crush all barriers now and to break with tradition and the status quo. The universe rockets forward this month, and you along with it.

Eighty to 90 per cent of the planets are above the horizon this month and there is also unusual power in your 10th House of Career. No question about it, you are a career-driven person this month. You've had enough of emotional security and catering to your family. This can get quite dull after a while. You want the bright lights, the glamour and the public recognition. You want 'to do something with life'. You will get as many challenges as you can handle and are worthy to receive. Those who have prepared themselves will get more fame and recognition than before. Those who are not yet prepared will nevertheless have opportunities to attain name and fame.

Your paths of greatest fulfilment are religious studies, higher education, foreign travel, your career, friendships and group activities.

Your health is excellent until the 24th, after then you should rest and relax more. The financial stalemate of the past few months is mostly but not completely over. Your earnings increase after the 24th.

Your new focus on the outside world will cause a long-term change in family relations and your domestic situation. The Lunar Eclipse of the 8th heralds this change. A modification of your marriage and social life in general is signalled by the Solar Eclipse of the 24th. A new balance between love and career will have to be found.

November

Best Days Overall: 8th, 9th, 10th, 18th, 19th, 27th, 28th

Most Stressful Days Overall: 6th, 7th, 14th, 15th, 21st, 22nd

Best Days for Love: 1st, 2nd, 3rd, 4th, 11th, 12th, 14th, 15th, 21st, 22nd, 23rd, 24th

Best Days for Money: 1st, 2nd, 3rd, 4th, 5th, 6th, 7th, 14th, 15th, 16th, 17th, 23rd, 25th, 26th, 29th, 30th

By the 4th, almost all the planets (with the exception of the Moon – which will cover every sector during the month) will have shifted to the East. Your days of people-pleasing, adaptation, dependence and ignoring yourself are ending. Whatever you needed to learn from being 'other-orientated' has been learned. On to the next stage – building your personal kingdom of 'Heaven on Earth'. It's time to think of yourself and your own needs.

Most of the planets are still above the horizon, showing that you feel that your duty to the world pre-empts your duty to your family, and that feeling at ease with society is more important than feeling emotionally at ease. You are thinking of the future more than of the past. The well-being of other people's families takes priority over your own.

Your paths of greatest fulfilment are higher education, foreign travel, religious studies, career, caring for other people's families, friendships and group activities.

Career activities are very successful this month. This is the year's peak time for your career. Your public status is boosted now and your prestige is enhanced. Your marriage partner is very supportive in your career, and his or her well-being is very high on your list of priorities. Your partner's career is also blossoming this month. Pluto, your Career Planet, makes a major, long-term move into Sagittarius this month and will stay there for many years to come. This is a positive career signal. You are being called upon to use your social, communication and networking skills in the world. In other words, the 'Powers that Be' recognize your true strengths and are asking you to use them. Career matters are more likely to be successful as you are working under your own steam.

After the 23rd you are involved in true bliss. Your 11th House of Friends becomes the most prominent sector of your Horoscope and you are preoccupied with things that you love to do: being with friends, taking part in group activities, becoming involved in media activities and creating within a group. Your fondest hopes and wishes come true this month – with a little help from your friends. Many new and long-term friendships are beginning now. These new friends can really help you in the future.

Your health is excellent all month.

December

Best Days Overall: 6th, 7th, 16th, 17th, 24th, 25th

Most Stressful Days Overall: 3rd, 4th, 11th, 12th, 18th, 19th, 31st

Best Days for Love: 1st, 2nd, 3rd, 4th, 11th, 12th, 13th, 14th, 20th, 21st, 24th, 30th, 31st

Best Days for Money: 1st, 2nd, 4th, 11th, 12th, 14th, 20th, 21st, 23rd, 26th, 27th, 28th, 29th, 31st

All of the planets are moving forward and nearly all of them – with the exception of the Moon – are in the Eastern sector of your chart. This is a month for personal action, achievement and progress. You set the pace, the tone and the trend of events. Your personal initiative makes things happen now. You give up 'people-pleasing' and work on pleasing yourself. If you are content with your life others will be content with it as well – a stunning realization. If you are personally happy the world will be that much happier. If you fulfil yourself the world in general will be more fulfilled. Begin with yourself.

Most of the planets are still in the upper sector of your chart. You are 'outer'-orientated rather than inner-orientated. You are concerned more with the future than with the past. You want to feel secure in your profession and in the world rather than in your emotions. You want recognition in society. Push your career now. Pluto, your Career Planet, has made a major move into your 11th House of Friends, Group Activities and Fondest Wishes and will stay there for many years to come. Networking and otherwise using your communication and social skills will boost your career. Join professional and industrial organizations connected with your career now. Your Career Planet in the House that rules 'fondest hopes and wishes' shows that your career fantasies are coming to pass.

Your paths of greatest fulfilment are friendships, career activities, religious studies, foreign travel, higher education, charitable activities and the enhancement of your image.

Your 11th and 12th Houses are the most active and prominent in your chart this month. Your 11th House rules group activities, your 12th rules spiritual wisdom and charity. Thus you are very much preoccupied with groups, professional and political organizations and charitable activities. Your dream life is hyperactive in a year of general hyperactivity. You are fighting a covert battle – perhaps a psychological battle – not for yourself but on behalf of the underprivileged. You are very much involved in clearing up a partner's health problem. Your partner's work-load is huge and the pace at work frenetic, especially later in the month.

Your personal health is excellent all month and will get even better next month. Your earnings are strong this month. Highly practical, workable earnings ideas come to you in dreams and visions.

Your love life is romantic and playful early in the month. Your partner or lover looks to entertain and amuse you. A romantic jaunt abroad is likely before the 22nd. After then your partner looks to serve your interests. Both of you are making sacrifices for the sake of the relationship as a whole.

Pisces

♓

THE FISH

Birthdays from
19th February
to 20th March

Personality Profile

PISCES AT A GLANCE

Element – Water

Ruling planet – Neptune
Career planet – Jupiter
Love planet – Mercury
Money planet – Mars
Planet of home and family life – Mercury

Colours – aqua, blue-green

Colours that promote love, romance and social harmony – earth tones, yellow, yellow-orange

Colours that promote earning power – red, scarlet

Gem – white diamond

Metal – tin

Scent – lotus

Quality – mutable (= flexibility)

Qualities most needed for balance – structure and the ability to handle form

Strongest virtues – psychic power, sensitivity, self-sacrifice, altruism

Deepest needs – spiritual illumination, liberation

Characteristics to avoid – escapism, keeping bad company, negative moods

Signs of greatest overall compatibility – Cancer, Scorpio

Signs of greatest overall incompatibility – Gemini, Virgo, Sagittarius

Sign most helpful to career – Sagittarius

Sign most helpful for emotional support – Gemini

Sign most helpful financially – Aries

Sign best for marriage and/or partnerships – Virgo

Sign most helpful for creative projects – Cancer

Best Sign to have fun with – Cancer

Signs most helpful in spiritual matters – Scorpio, Aquarius

Best day of the week – Thursday

Understanding the Pisces Personality

If Pisceans have one outstanding quality it's their belief in the invisible, spiritual and psychic side of things. This side of things is as real to them as the hard earth beneath their feet – so real, in fact, that they will often ignore the visible, tangible aspects of reality in order to focus on the invisible and so-called intangible ones.

Of all the Signs of the Zodiac, the intuitive and emotional faculties are the most highly developed in the Pisces. They are committed to living by their intuition and this can at times be infuriating to other people – especially those who are materially, scientifically or technically orientated. If you think that money or status or worldly success are the only goals in life, then you will never understand a Pisces.

Pisceans have intellect, but to them intellect is only a means by which they can rationalize what they know intuitively. To an Aquarius or a Gemini the intellect is a tool of knowing. To a well-developed Pisces it is only a tool by which to *express* knowing.

Pisceans feel like fish in an infinite ocean of thought and feeling. This ocean has many depths, currents and sub-currents. They long for purer waters where the denizens are good, true and beautiful, but they are sometimes pulled to the lower, murkier depths. Pisceans know that they don't generate thoughts but only tune in to thoughts that already exist; this is why they seek the purer waters. This ability to tune in to higher thoughts inspires them artistically and musically.

Since Pisces is so spiritually orientated – though many Pisceans in the corporate world may hide this fact – we will deal with this aspect in greater detail, for otherwise it is difficult to understand the true Pisces personality.

There are four basic attitudes of the spirit. One is outright scepticism – the attitude of secular humanists. The second is an intellectual or emotional belief, where one worships a far-distant God figure – the attitude of most modern church-going people. The third is not only belief but direct personal spiritual experience – this is the attitude of some 'born-again' religious people. The fourth is actually unity with the divinity, intermingling with the spiritual world – this is the attitude of yoga. This fourth attitude is the deepest urge of a Pisces and a Pisces is uniquely qualified to perform this work.

Consciously or unconsciously, Pisceans seek this union with the spiritual world. The belief in a greater reality makes Pisceans very tolerant and understanding of others – perhaps even too tolerant. There are instances in their lives when they should say 'enough is enough' and be ready to defend their position and put up a fight. However, because of their qualities it takes a good deal of doing to get them in that frame of mind.

Pisceans basically want and aspire to be 'saints'. They do so in their own way and according to their own rules. Others should not try to impose their concept of saintliness on a Pisces, because he or she always tries to find it for him- or herself.

Finance

Money is generally not that important to Pisces. Of course they need it as much as the next person, and many of them attain great wealth. But money is not generally a primary objective. Doing good, feeling good about oneself, peace of mind, the relief of pain and suffering – these are the things that matter most to a Pisces.

Pisceans earn money intuitively and instinctively. They follow their hunches rather than their logic. They tend to be generous and perhaps overly charitable. Almost any kind of misfortune is enough to move a Pisces to give. Although this is one of their greatest virtues, Pisceans should be more careful with their finances. They should try to be more choosy about the people they lend money, so that they are not being taken advantage of. If they give money to charities they should follow it up to see that their contributions are put to good use. Even when Pisceans are not rich, they still like to spend money on helping others. In this case they should really be careful, however: they must learn to say no sometimes and help themselves first.

Perhaps the biggest financial stumbling block for the Pisces is general passivity – a *laissez faire* attitude. In general Pisceans like to go with the flow of events. When it comes to financial matters, especially, they need to be more aggressive. They need to make things happen, to create their own wealth. A passive attitude will only cause loss and missed opportunity. Worrying about financial security will not provide that security. Pisceans need to go after what they want tenaciously.

Career and Public Image

Pisceans like to be perceived by the public as people of spiritual or material wealth, of generosity and philanthropy. They look up to big-hearted, philanthropic types. They admire people engaged in large-scale undertakings and eventually would like to head up these big enterprises themselves. In short, they like to be connected with big organizations that are doing things in a big way.

If Pisceans are to realize their full career and professional potential they need to travel more, educate themselves more and learn more about the actual world. In other words, they need some of the unflagging optimism of the Sagittarius in order to reach the top.

Because of all their caring and generous characteristics, Pisceans often choose professions through which they can help and touch the lives of other people. That is why many Pisceans become doctors, nurses, social workers or educators. Sometimes it takes a while before Pisceans realize what they really want to do in their professional lives, but once they find a career that lets them manifest their interests and virtues they will excel at it.

Love and Relationships

It is not surprising that someone as 'other-worldly' as the Pisces would like a partner who is practical and down-to-earth. Pisceans prefer a partner who is on top of all the details of life, because they dislike details. Pisceans seek this quality in both their romantic and professional partners. More than anything else this gives Pisces a feeling of being grounded, of being down-to-earth.

As expected, these kind of relationships – though necessary – are sure to have many ups and downs. Misunderstandings will take place because the two attitudes are poles apart. If you are in love with a Pisces you will experience these fluctuations and will need a lot of patience to see things stabilize. Pisceans are moody, intuitive, affectionate and difficult to get to know. Only time and the right attitude will yield Pisceans' deepest secrets. However, when in love with a Pisces you will find that riding the waves is worth it because they are good, sensitive people who need and like to give love and affection.

When in love, Pisceans like to fantasize. For them fantasy is 90 per cent of the fun of a relationship. They tend to idealize their partner, which can be good and bad at the same time. It is bad in that it's difficult for anyone in love with a Pisces to live up to the high ideals set.

Home and Domestic Life

In their family and domestic life Pisceans have to resist the tendency to relate only by feelings and moods. It is unrealistic to expect that your partner and other family members will be as intuitive as you are. There is a need for more verbal communication between a Pisces and his or her family. A cool, unemotional exchange of ideas and opinions will benefit everyone.

Some Pisceans tend to like mobility and moving around. For them too much stability feels like a restriction on their freedom. They hate to be locked in one location forever.

The Sign of Gemini sits on Pisces' 4th Solar House (of Home and Family) cusp. This shows that the Pisces likes and needs a home environment that promotes intellectual and mental interests. They tend to treat their neighbours as family – or extended family. Some Pisceans can have a dual attitude towards the home and family – on the one hand they like the emotional support of the family, but on the other they dislike the obligations, restrictions and duties involved with it. For Pisces, finding a balance is the key to a happy family life.

Horoscope for 1995

Major Trends

1994 was a year where you focused on things that were primarily non-material – and what the world would call 'impractical'. You concentrated on things like higher education, bible and religious studies, meditation, dream analysis and foreign travel. It was basically a happy, carefree year. But 1995 is a much more serious, work- and career-orientated year. Yes, you have read many books, absorbed many great ideas, seen many visions and dreamed many dreams. You have sat at the feet of masters and gurus and absorbed their wisdom. But now the 'word has to be made flesh'. All that you've learned and absorbed needs to be applied, made practical, tested in the fires of everyday circumstance.

This realistic application of the 'abstract' will do more for your personal growth than a million years of lectures and sermons. Lectures, sermons and books are indeed useful – as road maps and pointers in the right direction – but nothing substitutes for actually making the journey. For this will lead you into even deeper truth – experiential truth. You will learn and know things that no book could ever give you. You will understand the deeper context of what you have learned in 1994. 1995 is a year of trial and testing. You will be rewarded as much for your endurance and discipline as for what you know intellectually. Rejoice as the trials of everyday life consume all your book learning and leave you with the True Essence: knowledge that is workable and functional.

Health

Though your 6th House of Health is not a prominent House this year – indicating that there are no major health concerns on the horizon – still your overall vitality is not what you are used to. Two important, long-term planets, Saturn and Jupiter, have moved into stressful alignment with you. Pluto is also getting poised to move into a stressful alignment (this will happen by the end of the year).

You definitely need to be careful about your physical energy this year. You need to work harder and more efficiently. You must manage your physical energy the way a businessperson manages accounts. Ration and budget your energy. Budget it in such a way that the True Goals of your Heart are receiving their proper share and that wasteful activities are deprived of their share. This involves making many tough choices about your life. You need to decide what is and what is not really important to you and ration your energy accordingly. If you have your priorities straight, half the battle is won. If not, you must do some serious thinking.

In addition, never let yourself become over-tired. Rest and relax more. Apply the 'laws of rhythm' to your work and you will get more done with less effort. Working rhythmically means working to a relaxed 'go, rest, go' schedule. Alternate work and play. Alternate between different kinds of work. Give certain brain-cell groups time to rest before putting more pressure on them. Work for 20 minutes and then stretch, yawn and loosen-up. Then go back to work. Don't allow tension to build up in your body.

Talk less and listen more. Perceive more and think less. Learn to turn off your intellectual 'computer' when it's not needed.

Put the cosmic forces to work for you by aligning yourself with them. When the current is with you there is no need to work as hard. You can conserve your personal energy and let the cosmic currents carry you. You can do this by scheduling yourself astrologically, as described in the month-by-month forecasts below.

Increase your preventives against disease by scheduling regular visits with a chiropractor, reflexologist, herbalist or other natural health practitioner. This will prevent problems before they occur.

If you do all these things you will be amazed at how much sheer life-force is given to all of us and how much of it is just frittered away uselessly. You will have more than enough to achieve your goals and avoid illness.

Some of the good things about this Saturn transit over your Sun and Ascendant is that you are going to undergo a 'reality check'. Your physical limits are going to be revealed to you. This is good in that you can be more realistic with your body and exercise programmes.

This is an excellent year to start a dietary regime. Most of you are going to shed excess pounds this year. You are becoming leaner, sleeker and more efficient and effective.

Home and Domestic Life

Your 4th House of Home and Family is not a House of Power this year, Pisces. You are much more concerned with other things. The Cosmos neither obstructs nor helps you in your domestic plans. Your family grants you much freedom to pursue your goals. You can do pretty well as you please in the home, but you somehow lack interest in doing so.

Your relationship with your parents or parent figures is complex and ambivalent. On the one hand they support your career goals and do much to boost your public esteem.

On the other hand they do not help your personal self-esteem. Thus they will praise your new promotion or pay rise but put you down personally. Yes, they say, you are a big wheel in the world, but with us you are still a cheeky little kid. They still want to boss you around and belittle you in personal ways – the way you dress, the way you look, etc. It is always best to interpret this kind of behaviour in the best possible light. In most cases it is not meant maliciously. They just want to keep you humble, keep you from getting too big for your boots. In other cases it is just unconscious. No matter how old or successful you are – no matter how many employees you have under your command – you are still their little kid who must obey. They give you recognition for your work and achievement but not for who you are.

One of your parents is really expanding this year. This parent is optimistic, lucky, prospering and travelling. The financial picture is beginning to change for the better. He or she is probably moving or renovating the home. Later on in the year this parent is likely to undergo some cosmetic surgery to further polish up his or her image. This personal expansion makes him or her better able to help you in your career – and later on, probably next year, to help you financially as well. This parent is probably over-indulging in food and sensual pleasures and will have to spend some time 'cooling-off' later in the year.

If you are a married man, your partner is very fertile this year. Pregnancy is likely.

Man or woman, this year your partner takes over much of the burden of the home. He or she will beautify it, decorate it and otherwise make it bigger and better. Your partner's side of the family increases through births and marriages. Be patient when your partner's family meddles into your affairs good naturedly – they mean well.

Love and Social Life

Neither your 5th House of Love Affairs nor your 7th House of Marriage are prominent this year, Pisces. But the 11th

House of Platonic Friendships is. Thus you have great freedom in the social sphere. The Cosmos neither obstructs nor pushes you in any given direction. This configuration shows a lack of romantic interest on your part. In all probability this is because you are already in a satisfying relationship and have no further romantic urges. Your urge now – as it has been for many years – is toward friendships and intellectual contacts.

The status quo in love is favoured. Thus marrieds will tend to stay married and singles will tend to stay single. The good news here is that your partner is not obstructing your intense drive towards career success. On the contrary, there is much emotional, though not material, support for your ambitions.

For singles the most active romantic periods will be from 16th March to 3rd April, from 22nd June to 30th July and from 23rd August to 23rd September. The first and the last periods favour a significant relationship, while the middle period favours a more 'fun-and-games' type of relationship.

The love life of a parent or parent figure is blossoming right now. If this parent has been single, a marriage is likely. A fortunate and happy one.

Those of you working on your second marriage have probably found the right one in 1994. Those of you working on a third marriage are really in for a roller-coaster ride. Your love life is very unstable and your affections change with the speed of lightning. Nevertheless, if you persist, romance will be exciting. A third marriage this year is not especially recommended, though you will probably go ahead with it anyway.

Saturn on your Solar chart Ascendant can make you come off as cold, pitiless and controlling. You are not really this way – the Pisces character is just the opposite – but you are perceived this way by others. Lighten up a bit. Don't be too over-controlling with your partner. Make a special effort to grant others more freedom and to demonstrate your love. Duty, duty, duty can get quite boring to others. Have some fun.

Your friendships this year continue to be turbulent,

unpredictable, volatile and subject to sudden change. But all the rapid changes this year are happier than they've been in the recent past. You continue to make new friends easily and to lose them with equal ease. There's a lot of experimenting going on with your friends. All of this is leading you to the right sort of friends, friends who really and truly want to help you to make your fondest dreams and wishes come true. This is what the 11th House of Platonic Friendship is all about. Unencumbered by passion and sensual attachment, these friends can work impersonally for your highest good. True platonic friends are wonderful to have. It is their very coolness and detachment that gives them the vision to sense what you really want and to guide you to it.

You're making friends with someone older and more established than you are. He or she is helping you with your image or with your health. This person is going to be a long-term presence in your life, though not a romantic one. He or she values friendship over career and feels that your ambitions are misplaced. You will face quite a juggling act in order to appease both your ambitions and this friend.

Career and Finance

Your 2nd House of Money is not prominent this year, Pisces, yet there is no question that you will be earning more. You will be earning more without really caring about it. This is because you are focusing on your career and professional status. You know that – for now, anyway – money will follow a job well done and a boss who is satisfied. Pay rises and promotions are coming to you this year. You are more in the public eye than you have been in a long time. Your reputation is increasing positively. You are working harder and disciplining yourself as well. With these promotions and the pay rises come extra responsibility, extra work, extra duties and extra cares.

Saturn on your Sun and Solar Ascendant is going to prevent you from having too much 'hubris'. Though you are in the public eye (relatively speaking) and are being recognized for your achievements, keep a low profile. Personal flamboyance is not necessary and could probably undermine you.

You are being promoted based on real and substantive achievement – not for whom you know nor for your political connections. Keep up the achievement and you'll be fine. You have the capacity to reach career heights this year, for a power struggle in your company leaves a void that either you or someone friendly to you can fill.

Self-improvement

Your career and professional prestige are going to improve with almost no effort on your part this year. Of course you are working for these, but the opportunities come on their own. Many people work very hard and no opportunities come. What you need to make an effort with is your personal image and body. This will require some work and you are reluctant to put in the time, mainly because of your career responsibilities. Somehow or other you need to balance the two. Give each its due. Find a gym near your office or workplace, or find an empty spot at work where you can exercise and take stretching breaks. Merge your need to stay in shape with your need for success.

Month-by-month Forecasts

January

Best Days Overall: 5th, 6th, 15th, 16th, 24th, 25th

Most Stressful Days Overall: 12th, 13th, 19th, 20th, 21st, 22nd, 26th, 27th

Best Days for Love: 1st, 7th, 8th, 12th, 13th, 17th, 18th, 20th, 21st, 22nd, 23rd, 26th, 27th, 30th, 31st

Best Days for Money: 1st, 2nd, 7th, 8th, 10th, 11th, 17th, 18th, 19th, 20th, 26th, 27th

Though you are feeling burdened with cares and responsibilities you are making your mark on the world this month. The overwhelming majority of the planets are in the top half of your Solar Horoscope. This denotes ambition and the drive for 'outer', objective success. Attaining your place in society, both professionally and socially, is your dominating drive right now. You seem ready to – and in fact need to – sacrifice personal desires, inclinations and time with your family in order to pursue your career. A part of you is uncomfortable with this – but another part is elated.

Your sacrifices are not in vain. Your success in the world is meteoric this month. New vistas of achievement are opening up to you. Elders and authority figures demand much from you but they are giving much in return. The fact that they are giving so much – in terms of pay, prestige, promotions and perks – is their rationale for driving you so hard and expecting so much from you. You are working hard but are reaping the rewards. What more can you ask?

Mars, your Money Planet, is retrograde (travelling backwards) all month. Be cautious now about how you invest your new-found earnings. Avoid making major new purchases or financial commitments until you have given sufficient time to research these matters. It would be better to wait until Mars goes direct next month.

Socially you mingle with those above you in status – the rich, the beautiful and the powerful. Your private life is more complicated this month. First off, Mercury, your Love Planet, moves rather slowly and cautiously. Secondly it is out of bounds early in the month. Thirdly, it starts to go retrograde on the 26th. This suggests that you are in unknown social territory – mixing in circles that are outside your normal 'orbit' – and are treading your way cautiously until you learn the rules of the game. This caution seems wise indeed.

Although you attract love opportunities you want to move slowly with them. If you are in a current relationship you will have time to rethink it, correct it or dissolve it during Mercury's retrograde. If you are single you now have opportunity to take stock of your social life and decide what your real love goals are. At present you want your lover to be your friend as well. You are less interested in passion than in friendship. You also want someone who is in a position to fulfil your fondest dreams and wishes – and you will find him or her too. It would not be wise to schedule either a marriage or divorce until Mercury starts going direct again next month.

February

Best Days Overall: 1st, 2nd, 11th, 12th, 20th, 21st

Most Stressful Days Overall: 8th, 9th, 10th, 16th, 17th, 22nd, 23rd

Best Days for Love: 4th, 5th, 6th, 7th, 8th, 9th, 10th, 16th, 17th, 18th, 19th, 24th, 25th, 26th, 27th, 28th

Best Days for Money: 3rd, 4th, 5th, 13th, 14th, 15th, 22nd, 23rd

Like last month, most of the planets are in the Eastern and top hemispheres of your Solar Chart, making you unusually assertive and ambitious. You want your way and you get your way. You want your place in society and in your profession and you get it. Unlike last month, however, there are more planets moving forward, especially after the 16th. You will see much progress and achievement now. With the

Sun moving into your own Sign of Pisces on the 19th you can drop your fears and anxieties and set your plans into motion. It's really up to you now. You can create your conditions and circumstances, and the career of your dreams, and others will just have to accept meekly. Take the steps to do so.

Your work goals are being helped by secret powers. Take a creative and intuitive approach to all the things you need to do this month – and there is a lot to do. Let yourself be guided by a higher power. Your intuition in these matters is unusually sharp now. If you follow it you will do twice the amount of work in half the time. You must work *both* hard and cleverly. When you contemplate your work-load this month the feeling of being overwhelmed is understandable. But if you break the tasks down into small, achievable steps, you will be on top of things. At every moment there is something positive that can be done – even if it is only mentally visualizing the completed project.

Though your own health is excellent you seem preoccupied with the health of your partner and are doing much – probably in a self-sacrificing way – to ease the problem. The problem is short term. You will see progress by the 19th and by next month it should be gone. Your healing abilities and intuition are unusually strong this month.

Romantic relations with your partner seem complicated by health and work problems. Really these are your partner's problems and not yours. But indirectly you are affected. Your partner is perhaps devoting more time to work than to you. Patience and understanding are what's needed here. Marrieds need to work on the spiritual aspects of their relationships this month. Singles need to formulate more clearly their vision of perfect love and Mr or Ms Right. More romantic progress will be made by staying home and making this clear to yourself than by running after love in all the wrong places. How can you feel socially confident if you don't know exactly what you're looking for? Another question you should ask yourself – especially now – is, if Mr or Ms Right fell into my lap now, would I be worthy of it?

A lot depends on how you answer this question. More social confidence will return after the 16th.

March

Best Days Overall: 1st, 2nd, 10th, 11th, 12th, 19th, 20th, 28th, 29th

Most Stressful Days Overall: 8th, 9th, 15th, 16th, 21st, 22nd

Best Days for Love: 8th, 9th, 15th, 16th, 17th, 18th, 19th, 20th, 26th, 27th, 28th, 29th

Best Days for Money: 3rd, 4th, 13th, 14th, 21st, 22nd, 30th, 31st

Like last month, most of the planets are congregated in the Eastern hemisphere of your Solar chart. Thus you are self-assertive, independent and seeing clearly what your own interests are. You are in charge of conditions and circumstances. You are the Karma-maker rather than the Karma-payer right now. The urge is to be truly yourself and to let the chips fall where they may. Though this self-assertion causes some problems with a friend or an organization you belong to, it will pay off later on in the month.

Your paths of greatest fulfilment this month are career, spiritual and philanthropic activities, travel and higher education. With 80 per cent of the planets moving forward there is much action, achievement and rapid progress towards your goals. Enjoy.

This is also very much a month of getting your body and personal appearance in shape. It is a month to get involved in diet and exercise regimes. While this is not as pleasurable for you as career pursuits – for it requires discipline on your part – the long-term benefits are good.

With so many planets in your own Sign of Pisces the urge to self-indulgence and personal pleasure is understandably strong. Don't repress yourself but don't over-indulge either. Keep the middle way.

Mercury (your Love Planet) moves forward speedily this month, revealing your great social confidence and charisma. Mercury just loves being in the Sign of Aquarius - its position of exaltation - and this is another indication of happiness in love. This love is idealistic and self-sacrificing and it brings you greater spiritual fulfilment. People you meet now come from 'spiritual connections' made aeons ago.

After the 15th love becomes more physical. Your lover will do anything to please you and puts your interests above his or her own. There is an urge for total union - without any barriers or limitations - as if your partner wants to become part of your body and image, inseparable even from the smallest details in your life.

All this is only part of what the month is bringing you. When spring comes on the 21st, your career, professional status and earnings just rocket to the stratosphere. Mars (your Money Planet) starts moving forward after the 24th and gets involved in an unusually fortunate Grand Aspect with Jupiter (your Career Planet). The pace of success is rather dizzying.

April

Best Days Overall: 7th, 8th, 16th, 17th, 24th, 25th

Most Stressful Days Overall: 4th, 5th, 6th, 11th, 12th, 13th, 18th, 19th

Best Days for Love: 7th, 8th, 9th, 10th, 11th, 12th, 13th, 16th, 17th, 20th, 21st, 26th, 27th, 28th, 29th, 30th

Best Days for Money: 1st, 9th, 10th, 18th, 19th, 26th, 27th, 28th

You are shooting into the stratosphere of career success and public acclaim so rapidly this month that it is perhaps good that Jupiter, your Career Planet, goes retrograde. With so many career opportunities and offers coming your way you need to slow down and see where you are going. Earnings, too, shoot up rapidly and perhaps dizzyingly. Your tendency right now is to leap into investments or purchases too rashly and impulsively. Seldom have you had such financial confidence and fearlessness. You get your way in both career and money matters now – this is the joy but also the problem. Remember that you will be stuck with what you go after. Try to be more cautious and discriminating now. Realize that every gift and blessing has other, perhaps less beneficial things that go with it. Look for what comes with these career and financial opportunities and include them in your equations for decision-making.

The attainment of career and financial goals always leads to new spiritual quests. The feeling of 'What now, is this all there is? Is this why I am here?' begins to dominate. Spiritual life and philanthropic activities are always important to you, Pisces, but now, with Uranus making a major move into your 12th House of Spiritual Wisdom and Charity these things become even more important. Uranus also signals a major shift in your spiritual and philanthropic attitudes. You change which charities you support. You favour institutions that take a new and avant-garde approach to charity. Your spiritual life becomes more scientific. That is, faith alone and direct experience with spiritual realities are not enough for you. You want to discern the science behind all these things.

Better check your computers, phones, faxes and other communication equipment this month, Pisces, as the Solar Eclipse of the 29th is going to test them and reveal any flaws they might have. It is best to be prepared beforehand. The Lunar Eclipse of the 15th in your 8th Solar House of Elimination, Transformation and Other People's Money signals an important change in your partner's earnings. A temporary upheaval points up faults; this leads to making the necessary changes. If you are involved with investors an important adjustment occurs in your relationship with them. Some may leave to be replaced by others. Again, a temporary crisis highlights flaws and secret resentments. This will force positive changes.

Your health is excellent all month. Your love life is happy and you project great personal charm and 'sex-appeal'. Your personal glamour is unusually strong until the 22nd. Those who want a Pisces should support his or her financial goals until the 17th and his or her intellectual interests after then. Singles find love close to home.

May

Best Days Overall: 4th, 5th, 13th, 14th, 21st, 22nd, 23rd, 31st

Most Stressful Days Overall: 1st, 2nd, 3rd, 9th, 10th, 15th, 16th, 29th, 30th

Best Days for Love: 6th, 7th, 8th, 9th, 11th, 12th, 15th, 16th, 17th, 19th, 20th, 26th, 27th, 28th, 29th, 30th

Best Days for Money: 6th, 7th, 8th, 15th, 16th, 24th, 25th, 26th

The planets are still concentrated in the Eastern half of your chart, making you more concerned with personal interests than with other people's interests. You have more control over circumstances and conditions but you need to be more cautious in what you create now. Neptune, your Ruler, is retrograde.

In fact, 40 to 50 per cent of the planets are retrograde this month. The delays that you are experiencing personally are also being experienced by many other people. There is a general climate of stalemate, inaction and review now. Be patient. Use the delays constructively to further your goals and aspirations. There is always some improvement that can be made to your plans, projects, products or services; this is the time to make it.

The planets are more or less evenly distributed above and below the horizon this month, giving you a nice sense of balance and perspective about your career and domestic life. You see each as equally important and are trying your best to give each its proper due.

Your paths of greatest fulfilment this month are your career, ambitions, friends, group activities and money-making. After the 17th the pursuit of study and intellectual interests also bring you pleasure.

You are treading into unknown and unexplored territory in your love life this month and you will probably rue it. You are socializing with people outside your normal orbit. Your caution is well placed. Test the waters before you dive in.

Your social charisma could be stronger. Mercury not only moves slowly this month but on the 24th starts to go retrograde. A current relationship seems suddenly to go backwards. You find yourself right back where you started from. Give your partner the space to become sure about his or her feelings.

A cautious approach should be taken with family relations and with any major repairs around the house. By all means enjoy your family's company, but avoid making major commitments to family members until next month. The same is true for home repairs or purchases for the home. Your judgement in these matters seems unrealistic right now.

Finances are excellent all month. Social contacts are bringing you financial opportunities. Rest and relax more after the 21st.

June

Best Days Overall: 1st, 2nd, 10th, 11th, 18th, 19th, 27th, 28th, 29th

Most Stressful Days Overall: 5th, 6th, 12th, 13th, 25th, 26th

Best Days for Love: 5th, 6th, 7th, 8th, 9th, 16th, 17th, 25th, 26th

Best Days for Money: 3rd, 4th, 12th, 13th, 20th, 21st, 30th

Though it will be harder to do this month, you must exercise your genius of rising above circumstances and viewing things from a higher, more cosmic perspective. You must do it precisely because it is hard – for this will lead to growth and steer you through the challenges of the coming month. Solutions will become apparent to you from this higher vantage point.

There is a rare and stressful Heavenly Grand Square aspect in effect all month. Sixty per cent of the planets are involved in this – though different ones get involved at different times. This forces you to build a pattern from amid forces and people that are inherently antagonistic to each other. This requires wisdom and the willingness to suffer a few failures. Keep in mind that almost everyone around you – and in the world at large – is also being forced to do this work – but in different areas. In your case you must deal with the conflicts between your family interests and your career; between your need for emotional security and your need to be someone in the world; between your marriage or love life and the demands of your career; between friendships and your personal financial interests. None of these can be safely ignored. Each of these interests is legitimate. This is what makes things so complicated. This is what challenges your genius.

To further complicate matters – the Celestial Powers love to throw in some impossibilities to force us to grow – 50 per cent of the planets are going retrograde for most of the month. Many actions you would normally take are thwarted or delayed. When you try to negotiate between different parties your words are misinterpreted. Perhaps there is fear on one side of the issue which prevents a positive change from taking place. The cosmic message is that only cautious, well-thought-out changes which take into account everyone's interests and which take place by degrees will work. Your ability to rise above the situation will give you the almost superhuman patience you need to succeed.

One of the positive aspects of all these retrogrades is that you will have a chance to rest and relax more until the 22nd. You need this rest.

In romantic matters you alternate between extreme aggressiveness and undue timidity in your pursuit of love. Mercury (your Love Planet) is retrograde until the 17th, weakening your social confidence and charisma. Yet, Mars, the planet of aggressiveness and courage, is in your 7th House of Love all month. Perhaps your aggression and bravado are merely compensation for the lack of confidence you feel. Those involved with a Pisces this month please take note.

Your social judgement and confidence return after the 17th. You will then be better able to sense when to be aggressive or when not. Your aggressiveness will also begin to come from confidence and not fear.

July

Best Days Overall: 7th, 8th, 15th, 16th, 25th, 26th

Most Stressful Days Overall: 2nd, 3rd, 4th, 9th, 10th, 22nd, 23rd, 30th, 31st

Best Days for Love: 2nd, 3rd, 4th, 5th, 6th, 7th, 8th, 15th, 16th, 25th, 26th, 27th, 30th, 31st

Best Days for Money: 1st, 2nd, 3rd, 4th, 9th, 10th, 11th, 12th, 17th, 18th, 21st, 22nd, 27th, 28th

Though there is still plenty of delay for you to deal with, your life is getting easier. Authority figures who have been exacting and demanding are easing off for a while. Domestic flare-ups are winding down and problems are being resolved. Stalled domestic projects are going forward again, faster and more easily than before. Your health is excellent all month but especially so before the 23rd. Your health can be enhanced even further by keeping in harmony with children, exploring your personal creativity, having fun and, after the 23rd, starting a dietary regime.

Most of the planets are now in the Western sector of your chart, making you less assertive and more socially conscious. Success comes through adapting yourself to existing conditions rather than trying to change them. Self-assertion is made even more difficult by the fact that Neptune, your Ruler, is retrograde all month. Develop the social graces, put other people ahead of yourself and adapt, adapt, adapt. Your own needs will naturally be fulfilled in the most interesting ways.

The planets are evenly dispersed below and above the horizon of your chart. Thus there is a healthy balance between career interests and family demands. Your perspective on these things is just right.

Your paths of greatest fulfilment are your career, religious studies, foreign travel, studying foreign cultures, children, personal creativity and the achievement of work goals.

Your social urges are active and strong this month, but money seems to be the driving force. You seek social contacts to sell a product or service. Social networking aids your 'bottom line'. After the 22nd you earn money by making money for others and by eliminating wasteful expenses and overheads. Financial opportunities exist in defunct or bankrupt businesses which you can turn back to profitability. Your partner is doing well financially this month. Your partner's generosity with you, however, comes in fits and starts. Speculations are favourable and creative ideas are quickly turned to cold cash.

Your love life is fast-paced and active. Conflicts early in the month get resolved quickly. There are a lot of evenings out to entertainment venues this month. Singles are confused as to whether a current relationship is for real or just fun and games. Singles find love through family members, through parties and nightclubs – and, later on in the month, at the workplace and through or with health care professionals.

August

Best Days Overall: 3rd, 4th, 12th, 21st, 22nd, 31st

Most Stressful Days Overall: 5th, 6th, 19th, 20th, 26th, 27th

Best Days for Love: 5th, 6th, 14th, 15th, 16th, 17th, 26th, 27th

Best Days for Money: 1st, 2nd, 5th, 6th, 9th, 10th, 14th, 15th, 19th, 20th, 26th, 27th, 28th, 29th

The planets are shifting with ever greater weight to the top part of your Horoscope. Jupiter, your Career Planet, finally moves forward after many months of retrograde motion. Put these two facts together and they spell out ambition and the drive for outer success. These celestial indicators also show that these ambitious urges are expressed successfully. Career projects get unblocked and pay rises and promotions are in the stars for you. This is the time to sell yourself or your business to the public at large and to elders and superiors in particular. Elders and superiors are supporting your career efforts and granting special favours to you. However, have no illusions: you will have to earn these favours eventually or risk losing them.

The planets are slightly weighted in favour of the Western sector of your chart. This shows more social involvement and a greater social consciousness. Yes, you are concerned with others and their needs but you are far from being a doormat. You are uniquely able to maintain your self-identity and still relate to others at the same time. Your good will probably come to you through others this month, but should their co-operation not be forthcoming you have plenty of energy to go it alone. The problem is not one of energy but of being unclear about what your personal goals and desires are. This requires further study and contemplation.

Your paths of greatest fulfilment this month are the achievement of work goals, your love life, physical intimacy, your career and eliminating the undesirable from your life.

Your health is good all month. A long-standing health problem gets cleared up before the 23rd. Your health can be enhanced even further by a pure diet, emotional harmony with your lover and friends and by fulfilling your normal needs for physical intimacy. Though your health is good, try to rest and relax more after the 23rd.

This is far from being one of your strong earning periods. Nevertheless, with your Money Planet (Mars) in your 8th House of Elimination, Transformation and Other People's Money you earn now by helping others to prosper. In addition, large lump-sum payments come to you from insurance claims, royalties or stock dividends. Your partner is generous this month. Aim your financial guns at the reduction of debts and expenses now. Become leaner and meaner. Eliminate inessential things from your life.

Your love life is happy. Mercury, your Love Planet, spends most of the month in your 7th House of Marriage. Here it is very powerful on your behalf. Your social confidence is strong and there is a mood of romance in the air. You like a partner who is truly your opposite now. Yes, as a matter of fact, the over-achieving perfectionist who frets over every detail is just your cup of tea right now.

September

Best Days Overall: 8th, 9th, 17th, 18th, 19th, 27th, 28th

Most Stressful Days Overall: 2nd, 15th, 16th, 22nd, 23rd, 29th, 30th

Best Days for Love: 4th, 5th, 6th, 7th, 12th, 13th, 14th, 15th, 16th, 22nd, 23rd, 24th, 25th

Best Days for Money: 2nd, 8th, 10th, 11th, 17th, 18th, 20th, 21st, 27th, 28th, 29th, 30th

The retrograde of Neptune (your Ruler) and the dominance of the Western sector of your Horoscope are clear indicators for you to avoid power struggles, to put other people ahead of yourself, to avoid going it alone right now and to adapt yourself to situations rather than trying to change them. Until you are more certain as to what your personal needs and desires are, don't try to change what you consider to be awkward circumstances. The circumstances might actually be perfect when seen from a higher perspective.

The top half of your chart contains the overwhelming majority of planets. Thus you are career-orientated and restless for outer security. You've had plenty of emotional fulfilment of late, now you want some career fulfilment. This is happening over the next few months; in the mean time, prepare.

Your paths of greatest fulfilment are your love life, physical intimacy, your career and helping other people prosper.

Rest and relax more until the 23rd. After then your vitality improves. Your health can be enhanced by maintaining social harmony and a good rapport with your lover, purification regimes and a wholesome diet.

Love is an important priority this month and is favourable indeed. Love is sweet, tender and utterly romantic. Singles find a special someone this month. Only time will tell whether this is the real thing. Mercury, your Love Planet, moves cautiously for most of the month and on the 22nd starts to retrograde. Don't schedule that wedding just yet.

Finances are not a big priority this month. In fact – on a long-term level – the pursuit of merely personal profit is a path of stagnation for you. Focus on helping others and the world at large to prosper. Make sure that what you sell or produce is worth its cost. Don't load yourself up with excess possessions. Stick to what you need and can use. Money is earned more easily when you pool it with other people's cash. Shared finances prosper.

October

Best Days Overall: 5th, 6th, 15th, 16th, 24th, 25th

Most Stressful Days Overall: 12th, 13th, 20th, 21st, 26th, 27th

Best Days for Love: 3rd, 4th, 12th, 13th, 15th, 16th, 20th, 21st, 22nd, 23rd, 24th, 25th, 30th, 31st

Best Days for Money: 5th, 6th, 7th, 8th, 9th, 15th, 16th, 17th, 18th, 26th, 27th

Most of the planets are still in the Western sector of your chart this month – but this is soon to change. Neptune, your Ruler, finally moves forward on the 5th after many months of retrograde motion. After the 14th, 90 per cent of the planets are moving forward. Thus you are becoming ever more confident and assertive, ever clearer as to your real interests and more and more true to yourself. True, this month you still have to indulge in 'people-pleasing' and adapt yourself to alien conditions, but the need is rapidly diminishing. Whatever cosmic lessons that had to be learned through all of this are being learned and you're getting ready to do your own thing.

Eighty to 90 per cent of the planets continue to be above the horizon of your chart, and Mars joins Jupiter in your 10th House of Career on the 21st. There's no question about it, the bright lights and glamour of the world are calling to you. The drive to outer success is so strong now that you will banish any family member or emotional issue that blocks you. Outer security takes priority over inner security. Concern for other people's families takes priority over concern for your own. Your urge to exercise power is stronger than your need for personal happiness.

Your paths of greatest fulfilment are making money for others, eliminating the undesirable from your life, physical intimacy, religious studies, higher education, foreign travel and your career.

Though this has been a positive career year overall you haven't yet reached your peak. This will come in the following months. In the mean time, prepare yourself. Get all the education you need now. Get a clear vision of your career goals and your life's work. Then you'll be ready for all the good that is to come. Boldness in career matters pays off.

Finances are unusually good this month. A pay rise or promotion aids your 'bottom line'. Elders and superiors create financial opportunities for you. Your financial optimism is sky-high. Thus you earn money 'luckily' but tend to spend it rashly and over-generously. This is the month to buy the things – equipment, clothing or other paraphernalia – that will foster your career and public image.

The impasse in your love life is over after the 14th. You need to focus on the quality rather than the quantity of your relationships. Physical intimacy takes precedence over courtship.

November

Best Days Overall: 6th, 7th, 16th, 17th, 25th

Most Stressful Days Overall: 8th, 9th, 10th, 16th, 17th, 23rd

Best Days for Love: 2nd, 3rd, 4th, 11th, 12th, 14th, 15th, 16th, 17th, 21st, 22nd, 23rd, 24th

Best Days for Money: 4th, 5th, 14th, 15th, 23rd

Many noteworthy celestial events are taking place this month, signalling long-term shifts in your attitude and orientation and bringing on important events. First off, the planets are making a major shift into the Eastern sector of your Horoscope this month. By the 23rd nearly all of them will be there (the exception is the Moon). There will be periods this month when 100 per cent of the planets will be in the East. No question about it, your days of dependency, adaptation and worrying about how other people think of you are over with. This is a period in which you are called upon to build your own Heaven on Earth. Now is the time to create things as you would like them to be, customized to your personal specifications. You can have things your way now and others will assent. Moreover, this Eastern shift has not yet peaked – this will occur in March of 1996 – it is only just beginning (and gaining momentum all the while).

The planetary power is also overwhelmingly in the upper half – above the horizon – of your Horoscope this month, just about peaking there. Thus you are justifiably concerned with your place in the world and in society. Other people's families and other people's emotional security take priority over your own. You are concerned with families in general, not with your family in particular.

You are not looking back to the past this month but have your eyes fixed on the future. Enemies will no doubt accuse you of being high and mighty and of forgetting your origins. This charge is unfair. True, you are career-driven and ambitious, but you feel that your past is irrelevant and only the future counts.

This has been a year of being conscious of your duty to the world. This month you are even more so. Great career progress is being made. Fame, honour and glory are coming to you. You are getting involved with people of stature and power. Not all of you will make the front page of the *Times* this month, but each of you will have greater public recognition. There is tremendous support for your career goals and ambitions; elders and those at the top are granting you favours. Just remember the price-tag on all this – a sacrifice of many of your personal desires and inclinations, and a lot more work.

Try to rest and relax more after the 23rd. Your health can be enhanced by prayer and meditation and by maintaining harmony with elders and parents.

December

Best Days Overall: 8th, 9th, 18th, 19th, 26th, 27th

Most Stressful Days Overall: 6th, 7th, 13th, 14th, 20th, 21st

Best Days for Love: 1st, 2nd, 3rd, 4th, 12th, 13th, 14th, 22nd, 23rd, 24th, 31st

Best Days for Money: 1st, 2nd, 3rd, 4th, 11th, 12th, 13th, 14th, 20th, 21st, 22nd, 23rd, 28th, 29th

All the planets are moving forward now, and all of them – with the exception of the Moon – are firmly established in the Eastern sector of your chart. Thus the long interval of feeling dependent and powerless and of having to adapt to alien situations is very much over. There is a new you: assertive, independent, creative, in charge and personally influential. You have no one to please now but yourself. Your will is a 'law of the universe' and the universe obeys you. This a month of great progress, creativity and personal achievement.

In past months you've needed the good opinion of others, but now you face a more difficult challenge. You need to obtain the good opinion of yourself. You are in charge of your life and you are creating conditions now. Create them happily and wisely.

Most of the planets are still above the horizon of your chart, continuing to foster your ambitions in a year that has been fundamentally career-orientated. The past, where you've come from, your noble or humble origins are not important now – the goal is what counts. Keep your eyes on the prize.

Your paths of greatest fulfilment continue to be your career, physical intimacy, the re-invention of the self, group activities and friendships.

Rest and relax more until the 22nd. Plan your actions better to reduce a waste of energy. Your health can be enhanced by maintaining harmony with elders, superiors and friends. After the 22nd your health and vitality improve considerably.

Earnings are strong this month and boost your sense of self-esteem and personal freedom. You feel economically free to pursue your personal interests now. Your fondest financial dreams are coming true, with a little help from your friends. Social networking substantially increases your 'bottom line'.

Your lover is ever so slowly coming round to your point of view and begins to realize that he or she needs to fulfil your desires. You mix with the high and the mighty this month. Singles are attracted to administrators and to people of power. Your lover is ready, willing and able to help you in your career. Your social charisma is strongest before the 12th; you make new friends then. Singles are more likely to meet that special someone before the 12th than afterwards. However, with Saturn influencing Mercury (your Love Planet), you may not realize it at first.

The author wishes to give special thanks to STAR ★ DATA, who originally commissioned this work. Without their help – both financial and technical – this book could not have been written.

Of further interest . . .

SUN SIGN, MOON SIGN

Charles and Suzi Harvey

Most people know their Sun Sign and what it says about them. But just as important is your Moon sign, the sign associated with feelings and emotions. Taken together, the positions of the Sun and Moon in your chart form a remarkably revealing combination, giving you a far more accurate picture of your total personality than the sign sign alone. With the help of easy-to-use tables making it simple to discover your Moon sign, this book describes the 144 sun-moon types which are the key to a deeper insight into your own, and your friends' and family's true personality and psychology.

Charles Harvey is one of the top astrologers in the UK and has been president of the British Astrological Association since 1973. His wife Suzi has been a consultant astrologer for 12 years and is Editor of the *Astrological Journal.*

A LOVER'S GUIDE

Marjorie Orr

Is your love life predetermined by the stars? Will they lead you to the perfect lover? The key lies in understanding yourself and your mate – and astrology can help.

You are the product of both your sun sign (birthday) and moon sign (exact time of birth). Once you know these (there's a key to moon signs in this book) you can read each chapter to learn about:

★ What your signs say about your individual personality and qualities
★ How your sun clicks (or doesn't) with that of your mate
★ Your moon sign vs that of your lover
★ How your sun sign and your partner's sign complement one another

Each permutation can reveal endless insights into how well you will get along. You're Taurus, he's Aquarius? Probably not much hope. You're Aries, she's Gemini? Much better: sparks fly and passions rage!

Marjorie Orr is a psychotherapist and astrologer for the *Daily Express* and *Woman's Journal*. She is the author of *Star Quality.*

STAR QUALITY

Marjorie Orr

Who are the Aries actors, Sagittarius singers and Pisces politicians? Do you share your star sign with your favourite film star, or a member of the Royal Family?

If so, you will share many of their strengths, their weaknesses and their talents.

In *Star Quality*, leading psychological astrologer Marjorie Orr tells you what these strengths and weaknesses might be. For example, wouldn't you like to know

★ how each star sign rates as a wife, husband or lover
★ whether Taurus bosses are better than Libra, or which signs make the best slaves
★ how your Gemini child is likely to behave?

Each chapter concentrates on one of the twelve sun signs, and answers all these questions, as well as giving your horoscope up to the year 2000. The birth charts of three celebrities are analysed in depth for every sign.

Star Profiles include:

Madonna, Michael Jackson, Joan Collins, Arnold Schwarzenegger, Cher, Sean Connery, Princess Diana and Pavarotti.

SUN SIGNS
Sasha Fenton

Much has been written about astrology and, in particular, Sun signs. However, in this unique book Sasha Fenton turns her inimitable astrological skills to the subject, revealing once and for all exactly what you want to know about your Sun sign.

Sign by sign, the book fully explains the significance of each sign, including such details as the Elements and the Qualities of each sign. It dispels any confusions regarding cusps or Summertime, and compares well-known celebrities with yourself. It will leave you with vital knowledge about health, hobbies, shopping habits, possessions, work, sex and, most important of all, not what it is like to *be* a particular sign, but what it is like to *live* with one.

Together with Sasha Fenton's companion books, *Moon Signs, Rising Signs* and *The Planets, Sun Signs* will enhance your understanding of astrology, of yourself, and those around you.

Sasha Fenton is a best-selling astrologer whose books have sold over half a million copies world-wide. She is well known for her chatty, accessible style, and is the astrology columnist for *Woman's Own*. Her other books include *Super Tarot, Living Palmistry* and *Understanding Astrology.*

ASTROLOGY FOR LOVERS

Liz Greene

This comprehensive guide to life, relationships and lovers provides an accessible and readable introduction to astrology. Liz Greene, from her standpoint as a trained psychotherapist and astrologer, explains the principles of astrology, debunks popular myths and shows how an understanding of the subject helps in forming lasting relationships.

This book deals with complex ideas clearly, provocatively and compassionately. It shows, for example, how to interpret your own and your partner's astrological signature in order to understand the complex patterns that make up each individual's personality. There is also valuable advice on recognizing the difficulties your choice of partner may pose, and how to deal with them.

RELATING

Liz Greene

Since it was first published in 1977 this book has becoome a classic of modern astrological literature. Liz Greene's insights are as fresh and exciting as ever and the ideas she explores about the nature of relating have increased relevance today.

She shows how to use basic astrological concepts symbolically and practically, in a framework of Jungian psychology, to illuminate the ways in which people relate to each other on both conscious and unconscious levels.

Relating remains a key text for any reader interested in the psychological dimensions of astrology; but it is also a book for anyone who wants to know more about themselves and the way they relate to others.

'If you only read one astrology book this year, make it Liz Greene's *Relating* . . . Even if you plan to read only one book of *any* kind this year, *Relating* would still be an excellent choice' HOROSCOPE MAGAZINE

'A thoughtful and scholarly book which marries the profundities of Jungian psychology with the age-old science of astrology to provide fresh insights into ourselves and our relationships' PSYCHOLOGY TODAY

'A remarkably good book and highly recommended . . . this book deserves to be on every astrologer's shelf, if not on the shelf of anyone who cares about his or her relationships with others' PREDICTION

YOUR CHINESE HOROSCOPE FOR 1995

Neil Somerville

Chinese astrology is an ancient and increasingly popular subject, a system of character analysis and prediction which has inspired renewed interest in the West.

In this best-selling annual guide, Neil Somerville introduces the 12 signs of the Chinese zodiac, and outlines the main qualities and weaknesses of each. In addition, he reveals how the Five Elements influence the signs, and provides prospects for 1995, the Year of the Pig.

All you need to know is the year you were born; then you can discover a wealth of information about the hidden depths of your character.

Whatever your sign, you'll find plenty to interest you in this informative and amusing guide. Not only can you learn what lies ahead for you in 1995, but also how you relate to other signs, what your ascendant is and which famous people share your sign. Find out what the Year of the Pig holds in store for you!

SUN SIGN, MOON SIGN	1 85538 159 1	£6.99	☐
A LOVER'S GUIDE	1 85538 315 2	£5.99	☐
STAR QUALITY	1 85538 179 6	£4.99	☐
SUN SIGNS	1 85538 021 8	£4.99	☐
MOON SIGNS	1 85030 552 7	£5.99	☐
RISING SIGNS	1 85030 751 1	£4.99	☐
THE PLANETS	1 85538 352 7	£5.99	☐
ASTROLOGY FOR LOVERS	1 85538 358 6	£8.99	☐
RELATING	0 85030 957 3	£7.99	☐
YOUR CHINESE HOROSCOPE FOR 1995	1 85538 386 1	£4.99	☐

All these books are available from your local bookseller or can be ordered direct from the publishers.

To order direct just tick the titles you want and fill in the form below:

Name: _____

Address: _____

_____ Postcode: _____

Send to: Thorsons Mail Order, Dept 3, HarperCollins*Publishers*, Westerhill Road, Bishopbriggs, Glasgow G64 2QT.
Please enclose a cheque or postal order or your authority to debit your Visa/Access account —

Credit card no: _____

Expiry date: _____

Signature: _____

— up to the value of the cover price plus:
UK & BFPO: Add £1.00 for the first book and 25p for each additional book ordered.
Overseas orders including Eire: Please add £2.95 service charge. Books will be sent by surface mail but quotes for airmail despatches will be given on request.

24 HOUR TELEPHONE ORDERING SERVICE FOR ACCESS/VISA CARDHOLDERS — TEL: **041 772 2281**